# Uneasy
# Rider

# Uneasy Rider

## Travels Through a Mid-Life Crisis

Mike Carter

EBURY
PRESS

917.304

1 3 5 7 9 10 8 6 4 2

Published in 2008 by Ebury Press, an imprint of Ebury Publishing
A Random House Group Company

Copyright © Mike Carter 2008

Mike Carter has asserted his right to be identified as the author of this
Work in accordance with the Copyright, Designs and Patents Act 1988

The Random House Group Limited Reg. No. 954009

Addresses for companies within the Random House Group can be found
at www.randomhouse.co.uk

A CIP catalogue record for this book is available from the British Library

The Random House Group Limited supports The Forest Stewardship
Council (FSC), the leading international forest certification organisation.
All our titles that are printed on Greenpeace approved FSC certified
paper carry the FSC logo. Our paper procurement policy can be found
at www.rbooks.co.uk/environment

**Mixed Sources**
Product group from well-managed
forests and other controlled sources
www.fsc.org  Cert no. TT-COC-2139
© 1996 Forest Stewardship Council
FSC

Printed in the UK by CPI Mackays, Chatham, ME5 8TD

ISBN 9780091922689

To buy books by your favourite authors and register for offers visit
www.rbooks.co.uk

For Norma

# SPECIAL THANKS

To my editor Andrew Goodfellow, for approaching me in the first place and for having blind faith. To Simon Shore, for your patience, insight and encouragement – and for the Borough Market Scotch eggs. I owe you much. To Joanne O'Connor, who commissioned the original weekly column in the *Observer* and actually ran it, as opposed to just pretending to and not telling me until I got back. To Carole Cadwalladr, for refusing to let me back out. To Isabel Tamarit, for giving me a quiet place to work when I needed it most. To Wendy, Gordon and Paul – your capacity for love and support never ceases to amaze me. To all the bikers I met on my trip. You really are the nicest bunch of people in the world. To the Aussie Honeymooners, for restoring my faith in coupledom. To Kevin and the gang at BMW's rider training centre in Wales for all your help. To Mrs Chrysanthi, for Ilias and for taking me in. Rest in peace. And finally, to Pete. I hope we are at last getting to know one another.

# PROLOGUE

# 42

The nadir of a man's life is 42. I don't know why, exactly. The frustrating thing about a nadir is that you cannot know precisely when you have reached it. That only comes later.

There are plenty of surveys that confirm it to be true, though. You can find them if you're looking for them. I was coming across them everywhere: magazines in doctors' waiting rooms, newspapers discarded on trains, television, radio; all concluding that the absolute rock bottom, the pit of despair, the precise moment when a man runs out of steam, suffers a catastrophic crisis of confidence, hits ground zero, call it what you will, occurs at age 42.

It's amazing when I started looking more personally how much misery I found attached to men and the number 42. It was the age my dad walked away from my mum and his family. A teetotal uncle started drinking heavily in his 42nd year. A good friend had a heart attack aged 42. An acquaintance shot himself at, yes, 42. Elvis. He was 42. Nearly all my male fortysomething friends and colleagues appeared to be going up the wall, tearing out what was left of their hair. None of them seemed particularly happy. Most reported a slow, creeping sense of futility to their lives.

From my completely unscientific analysis, it seemed to me

that men might reach some kind of crossroads at aged 42. There were no signposts at this junction, no clues as to where to go, just a terrible restlessness and a desire to be somewhere else. One night men go to bed and all is well with the world. Then they wake up and everything has gone to shit.

In April 2006, I turned 42.

# 1 Party

The morning after the *Observer* newspaper Christmas party seemed different from previous years. Laying in bed, head throbbing, I replayed sequentially the evening's events, frame by frame, waiting for the frame that would bring the replay grinding to a halt; the frame that would have to be analysed closely, stared at in horror.

Twelve months earlier, the frozen frame had involved me calling a Cabinet minister a name that Dennis Skinner would have baulked at; a frame that contained, apart from me and the minister, obviously, a dozen of my colleagues doing a good impersonation of Munch's *The Scream*.

Or the do a few years back, when my colleagues were invited to present their party pieces, and we had recitations of Kipling and polished light opera pieces and, if I recall correctly, a rather good mime. And then we had the bloke who hadn't prepared anything but who didn't want to miss out, who blew a condom up on his head while attempting to juggle three limes. This had failed to capture the audience's imagination quite as much as the Gilbert and Sullivan.

But each frame flickered by and the people were laughing with me, and nobody stormed off in a huff, nor did I try to shag a work-experience girl, nor throw up, nor attempt to dance. I appeared not to have told anybody about fictitious awards or trophies I'd never won nor, indeed, pull a prophylactic over my head and reach for the bar fruit.

There was a scuffle, a few hands straying over backsides inappropriately, animated returnees from the toilet with the sniffles. But, glory be to God, I was never in those scenes. Maybe I was becoming the sophisticate I always suspected I might be.

There was a section missing between midnight and the taxi ride home, of course, but no alarm bells were ringing. I could walk into work safe in the knowledge that, if there was somebody at the party who'd set the bar for idiocy, a giant sozzled prat against whose antics we could all offset our own misdemeanours, for once it wasn't going to be me.

So later that day, in the office, when my editor walked up to me and asked when I would be leaving, accompanied by a little twist of the right wrist, those hitherto silent bells started to twinkle like windchimes on a gentle breeze.

When another male colleague approached, eyes like saucers, shook my hand and slapped my back in the wildly heterosexual manner of a beer commercial, I had a full Westminster-Abbey-after-a-coronation going on. The motoring editor was next to present himself. 'Sensational stuff,' he said, also twisting his right wrist. 'Dangerous, sure, but what a trip! I only wish I could come with you.'

But where exactly was I going? I urgently needed to sit down and probe once more the Stella-fuelled fog swirling round, crawl back through that tape. Oh, God. What had I said? What had I done?

Young people of an idealistic nature are generally attracted to a career in newspapers by the spirit of Bob Woodward and Carl Bernstein. What they find are Lord Copper and William Boot. Rumour and drunken misunderstandings are as likely to shape the paper's content as a leak from the Treasury or the outbreak of war in some distant former colony. When an editor has an idea they think is worthwhile, or is presented with such an idea at morning conference, say, from where my colleagues had just emerged, it becomes utterly inviolable. As I searched for some Nurofen, the word Ishmaelia bounced around my addled brain.

I didn't have to wait too long to find out what was going on. Apparently, in that drink-fuelled witching hour, where everything is possible and the world is just one big casserole of love and opportunity, I had announced that in a few months' time I was going to take a motorcycle on a six-month road trip. (And not just any old motorcycle, but a big one, specifically a BMW R1200GS. This had required zero imagination on my part: I had just read *Long Way Round* and this was as near as dammit to the bikes that Ewan McGregor and Charley Boorman had ridden.)

I was going to take off around the world, give up the grind of London life, go where the road took me. Oh, how glorious it would be, I'd said, a sentiment shared by my sober and enthusiastic travel editor who had declared, in front of many equally enthused witnesses, that I was to write a column about my travels.

'Thassh fugging great thassh is,' I'd replied, apparently. 'More Stella, anyone?'

Alas, what I had neglected to share with my colleagues was that I hadn't been on two wheels since an inglorious three-month teenage chapter involving a Lambretta, four crashes and an 18-month ban for drunk-driving.

So, I was in a pickle and no mistake. The last thing a man having a midlife crisis wants to do is admit that he's been writing cheques with his drunken mouth that he has no means of cashing.

The type of person who just takes off into the unknown for six months on a large motorcycle would surely otherwise be found performing emergency heart surgery with a coat hanger on an aeroplane over the Atlantic, or hacking off their own foot with a biro in a rockfall. They tend not to consistently get on the Circle Line going the wrong way. This was the sort of thing that Other People did: Better People, Braver People and, ultimately, Deader People.

However, interestingly, as word started getting around of my proposed trip, my stock seemed to have risen, especially with men and women of a certain vintage, as if I'd become a poster boy for the middle-aged and disaffected. They'd stop me by the water cooler, chat to me in the lift, come over to me in the canteen. Even the editor now knew my name. 'So, Carter, when are you leaving on this shagathon?' he'd bellowed across the office.

But if I was now some kind of proxy for the projected fantasies of others, I was also the recipient of their fears and frustrations. A typical exchange ran thus:

Friend/colleague/stranger at bus stop: 'Wow, that sounds amazing. I'm jealous. I'd love to come with you.'

A beat.

F/C/SABS: 'I had a good friend, about your age. He bought a motorcycle, did something similar.'

Me: 'Oh, yeah. How'd they get on?'

F/C/SABS: 'Killed.'

Always dead. Usually decapitated, the head still in the helmet found in a nearby field, the story told with such relish and in such gruesome detail that it would be easy to conclude they were enjoying the telling. I had no idea that every single person in the entire world had lost a good friend to a foreign motorcycle adventure.

I'd be lying if I claimed that such constant warnings of impending decapitation didn't unnerve me. But, if *in lager veritas*, I'd been attempting to reclaim a waning virility, trying to spice up a life that had become little more than a sleepwalk through the shadows, then how to backtrack with any dignity? I might as well have knocked up a sandwich board that read: 'Loser, with hairy nostrils, a broken marriage, no kids, brittle confidence, stagnating career, bad back and, now, no bottle.' As Tim from *The Office* said so eloquently: 'Form an orderly queue, ladies.'

As providence would have it, at the time I was reading *The Scottish Himalayan Expedition* by W. H. Murray, written in 1951. Talking about the doubts he'd had prior to departure, he'd written: 'The moment one commits oneself, then providence moves too.'

Of course, Mr Murray would have had to rely on the traditional form of providence, all cosmic forces and serendipity. Whereas all I had to do was key a few words into Google. And so it was that I discovered that BMW had a residential rider training school just outside Neath, South Wales, where, in the space of five days, they take you through your compulsory basic training on a 125cc Honda, then on to BMW 650s for your Direct Access course. This would lead, on day six, to your full motorcycle test.

My hand hovered over the phone for a few seconds. Then I picked it up and dialled the number. A few weeks later I was on a train heading west away from Paddington.

# 2 It came to Pass

Kevin Sanders ran the training school. He was 42. But if he was currently at the lowest ebb of his life, he was doing a good job of putting on a brave face. This man loved motorcycles. He spent six months of the year sharing his passion with pupils at the school, and the other six months on the road, guiding two-wheeled expeditions through the Americas.

Kevin's assistant was called Emmett. A year or two previously, Emmett had taken a sabbatical from a well-paid job in the City to join one of Kevin's tours. On his return to the UK, Emmett quit his job and moved to Wales to work with Kevin. They had the perma-smile of evangelists.

The school's training routes took in the Brecon Beacons, with the headquarters in the former mining town of Ystradgynlais, light on vowels but heavy on pensioners crossing the road without looking, thus very handy for practising those emergency stops.

During the week, I learned about the correct line to take around corners, how nearly all braking on a motorbike is done with the front brake, and I practised until I was dizzy doing tight-circled U-turns, the inability to complete one of these without putting your foot on the ground was the prime reason for failing the test.

'Head up!' Kevin would shout, following another failed

14

U-turn. 'You have to look where you want to go. The bike will follow you round. It's a natural law. Have faith.'

But most of all, Kevin and Emmett drummed into me time and again the vital importance of using what is known as the 'lifesaver', the last-second glance over your shoulder before making a turn to check the mirror's blind spots. Did Steve McQueen have to go through all this? Would Jack Nicholson have refused to jump on the pillion seat until Peter Fonda had demonstrated his emergency stop? I doubted it.

After five days of whizzing around the Welsh countryside, it was time for the test. My fellow learner Derek (about my age, if you're asking) and me pulled on our Day-Glo gilets and, like a couple of chicks, followed mother-hen Kevin towards the glitz and glamour of Neath on a wet Thursday morning.

Over a pre-match coffee in Burger King, sitting next to some hooded youths, Kevin went through his final pep talk. My mouth was parched with nerves. I considered how the next hour would decide one of two very different directions my immediate life could take. If, on the one hand, I failed my test, as nearly half of entrants do, I could invoke providence and abandon my trip. 'Damn those U-turns. I guess it just wasn't meant to be. Now, where's the Circle Line?'

However, the prospect of having to go back to the office as a failure who tripped over his laces before the first hurdle even arrived was not particularly enticing.

On the other hand, if I passed, within a few weeks I would be hitting the road and heading into the unknown. I wasn't sure, at that moment, which outcome I'd have preferred.

I sat in the examiner's office, listening to the muffled sound of a phone conversation next door through the thin Portakabin walls. Five minutes passed. Then 10. Fear filled my heart. Sweat filled my riding suit. I read and reread the various safety and community messages on the noticeboard. Motorcyclists make up five per cent of road traffic, yet account for 21 per cent of fatalities, apparently. Thanks for that. Also, the local youth orchestra was on the lookout for a new French horn player owing to the incumbent moving abroad. Fifteen minutes. Twenty-one per cent, tsk, tsk.

I started thinking about the possibility of failing again. I don't like to fail, but for some reason I'm completely ambivalent about success. The result is a perpetual stasis. A no-win situation. It is a curious perversion that for years I was convinced was mine, and mine alone. But then I read Groucho Marx's line about not wanting to be a member of a club that would have him for a member, and I realised that there were at least two of us. It's a conumdrum, all right, but put into some perspective that morning by the travails of the local youth orchestra.

The muffled talking next door stopped and a large man of military bearing dressed in full leather creaked into the room wearing an unfeasibly big helmet complete with call-centre mouthpiece.

'Mr Carter?' he enquired, looking at his clipboard, then scanning the otherwise empty room.

'That's me,' I tried to say, stumbling to my feet, but actually said something like 'haaaaashme' in the style of an asthmatic drunk, owing to the fact that my legs were no longer working and my tongue was stuck to the roof of my mouth.

'I am your examiner. Mr Pass,' he said, offering his leather-gauntletted hand. The words of W. H. Murray flickered once more across my mind.

'Is that really your name?' I asked, looking for the cameras.

'Yes,' came a voice, deadpan, from somewhere beneath the helmet, in the manner of a man who hadn't heard anybody point out the absurdity of his name. Well, not for 10 minutes anyway. 'Shall we start?'

I managed to dodge the souped-up Novas and weekday shoppers of Neath, and when we eventually pulled back into the riding school, Mr Pass went through the litany of cock-ups that I'd managed to squeeze into 30 minutes of riding.

These included failure to indicate, failure to execute life-saver and failure to resist taking the piss out of his name. Though the latter was not officially listed on the charge sheet.

I was braced for 'You're a disgrace, Carter, what are you? Drop and give me 20.' But instead he said, 'You've passed' and I thanked Mr Pass for passing me and uttered something about being happy that I'd avoided Mr Fail's shift, which went down about as well as my original comment.

I wanted to do something girly like squeal or leap into the air or kiss Mr Pass on the helmet, but instead settled on a restrained, gloved manly handshake.

We wandered back to the Portakabin for the debrief, where, having allowed me to wallow for at least five minutes in naked self-congratulation, the voice of Groucho piped up to say 'big deal' and the local youth orchestra was still mourning the loss of its French horn.

Kevin was waiting by the gates like a concerned parent after the first day of big school, full of praise and pride in his pupil. Derek roared up after his test and, so excited was he that he'd also passed, forgot some of the fundamentals of riding and physics – and only having had four days' worth of lessons.

He removed both hands from the handlebars at 30 mph and, punching the air in triumph – which, fair enough, Evel Knievel used to do, but usually after leaping over 3,000 buses, or the Straits of Gibraltar – first wobbled, then crashed the school's brand-new hitherto unscratched BMW spectacularly in the gravel at our feet.

Thus came the final lesson of the day: motorcycles make one hell of a noise when they crash. It was a racket I would be hearing again a few times in the not-too distant future.

# 3 The bike

Late April, two months later, and I was back on a train again heading west out of Paddington. My bike and luggage were ready and I'd arranged for them to be delivered to Kevin's place so that he could help me fit the panniers and familiarise me with the bike. I'd never actually seen a BMW R1200GS up close before. It was gun-metal grey and extraordinarily beautiful, with a front mudguard sticking out like the tongue of an exotic palm, and exposed engine parts strapped on to a criss-cross frame that made it look like it belonged to Mad Max or a Power Ranger. I peered at the speedometer. It went up to 140 mph.

It was also huge. So tall in fact that I had to do 20 minutes of astanga yoga before my hamstrings were supple enough to even contemplate getting my leg over.

Once in the saddle, I had a flashback to sitting on a camel as a youngster at Dudley Zoo. I couldn't wait to get off that camel. And it only went about 5 mph.

Kevin and me headed off into the Brecon Beacons and he went ahead to show me some advanced riding lines around corners. He was like an artist, effortlessly making smooth, flowing shapes and curves like a Michelangelo or a Picasso. Kevin and the bike seemed like one and the same thing. I followed, twitching and stuttering, making shapes and curves in the manner of Rolf Harris with the DTs, the bike and me as awkward as if on a first date.

After a few hours, we stopped at a petrol station for a coffee and I felt like a dog who'd just picked up in the air that its owners were about to leave for a holiday without it. I knew that any minute Kevin was going to put down his cup, yawn or stretch, or look at his watch and say, 'Is that the time?' and announce that he had to get back to the school. He would put on his helmet and his gloves and shake my hand and disappear past the mucky mags and the bags of dolly mixtures and I would be alone for the first time with an enormous motorcycle, a full set of luggage and the awfully long 200-mile road home to London.

Kevin duly looked at his watch and stretched. As he disappeared, the rain arrived, first in apologetic streaks, then in fat two-fingered torrents. For the first time, this all felt very real. I considered staying in the garage, perhaps for ever, getting a job ordering the dolly mixtures and stacking the mucky mags and perhaps marrying the woman behind the till, who was about 65, but comely from a certain angle, all things considered.

Eventually, I wobbled away along the A roads, pizza-delivery boys and milkfloats whizzing past, a queue of farmers in their tractors getting frustrated behind me.

I felt terrified and euphoric in equal measure as I started to grasp the bikers' saying that Kevin had told me: 'Only a motorcyclist knows why a dog sticks its head out of a car window.'

During training, I had always been with somebody, and although this hadn't made me less vulnerable, it had certainly made me feel more capable, more confident, less alone. That was the overwhelming thing I felt right then. Alone.

On that rain-soaked journey, I had plenty of time to reflect on what had brought me to this point.

Okay, I'd previously told you that life seemed dull, monotone, and that I had been gripped by midlife onset grumpy syndrome, as random as if it were a plague that had descended unbidden from the sky. But there were specifics to my particular strain of midlife crisis. If, to simultaneously paraphrase and murder a famous Russian grumpy, all happy middle-aged people are alike, then all unhappy middle-aged people are unhappy after their own fashion.

Ten years previously, I had met a woman and fallen in love for the first and only time. Within days, we moved in together and for the next seven years I'd lived in unmitigated bliss. She was the best friend I'd ever had, the person who – ready, cliché fans? – made me feel wonderfully, completely whole. I was fearless, reborn. That she was stunningly beautiful only added to the peachy sense of self-satisfaction that life wasn't treating me too badly.

Sometimes I used to watch her sleeping and will her to wake up, as if any time away from her was a waste of something rare and precious. Reading back those words now, it's probably just as well she hadn't woken up, lest she'd screamed and brought the neighbours running. We got married. We were going to start a family. I had the perfect life.

Then she left me. What's that about giving the gods a good old laugh by telling them your plans? There weren't really any rows, no slow decay, just a flick of a switch and a relationship consigned to the rubbish bin in perfect time with the cadences of disposable modern life: memories of my marriage frozen for rose-tinted eternity like an untimely death.

In desperation, I gave her a copy of Yeats's 'He Wishes For The Cloths of Heaven', but I might as well have given her the instructions for the dishwasher to read. She didn't tread softly on my dreams, she riverdanced. I learned then that when a woman has fallen out of love with you, there is no way back.

But where could I go while I was waiting to fall out of love with her? Well, there was Threshers, and I thank them very much for all their support during that difficult time. Then there were the marathons to run, the endless hours lifting weights in the gym, the big Himalayan peak to scale;

anything to try and eradicate the creeping sense of emasculation, the feeling that, as a man, I had failed.

There was a new-found sense of delight I got poring over the car-crash relationships of the tabloid fodder. There were the messy fumblings with other women that always, frustratingly, felt like an infidelity. And there was a terrifying trip to the Land of Misogyny – and, boy, is there a big old gang of guys living there willing to radicalise you to the cause.

I didn't recognise myself any more. The values and views I'd held my entire life – about loyalty, commitment, women – had been turned upside down. Somebody had stolen my script and replaced it with this piece of shit. I was 40 and stuck, watching as my friends had babies. I aged overnight. My courage was gone, my shoulders were hunched. I knew that tomorrow would be just like today. Bitterness had me by the throat; there was a joyless, corrosive futility about everything I did. Oh, happy days.

But most of all, I filled that time with reading. I read about relationship breakdowns, trying to find some peace, some answers. Then, slowly, as a year's separation turned into two, it started to dawn on me that what was keeping me stuck was not just the failure of my marriage, but the fact that it had happened as I hit middle age.

One day, when the sun was shining and the birds were singing and I was inside a dark room googling 'middle-aged', I came across this quote from Saki: 'The young have aspirations that never come to pass, the old have reminiscences of what never happened. It's only the middle-aged who are really conscious of their limitations.'

It hit me like a thunderbolt. It was true. I had lost all of the idealism and optimism that had driven the first 20 years of my adult life. I had stopped dreaming, fantasising about what was possible in the future.

Weirdly, I had also suddenly become very sensitive to noise, and smells, and annoyed by everything anybody did.

And I mean everything and anybody. I started agreeing with Peter Hitchens and Melanie Phillips, watched *Grumpy Old Men* for its lucid and sage commentary on contemporary life, and everything I ever read that postulated that the world was going to shit in a handcart would only confirm my views. Hoodies? National Service would sort them out. Footballers? Bunch of overpaid tossers. Terrorists? Forget that 'other people's freedom fighters' bollocks. String 'em all up.

At the same time as I was turning into a Tory, it had also become suddenly very important that younger women found me attractive, as if invisibility and undesirability to them would effectively mean I had ceased to exist.

With this new turbo-charged libido, I tried to catch their eye in pubs or on the street, and actually felt myself sucking in my stomach and puffing out my chest.

During that beat when sexual possibilities are considered, a young woman might once have returned my gaze for three seconds. Now it was down to one or less. It was the spirit of Groucho again: when once I might have attracted their attention, it wasn't that important. Now I rarely could, it was life or death. It wasn't even that I wanted to sleep with them. Honestly. I just wanted to think I might be able to.

One night I went to bed the picture of physical health. When I woke up the next morning, my hairline had receded an inch and my back and right knee had gone. In the surgery's waiting room, I flicked through the men's magazines and for the first time noticed the ads for trichology clinics. The 'before' shots, with the follically challenged model sitting alone and pensive and staring at the floor, looked like the new me. The 'after' shots looked like the old me: full-beam smile and getting jiggy with some attractive young filly. I punched the number into my mobile.

The doctor's diagnosis about my back and knee was blunt as she wrote out a prescription for diclofenac.

'This is very normal for somebody your age,' she'd said.

My age? It was the first time that anybody had linked something that was happening to me physically as age-related since my balls had dropped. Really, I had no idea. I had always paid as much attention to moaning middle-agers as I had to ads for Stannah Stairlifts or walk-in bathtubs. Surely the midlife crisis was just an excuse that men used to justify shagging the Lithuanian au pair and getting a Harley, and women to go to Harley Street for a face lift before heading off to Naxos to shag a waiter with a big moustache and a predilection for stretch marks. It was all one big joke, right?

But a quick google of 'midlife crisis' threw up an entire cyberverse of misery and advice, not to mention countless support groups whose members submitted heartbreaking posts of families ripped asunder by some truly outrageous spousal behaviour. When I say spousal, most of the posts were from women. 'He's gone mad,' they'd distil down to. 'Become a stranger overnight.'

I did a quick audit of my male friends, all of whom were roughly the same age as me. One, K.D., had recently given up his high-powered, well-paying job at a national newspaper and was heading for the States. He had no work permit, and was planning to drag his wife and family with him.

'Mike, I feel like it's my last chance to do something with my life,' he'd said when I asked him why he was doing it.

'Last chance!' I'd replied. 'You're only 40, at the top of your game.'

'I can't explain. It's like a switch has flicked, feels like time's running out.'

Another friend had recently walked away from his family and was living alone with no electricity or running water in a hut in a Welsh forest.

A few had decided to give their rugby/football careers another go after a break of a decade and were spending Saturday evenings they'd previously devoted to their families in various A&E departments.

There were affairs with younger women and ridiculous physical challenges (and often a combination of the two), and new bleach-blond hair and punishing gym routines and tight T-shirts to display the punishing gym routines. One or two of the most pitiable figures had even gone out and bought large motorcycles.

As for the others, they seemed to report the joyless, corrosive futility in their lives that I had been experiencing. Marriage and parenthood, after the initial euphoria, had often become suffocating, routinised, dull, they said. Rather than the isolation I'd been feeling post-divorce, the married people talked of suffocation.

Some of them were taking industrial quantities of cocaine or drinking like crazy men in the last-chance saloon. All reported detesting their jobs with a passion. Many were simply sitting out the storm, confident that one day it would pass.

But one thing everybody seemed to agree about was that something had changed for them, inside of them, that, like K.D., there was this intense pressure to try and become the man you'd always imagined you'd be at 40. As if once you passed that notional landmark, the opportunity for reinvention, to be somebody else, the glittering star you always thought you were, is gone for ever.

But why now? What was this pressure and where had it come from? There was nothing really wrong with my life. Nor the lives of my friends. We had nothing to complain about. But sitting down and telling ourselves that didn't seem to help.

'It's not about having what you want,' one friend told me, 'it's wanting what you've got.'

'That's very profound,' I'd said.

'Sheryl Crow,' he'd replied.

Another talked about the start of the movie *Fight Club*.

'I can really relate to that now,' he said. 'That deadness,

that numbness. That sense of trying to walk up the down escalator. When I first saw it a few years ago, I didn't understand. But I watched it again the other night. I totally get it now. Why Edward Norton would want to hang out with the dying, how it was the only way he could feel alive.'

'I'm not going to punch you.'

'I'm not asking you to.'

I carried on with my research. I became a misery magnet.

'The second half of a man's life is made up of nothing but the habits he has acquired during the first half,' wrote Fyodor Dostoevsky. And, as I don't personally know anybody as smart as old Fyodor, I think I'll give him the last word.

Actually, there's Carl Jung, who my money would be on in a pub quiz. 'Wholly unprepared, we embark on the second half of adult life ... worse still, we take this step with the false assumption that our truths and ideals will serve us hitherto,' Jung said, when the correct answer was in fact Kevin Bacon. 'But we cannot live the afternoon of life according to the programme of life's morning: for what was great in the morning will be little at evening, and what in the morning was true will at evening have become a lie.' Quite. Whatever that means.

The answer was as clear to me as the hairs sprouting out of my ears. I had lost my way. Reached the end of something, stuck in that tricky lunchtime period reflecting back on a glorious morning's studying with no idea how to find out where the afternoon's lessons were being held.

Ultimately, of course, I had an inkling that the afternoon would find me if I just sat still long enough, but what fun would that be?

No, what I needed to do was travel again. Not with the naivety of youth, when, as a young man, I was genuinely surprised to see my own reflection staring back at in the loo at JFK. Nor with the safety of a package holiday. But by exposing myself to risk and failure (and possibly a punch in the face), to set myself challenges and put myself into situations that would test me on emotional and physical levels. In short, to stop existing and stop moaning and start living again.

Obviously all that latent desire had needed was the requisite combination of Stella Artois and a bunch of witnesses.

Now I just needed to work out where I was going.

# 4 Planning

I eventually made it home to London on that sodden late April day. Exhausted from the concentration and the driving rain and the hell that is the M25 in rush hour, I pulled up outside my flat, dismounted and made to heave the gargantuan 250-kilogram beast up and over on to its centre stand.

My foot slipped off the wet metal pedal, the bike twitched momentarily towards me and then began to fall away as surely and as smoothly as a felled oak. Applying Canute's theory of natural law, and eschewing the upstart Newton, I tried to hold it but the next second there was a violent, ungodly noise of crunching metal on concrete, a wrenching of some unspecified lower vertebra and me spreadeagled prostrate on the dead bike, tangled up in the wheels and the bungee cords and holding down the handlebars for the count of three.

A passing group of young women stopped.

'Are you okay?' one of them asked, holding my gaze back for just a second, or maybe less. 'Would you like some help?'

I refused her offer with a cheery, dismissive wave and lay there for a moment or two longer until they had disappeared around the corner.

I set my departure date for 5 June. This would leave a month for planning. Well, I say planning but, in truth, this was never my strong suit. I once prepared for a Caribbean holiday by getting steaming drunk the night before, collapsing into a coma, and then randomly stuffing things into a bag as the cab for the airport tooted outside my flat. I cannot recall whether my Aran sweater, the rubber Margaret Thatcher mask or my West Bromwich Albion scarf ever made it to the beach.

On another occasion, and it would seem that drink was involved here as well, I agreed to go sailing the next day with a man I'd only just met in a Queensland bar. Never mind that I'd not sailed before in my life. Never mind that 'going sailing' involved a two-week voyage of 1,000 miles across the notorious Tasman Sea to New Zealand, with me the only crew and the skipper a certified lunatic (who, come to think about it, had just turned 40 and had recently left his wife). Never mind the fact that I didn't even want to go to New Zealand.

I digress. For some people, the planning element would be a glorious stage: all that poring over maps, flicking through guidebooks, deciding on routes, finding out about visas, reading motorcycle maintenance books. For me, and I hang my head in shame here, I couldn't be arsed.

I tried for a short while to contrive some route, some shtick, some structure to my trip. Most journeys seemed to have a hook, a raison d'être, a goal, something that the traveller could respond with when asked the inevitable question: why? Somehow the response 'because I'm a miserable old fart and bored shitless with my life' lacked the punch of 'because it's there'.

I thought about the great historic journeys, to the Poles, along the Silk Road, around the world in 80 days or across the Alps on an elephant. And I thought about the classic modern journeys, to the Poles, along the Silk Road, around the world in 80 days, and round Ireland with a fridge.

But the more I tried to create some kind of shape, a framework, the more it seemed rather apposite for a man in his early forties who may or may not be having a midlife crisis to set out on a journey uncluttered by appointments with monuments and landmarks, free of itineraries and goals. A map can be a useful tool if you know where you are. Otherwise you might as well just start walking in any direction.

Besides, I reasoned, it's no use just warming your hands on the idea of providence. Surely it can only work when we let go completely.

So finally, I had a plan, which was no plan, which seemed as good a plan as any. I would go to Calais – which to the more pedantically minded is a plan, I grant you, but so is getting out of bed in the morning and that much structure I would need, else I spend the next six months in my pyjamas in Wandsworth – and turn left and then just keep going till I ran out of land in the north.

Afterwards, I would head south and east as far as I could without needing visas, which by my reckoning was Mount Ararat on the Turkey/Iranian border, then west again until the sea, which was the Iberian peninsula, and then north and home.

A rough calculation had this journey at around 20,000 miles. I gave myself permission to stop if I fell in love, got a job, joined a cult, or got killed. But within that loose framework, I would navigate by instinct, listening to people's recommendations, being open to suggestions.

There was only one definite place I needed to go. An island in the Mediterranean where I wanted to meet up with an old friend. He was flexible on dates, though. He'd been waiting for me to come and see him for a few years now. A few more months wouldn't make much difference.

I released a wedge of equity from my apartment so money shouldn't be an issue. Soon after, I rented it out so for six months, so if I bottled it and came home early, I'd have nowhere to live, an incentive of sorts to keep going when the going got tough.

I systematically dismantled my life in London and disentangled myself from the standing orders, gym memberships and commitments that meant I belonged somewhere.

I could feel myself putting some distance between myself and my friends and family. It felt like I was severing the guy ropes that had been keeping me tethered. I was floating free. It was terrifying. Just like the point on the runway when the pilot announces V1, the speed after which aborting the take-off is impossible without crashing, I was past the point of no return.

# 5 The map

How foreboding are those cliffs? A million journeys have begun with them. I had never managed to feel elated watching them recede. They always mark beginnings, of course, and even if that start point is a week in the Dordogne, or an afternoon in the booze section of the hypermarket, it is still a letting go of the known. And if letting go of the known is always unsettling, then what I was doing was enough to want to make me curl into a foetal ball.

Standing out on the deck of the ferry's stern under a low, grey ceiling of cloud, the thought occurred to me that I might never see those cliffs again. No, that's not quite what I was thinking. The thought I had was that the next time I saw those cliffs, they would in all hope look completely different to the sad, stained, grey slabs of chalk that reared up before me then. I had invested much in the fantasy that the next time I saw them, they would be blindingly, brilliantly white in the afternoon sun.

The *Rodin* shuddered into life and slipped quietly through the gap in the harbour walls. I stood there for as long as it took for the cliffs to sink into the Channel.

I walked down the stairs to the restaurant, bought a coffee and picked up an abandoned copy of *Hello!*, I read about Kerry's latest love rat, and Victoria's newest eating regime, and attended the wedding of Lord somebody to a soap star who'd been in *Hollyoaks* but was now in *The Bill*, and visited a safari lodge that was so mind-blowingly amazing that even Michael and Catherine had been there, their patronage being so key to its mind-blowing amazingness that it was the fourth paragraph before any animals made an appearance. It had fab hot-stone massages, though.

I would love to be able to say that I didn't know who any of these people were. But I had somehow become on first-name terms with them all; knew more about their trials and tribulations than those of some members of my family. I don't know how this happens. Imagine the world if we osmotically absorbed really useful information.

The proliferation of those mags represent so much that I'd grown to dislike about the change in British life over the past decade or so. (I forgot to add this to my collection of middle-aged beefs earlier.) But it's a perverse thing that when faced with change, the known, even if you're trying to escape it, becomes charming, endearing, important. A part of me felt like I was going to miss Kerry and Victoria and the triumphs and travails of being a modern toff.

Somebody had obviously moved Calais a lot nearer to Dover, because whereas the journey used to take around 90 minutes, that day it seemed more like 90 seconds. For no sooner had I started reading about Tara's victory over her cocaine addiction, than the spectacularly ugly Apollo Five clocktower that tops of the equally ugly Flemish-Renaissance-style town hall of Calais was being framed in the restaurant window. I tucked *Hello!* into my jacket and made my way to the car deck.

This was it, then. The big push. As the *Rodin* throbbed and bumped against the quayside, I tried to undo the straps that had been fixed across the saddle by the loading crew. Seeing me struggling, one of the crew came over to help.

'Where are you off to?' he asked me as he effortlessly flicked open the catch and the bike was unleashed. I told him.

'I had a mate who did the same thing,' he replied.

'Oh yeah?' I said.

Before he had the chance to tell me the gruesome details, I fired up the ignition, put on my helmet and rode off down the ramp.

I tried to turn left at Calais as per my provisional plan. But unless there is more than one vast, ugly Flemish-Renaissance-style town hall in Calais, which you would have to doubt, then I was failing.

Riding along, I looked studiously again at the map in the cellophane pocket of my tankbag. I looked less studiously at the red traffic light a few yards ahead of me.

With a whoosh of air and an ungodly squeal, a truck driver slammed his foot on the brakes, swerved, and missed me by a margin that micrometers were invented to measure. His enthusiastic curses – whether they were in French, Spanish, Polish, or some other European tongue, I could not state with any certainty – tailed off behind me along with the stench of burned rubber. I spotted a Flemish-Renaissance-style town hall away to my left and, up ahead, a road sign for Dunkirk.

After telling me about dead motorbikers, the second response of people on hearing about my trip was always to ask where I was planning to stay on my first night on the road – assuming I still had a head by then.

It was vital, apparently, to have a specific place to head to on that first difficult evening; maybe a nice room in a chateau, or a friendly gîte recommended by someone whose judgement you valued, all to assuage the fear and loneliness and doubt that will envelop you and make you wish that you had been decapitated. Everybody knew this bit of obvious travel advice. It came just after 'Thou Shalt Talk Loudly To Foreigners' and before 'Drinketh Not The Tap Water' in the 10 Travelling Commandments.

I hadn't, of course, and as I picked up the road to Dunkirk, I could imagine my friends telling future nascent bikers about their mate Mike who was wiped out in Calais by a truck and, get this, he didn't even have anywhere booked for the first night!

What providence had lined up for me that evening was a salemen's motel just off a roundabout on the outskirts of Dunkirk. The man at the front desk prodded the registration form at me across the counter with the tip of his pen and rolled his eyes as I asked such unnecessary and tiresome questions such as whether breakfast was included in the price and, if so, from what time. I also enquired as to whether my bike would be safe in the car park.

'*Peut-être*,' he replied.

I asked him if the restaurant was still open. With my poor French, I must have mistakenly asked him if he had any photographs of his wife naked, because he said '*Non!*' with such undisguised contempt before disappearing through a door that I almost started to cry.

Looking out of the window at the dark industrial estate beyond and calculating that the nearest open food outlet – what with it being 9.30 p.m. and this being France – was probably in Kent, I took up a place on a stool at the bar, ordered a beer and started to make my way through a large bowl of peanuts.

The young man sitting on the bar stool next to me had neither beer nor peanuts. Nor much of a civil tongue, judging by the way he started shouting at the bartender.

'Just give me a fucking beer, arsehole,' he yelled. He was from Valencia, which I didn't know at that precise moment, but I did a few seconds later when he turned to me and slurring, sotto voce, told me as much, as if this would explain everything. I made a wild guess that this hadn't been the first time he'd been refused a beer that evening.

The bartender disappeared and the Spanish guy, after reaching over and helping himself to one of my cigarettes, asked me to buy him a beer. He winked, tried to touch his nose and missed.

'You are English. I love the English. You know how to drink. Not like these arseholes,' he said, pointing out of the window to the whole of France. 'We must stick together.'

Sensing that forming my first alliance on the road with this man could only lead to tears and possible eviction from the motel, if not the country, I succumbed to the irresistible lure of the Delights of Dunkirk leaflets in the revolving bar-top stand and busied myself learning fascinating facts about the local miniature villages, cheese emporia and llama farms.

The bartender returned with the man from the front desk who, clearly more interested in drunken Spaniards than sober English motorcyclists, was soon trumping 'fucking arsehole' with 'fucking prick', until it rapidly degenerated into a Derek and Clive sketch. Why a Spaniard and a Frenchman in Normandy would choose to abuse each other in English was never explained.

After ten minutes, the electric doors of the lobby swished open and revealed a six-man wall of gendarmes in full riot gear, batons drawn. After a few more exchanged pleasantries, the police charged the Spaniard, who went down fighting like a dervish. In the melee that followed, first the Delights of Dunkirk display, then my beer, then me, ended up on the floor as the gendarmes finally subdued their man, who only had time to glance at me with a betrayed look in his eyes before being dragged off towards the doors. They swished open, and then swished closed behind them. From out in the car park, I could hear the odd muffled 'don't touch me, arsehole' and the occasional dull thump.

I picked up my bowl of peanuts, mercifully intact, to finish in my room, where I would find out how Tara had been getting on battling her drug demons and then, afterwards, open my *Lonely Planet* and research places to stay tomorrow night.

My eyes were closed and I was in bed in my flat in London. My eyes were open and I was no longer in London, but where

I was exactly remained unclear. Then I remembered. I felt sick. The first full day on the road and all I had to do was decide which road it should be. If choice creates anxiety, I was crippled by an entire world of options.

I went to the bathroom and looked in the mirror. I saw myself and for a second I felt disappointment, annoyance even. I'd done it again.

I showered, then methodically loaded my two aluminium panniers, my tankbag and holdall. The only thing that was left over was the frying pan, its awkward shape and long handle making it almost impossible to fit anywhere. Perhaps if I'd bought one of those camping pans with detachable handles it would have been easier but, with typical foresight, I'd just picked this out of my pan drawer at home.

I didn't even know why I'd brought it along. I hadn't packed a camping stove. Back home, I'd had visions of me sitting in a wadi somewhere with random Bedouin tribesmen, cooking up a full English over hot coals while regaling them with my amusing stories of daring and courage.

Who was I kidding? I put the pan in the desk drawer, next to the Gideon Bible which, if nothing else, might give the next guests something to think about.

I made my bed. Then I unmade it, just a little bit. Because that was not my job any more. Then I turned on the TV and watched a programme about squid. Then I took another shower. Then I counted all the matches in the complimentary box on the desk. By now it was 11 a.m. The latest check-out time. I knew this because it was the one piece of information the guy at the front desk had offered freely, even giving me a hint of a smile.

I had to go. I picked up my stuff and walked slowly down the corridor and out to the car park. Standing by my motor-bike were three shaven-headed middle-aged men. Besides the three shaven-headed middle-aged men were three Lambrettas. The Lambrettas were missing side panels, the odd saddle, running boards and other bits deemed necessary by the designers at Lambretta but apparently considered surplus to requirements by the three men.

'All right?' one of the shaven-headed men said.

They were from Lancashire, I discovered, and heading home after two weeks on the roads of Europe together, an event they've undertaken annually since their teenage years. Every year, they told me, it got harder to justify to their partners and their kids, and they got no end of grief for it.

'Used to be five of us,' said one of them. 'This year two guys had to pull out. One couldn't get the time off work. The other's missus has run off and he's in a bad way. Us three will never stop, though.'

He scanned the others for affirmation. I noticed one had turned away to fiddle with something on his scooter.

The other two looked over my bike, but I could tell they were not particularly impressed by the gleaming, monstrous slab of Bavarian engineering with its comfy saddle and all its bits from the factory still attached.

'Where are you heading?' asked one.

I told him.

'What, you've got absolutely no idea? That's mental.'

My chest puffed up and I felt a tad heroic when I replied, yes, that's right, I would go where the road took me. I was completely free and in search of adventure, hard liquor and loose women. Two of the guys, standing now with arms crossed, regarded me wistfully. The other one was still looking at his scooter.

The act was hard to sustain, so my chest depuffed as I confessed to only having just passed my test and feeling very nervous, and admitted also that I did have a rough plan of action, but that it was very flexible, though hard liquor and loose women would hopefully play a part. Arms uncrossed.

One of the guys went off to his scooter and returned with

a length of frayed and oil-stained blue rope, which he said might come in handy if I ever needed a tow.

'But I have BMW Roadside Assistance,' I didn't say, because Peter Fonda wouldn't have and, anyway, it would ruin this little scene. I accepted the rope somewhat ceremoniously, with a little bow, as if I'd just been made a Freeman of Dunkirk.

I suspected that the tow-rope thing was a little rite for the novice, because who ever heard of getting a tow on a motorcycle? And that here was the equivalent of the apprentice being sent out for a tub of elbow grease, or a new bubble for the spirit level. So I gave them an ambivalent smile, which I hoped might be interpreted as either knowing or unknowing.

'You married?' the rope guy asked me. I hesitated for a second, trying to decide how much of myself I wanted to share. I then told them I was just divorced, and as I said the words I was aware that a hint of sadness had flashed across my eyes.

We stood around for a few seconds in silence. Then the second guy went off to his Lambretta, fished around in his holdall for a while and returned.

'I won't be needing this at home,' he said, holding out something in his hands. 'Any use to you?'

I looked down. It was a lumpy, misshapen frying pan, somewhat bigger than the one I'd just dumped. I also noticed that, like mine, it did not have a detachable handle.

I was on the verge of explaining what had just happened, and we could all have had a good laugh about it. But there was something in his eyes; something that seemed to be imploring me to take the gift, as if this act of faith would find ample reward somewhere along the road.

'This must be fate,' I said to him. 'In my room, I was just cursing the fact I'd left mine behind.'

'Lucky for you,' he said.

'Yeah, dead lucky.'

There were follow-up questions, about whether I had kids, and what had happened to my marriage, which I wanted to stonewall, but found myself talking about frankly with these three strangers from Lancashire.

The third guy went over to his Lambretta and returned with a heavily creased and poorly folded map. He handed it to me with solemnity.

'We were given this by a biker from Newcastle who was heading home just after we got off the ferry,' he said. 'It's given us some great times. Maybe you should have it now.'

I looked down at the map. It covered northern Europe and Scandinavia. On it were drawn a load of crosses, some in black ink and some in blue, places where the guys had stayed or found adventure, perhaps? Or maybe where the Geordie had buried some treasure. I accepted the gift with another little bow.

The nearest cross to Dunkirk was some 200 miles to the east, from where, presumably, the three men had latterly come. Had providence sprinkled her pixie dust? I lashed the knackered old rope to my panniers and stuffed the battered frying pan down my jacket. I was off to Amsterdam.

# 6 Reds

I arrived in the Dutch capital under a late afternoon sky the colour of a nicotine-stained ceiling. It was my first time in Amsterdam, but it was one of those places I'd seen so often and heard so much about that it all felt and looked very familiar. I rode through Dam Square and along the bank of one of Centrum's canals.

Fat rain started to fall. I parked the bike and took shelter under a canal-side café's pavement tent. On the table next to mine, a group of vermilion-faced Scouse lads were hoovering mountainous portions of apple pie topped with whipped cream.

'This has got to be the best fugging city in the world, eh,' said one, whose name, according to his shirt, was Gerrard. The giggling started. Soon they were laughing so hard that one, whose name was Riise, actually fell off his chair. I thought that only happened in cartoons.

With no waiter forthcoming, I walked out of the tent and into the café on the opposite side of the road. The myriad stairways leading off in every direction were wallpapered with black and white geometric patterns. I took some steps leading down into a Stygian room, the air a sweet, thick fug of smoke. Hoping I was addressing a member of staff and not a coat-stand, I ordered a coffee. 'Anything to smoke?' said a voice through the pea-souper.

'No thanks, man. I'm cool,' I replied.

There was a muffled laugh from somewhere.

I drank a coffee, and then another. Feeling restored, and somewhat relaxed, I stumbled around in the dark for a while, trying to find the stairs which, once I was on them, I knew logically to be going up, because I was moving towards the light in the street, but which felt strangely like they were going down, because I had the sensation of being about to fall forwards.

I could just about make out the geometric patterns on the walls. It felt like I was in an Escher painting. This struck me as being just about the funniest thing that had ever happened in the world.

It was so funny that when I got back to the tent, I told Gerrard about it. He thought it was very funny too, and he laid it off to Riise, who fell off his chair again.

'I don't suppose any of you need a frying pan, do you?' I asked, pulling it out of my jacket.

Poor Riise. He looked like his head was about to explode.

After a while I left the tent and started walking down the street, breathing the air deeply into my lungs. I turned right into a narrow alleyway, on either side of which were doors like on a prison corridor. But instead of metal, the doors were of glass, and framed within each one was a stunning woman, all naked breasts and Day-Glo thongs, the colours burning bright through the gloom like neon paint in a ghost train.

I walked along the row and tried to meet their smiles. But all I felt was deeply ashamed and self-conscious. None of this seemed funny any more.

For some reason, I remembered my dad smacking my 13-year-old head very hard after I had wolf-whistled at a girl out of the car window, with dire threats of worse to come if he ever caught me doing something similar again.

Women, he had said, were not there to be leered at or sexually objectivised by the likes of me. Well, in his defence, it was the seventies. For the prosecution, it was just before he started a string of affairs and walked away from my mum and his kids. I'm not sure I took anything he had to say on the subject of women too seriously after that.

What I would have loved that day in Amsterdam was to have met those girls' smiles, lighten up. Where would the harm be? Wasn't this precisely the kind of thing a fortysomething man on a motorcycle adventure was supposed to do?

Everybody else seemed to be getting it, including Gerrard, whom I noticed negotiating with one of the girls and, shortly afterwards, stepping across the threshold.

I turned around at the end of the alleyway and walked back along it. I forced myself to look right into the girls' eyes, examine their bodies as if I were at the National Gallery, ask how much. But all I saw, above the pink thongs and the pneumatic breasts and the million-dollar smiles, were lifeless eyes and dreams that began in Latvia or Nigeria or Ukraine, and ended up here, on a filthy wet afternoon, standing in their pants getting leered at.

I returned to my bike and left Amsterdam. Slipping on the wet tramtracks and dodging the cyclists, I took the first main road I could find. After about 30 minutes, I pulled over for a cigarette and dug out the Lambretta boys' map.

Amsterdam hadn't exactly been a hoot, but at least I had seen a man laugh so much that he'd fallen off a chair. You can't put a price on that. Thirty miles to the south was a cross marked on Utrecht.

Gerontologists in Utrecht would be fighting over the sparse resources. With Holland's greatest concentration of students, entering the city was like encountering the world's biggest critical mass cycling action. They all seemed in a fearful hurry, as if Godzilla had decided to take his annual holiday in the North Sea and had been spotted coming this way for an ice cream.

The bikes clattered over the cobbles, often with pillions sitting sidesaddle on luggage racks, chatting away on their mobile phones, whizzing along.

Businessmen in smart suits were on two wheels, too. But weirdly, all the bikes were totally, uniformly, rubbish; old sit-up-and-beg numbers that most people in Britain wouldn't be seen dead riding. Perhaps a moratorium on flash had been included in the famous treaty. Who knows? But it was something I'd noticed about the cars and houses in Holland, too: they all seemed, well, quite modest. I don't think I'd seen a palatial dwelling or expensive sports car since crossing the border. It seemed in stark contrast to modern Britain.

With families promenading along the canals, bristling with shops and bars, and shiny young students training for the Tour de Randstad, Utrecht seemed a peach of a little city, basking in the early evening sun. But the thing I liked best about Utrecht was that it wasn't Amsterdam.

I found a sign for a B&B in one of the old townhouses that lined the canal, and pulled the chain. A bell echoed from within down what sounded like a very big cave. I stood on the pavement for five minutes and was about to leave when I heard a window opening above my head. I looked up, and there was Barbara Cartland saying, 'Hello, hello. I'll be down in a minute.' I'd found the only old person in town.

The minute turned into two, then five, then ten until, eventually, the front door creaked open and Andreas introduced herself, a vision in painted-on eyelashes and a lilac teepee that by rights belonged in a German opera.

'I'm sorry I took so long. I had a hip operation recently, but it went bad and now I walk like a duck,' she said. She invited me to enter, then walked ahead like a duck.

She showed me to my room. Instead of a wardrobe, there was a vast metal contraption that looked like a walk-in safe. Dotted around the room were plastic Greek urns full of silk gerberas and miniature statues of Eros and David. On the laminate wood walls hung swathes of fabric and a teddy bear wearing a Santa hat. It was like a cross between the Palace of Versailles and Poundstretchers. Andreas said farewell and turned to go back to her room. I figured she'd make it just in time to sort out breakfast.

The next morning, I climbed the stairs to the first-floor dining room. There was only one place set, so I concluded that I was the only guest. I'm quick like that. Beyond the sealed French windows there was an immaculate garden full of topiarised pheasants, manicured shrubs and florid perennials, riotous in the morning sunshine.

Inside the room, it was all dust-covered silk flowers in chintz vases sitting atop plastic Doric columns. It was as if nature belonged outside and only facsimiles within. The closed windows baffled all sound from the world. An oversized clock on the wall showing the movements of the sun and the moon ticked loudly. It was the only noise.

Andreas waddled in. This morning she was wearing a rather splendid purple kaftan and a red plastic rose in her white nest of hair. As well as the starburst eyes and aubergine lips, the rest of her make-up was immaculate, and must have added at least an inch to the circumference of her head.

She looked gorgeous and if I were not a gentleman, and somebody was holding a gun against my temple, I would have guessed her age to be somewhere between 60 and 132.

With a flourish, she put my breakfast on the table in front of me. It consisted of two fried quails' eggs on tiny slivers of toast, with a side garnish of caviar. She returned with a champagne flute full of lemon mousse with a chocolate flake sticking out of the top.

As this was my first ever breakfast in Holland, I wasn't in a position to tell whether this was in any way typical fare. Something told me that it probably wasn't.

Andreas sat down opposite me and watched as I popped the first egg into my mouth. 'Good?' she asked.

'Very good,' I said.

I put a teaspoon of caviar on the second, popped it into my mouth and swallowed.

'Good?' Andreas asked.

'Very good,' I replied.

There was a period of silence. Apart from the clock.

I asked her how long she had been running the guest-house.

'For 50 years,' she said. She explained how she'd been born and brought up in Amsterdam, but left the city to follow her dreams of training as a beautician in Switzerland.

'As I was leaving, I told everybody there what I really thought of them. Then the clinic in Switzerland cancelled my place. But I still had to leave Amsterdam, because I burned my bridges. So I came here.'

She told me that she'd lived in the house with her husband for a long time, but that he'd died 25 years ago.

'I'm sorry,' I said.

'I wasn't. He was a bastard,' she replied. 'A drunken, violent bastard.'

'Oh,' I said, and scooped a piece of lemon mousse into my mouth with the chocolate flake.

Andreas said she'd lived alone ever since.

'Even though I have been here 50 years, they still treat me as an outsider,' she said. 'But it is nothing more than a village. I am better off without them. Without a man. Without anybody.'

More silence. More ticking.

'Thank you,' I said, after eating the last of my mousse.

'You're welcome,' she replied.

I returned to my room and turned on the tear-dropped chandelier, better to see the map I'd spread out on the velour purple bedspread, embossed with golden fleur-de-lys. There were crosses on Cocksdorp and Assen in Holland, and Wankum in Germany, which suggested to me that here was an itinerary devised not entirely uninfluenced by the spirit of the third form.

But I couldn't visit every cross. There were dozens of them. I knew that the Lambretta boys had been travelling for a fortnight, but what about the Geordie? He might have been on the road for months, years. What if he was a travelling salesman? How was I ever going to get to Mount Ararat and back if six months down the line I was still pootling around towns with comedy names in North Rhine-Westphalia?

I looked beyond Holland and Germany and saw that there was a cross on Copenhagen, some 350 miles away. That suited me. I had once been madly in love with a girl who lived in Copenhagen. Four weeks previously, in fact.

I started packing. I laid out all my stuff on the bed. I had a decision to make. I couldn't ride for the next six months with a frying pan stuffed down my jacket. But, clutching somewhat at straws, I was still convinced that it might have mystic properties, that there would at some stage be a cosmic confluence and everything would become clear why I needed it.

So something else had to be jettisoned. I packed the frying pan into my panniers and carried all my gear out to the bike. As I strapped the last bungee cord over the holdall, Andreas appeared outside to say farewell.

'Thanks for everything,' I said to her. 'I'm leaving this behind. Any use to you?'

I held out my CamelBak.

'What is it?'

'It's a rucksack containing a bladder. You fill it with water which you drink through this tube. It's really good if you go jogging or hiking.'

'Thank you,' Andreas said, slipping the CamelBak over one shoulder.

I fired up the bike and made to slip out into the Tour de

Randstad. I turned back to say goodbye to Andreas for the final time.

'I hope you find what you are looking for,' she said.

'Thank you,' I replied.

It was a bit of an odd thing for her to say, as I hadn't told her I was looking for anything.

# 7 Margaret

I rode to the north of Holland, across the vast man-made Afsluitdijk, a dyke built on top of millions of tons of boulder clay, sand and basalt rock. The 20-mile-long dual carriageway felt like it was floating on the North Sea, with nothing but water on either side as far as the eye could see.

A biker heading towards me waved. Back in the UK, bikers don't tend to wave much. I'd noticed that many of them appeared to have cramp, though, as they always seemed to be stretching their right leg when passing.

I hadn't thought too much about it until hitting foreign roads, where every single biker coming in the opposite direction waved. Well, when I say waved, what they actually did was thrust out their left hand in a kind of half-cocked salute, as if Mussolini was poised to pat a small boy on the head. It was like a giant fraternity of biking fascists on the continent. Perhaps British bikers were just too miserable, or cool, or right-on, to do anything so demeaning as say hello.

A biker overtook me. He seemed to have cramp in his right leg, too. His number plate was German, so the British theory was shot. Then the euro dropped. On a bike, if you remove your right hand from the throttle, your drop of speed is almost as rapid as if you were braking. Thus bikers in Britain, and bikers overtaking abroad, have to resort to kung-fu kicks while our continental cousins, and bikers overtaking in Britain, are free to wave like Il Duce with a yo-yo. Still awake?

Unwilling to embrace the fascist salute, I had started off by waving back like the Queen. But realised, after nearly having my arm ripped out of its socket, why bikers keep their palms flat. Every day was a school day on a motorcycle.

There had been a cross on Groningen in eastern Holland, so as I was passing anyway, and low on fuel, I pulled off the motorway and meandered through the city's streets for a while, keeping my eyes open for ciphers and, failing to find any, petrol pumps.

I filled up the bike and pulled away. The engine noise seemed louder than usual, but I got lost trying to find my way out of Groningen and forgot to be worried.

As I headed east, I thought about Margaret. I had met her while I was on an assignment in Yemen earlier that year, a Danish journalist working in Sana'a during the cartoon crisis when all around her were burning the Danish flag and re-decorating the external walls of various infidel embassies with Danish dairy products. What a gal!

I was utterly convinced I was falling in love with her, all Scandinavian loveliness and big Danish eyes of perpetual surprise. She was gorgeous, certainly, but there was some-thing else about her, a familiarity, an affinity, as if I somehow already knew her. We flirted and danced around each other and everything was easy.

I had only spent one evening with her in Sana'a, but after-wards I'd lain in bed awake all night, staring up at the hotel room ceiling with a huge grin on my face.

But then Margaret came to stay with me in London on her way back to Copenhagen and there was nothing there at all. We were two strangers, listening to different tunes. She'd gone home after a week and I'd been confused. It had been the first time I'd felt so strongly about anybody since my marriage broke up.

Had I simply become like an abandoned newly hatched chick, so desperate for love that I'd cling on to the first thing

I latched on to? Maybe it was me that was weird in London, my home city. Perhaps if I went to Copenhagen, things would be different.

I crossed the border into Germany and on to the autobahn. Everything went into fast-forward. I glanced in my mirror to see an empty fast lane, indicated and did my life-saver check, only for a Merc or a Porsche to come whooshing past, doing the kind of speed that should really be reserved for salt flats.

There were only two ways to deal with this: pull into the slow lane and leave the Teutonic lunatics to their business; or get with the programme. Soon, I was pushing 120 mph and any twitching of my neck to look in my mirrors resulted in my head rotating like a barn owl's.

I recalled when I was first learning to ride a motorbike, all those days ago, and feeling when I first went over 50 mph that my body was going to be sucked inside out. And here I was, doing nearly two and a half times that speed, weaving in and out of the traffic, all my senses acute, the world all blurry.

But the bike was still noisy. Then another euro dropped. Just before I left home, a nice chap from a company called Green Leopard had visited my flat and poured silicon into my ears. I believe that there are places frequented by judges and Tory MPs where that kind of thing is quite normal, but in this instance I was just procuring a set of custom-made earplugs, a vital piece of kit, according to Kevin Sanders, to prevent me from going deaf and/or mad from the constant wind and engine noise. Those earplugs, a rather natty zebra stripe, were no longer wedged into my lugholes, but sitting atop a petrol pump in Groningen.

But it was too far to go back. I would just have to face the prospect of going deaf and/or mad. And the Groningen garage would have to figure out how a pair of waxy, zebra-stripped silicon blobs fitted into the grand scheme of things.

As I arrived in Copenhagen, there seemed to be some kind of beauty pageant on bicycles going on. I parked the bike, grabbed a chair at a streetside café and watched. Wave after wave of strapping Aryan women pedalled past, every one of whom would make Helena Christensen look like the ugly mate.

But this was no beauty pageant. This was just Copenhagen. All the women seem to chain-smoke, drink endless bottles of beer and look like supermodels. How wonderful, wonderful was that? Carlsberg don't do cities. But if they did, they would look like Copenhagen.

The waiter leaned forward and asked me something.

'Huh?' I said. I had a terrible ringing in my ears.

He pointed at the empty coffee cup and then made a little sipping motion from an imaginary cup.

'Oh, no thanks,' I replied. 'I've got to go.'

I'd called Margaret that morning to ask whether it would be okay to come and stay for a few days.

'When?' she'd asked.

'Tonight,' I'd said.

I'd told her that I had a map and that Copenhagen had a cross on it and, seeing as I was in the neighbourhood, it seemed like a good idea to come and say hello.

'Are you in town now?' she'd asked.

'No. Utrecht,' I'd replied.

'Utrecht in Holland?'

Margaret looked as beautiful as before. If anything, more so. Those eyes were on fire. In my mind, I imagined I looked quite the heroic figure pulling up on my motorcycle. I leaped off to embrace her. This felt like the proper script again, after the strangeness of London. I pulled off my panniers and followed her up the stairs to her apartment. There was only one bedroom, so Margaret pointed towards the sofa. I unpacked my stuff.

'What's with the frying pan?' she asked.

'Don't suppose you've been looking for one, have you?' I said.

'I have a pan,' she said.

I told her about the Lambretta boys and the map and how it was possibly fate that brought me to see her. She laughed and touched my arm.

She made tea and we sat and talked, about Sana'a and London and the documentary she'd just got funding for to make about Somali warlords, and music festivals she'd been to since she'd returned to Copenhagen. Margaret was into music in a big way. Margaret was unbelievably cool. She was like the goddess in the sixth form, and me the prepubescent oily tic. She would always go for the guy with the Capri.

'How's the love life?' I asked her.

'I met a guy, but we broke up last week,' she said.

'Sorry to hear that,' I lied.

Margaret went off to her bedroom and returned with a photograph.

'Remember that guy in New York I've been dating on and off for years that I told you about?' she said. 'Well, this is him.'

She presented the picture to me. It showed Margaret and this guy with their arms wrapped around each other. The guy was considerably older than Margaret. And he was famous, really famous. A rock-and-roll megastar. I recognised him immediately, but had no idea who he was. I don't know much about music. If it had been Tara or Kerry or Posh, I might have stood a chance. But this guy didn't share his life with *Hello!*. He was far too cool.

If there was ever a chance for the magic of Sana'a to be rekindled, I believed that to have been the moment when it was finally extinguished. If I could have reeled off a list of my favourite songs or unplugged underground gigs I'd been to in smoky basement bars in Berlin, or Rio, I think I might have at least remained a possibility in Margaret's eyes.

But I just stared at the photograph for too long without saying anything. Finally, I just spluttered something about how I really should know this guy's name.

'Not necessarily,' she said.

We went out for a curry that night, just the two of us. The Indian waiter came over to take our order and spoke in Danish to Margaret. I told him how impressive his Danish was, but he didn't speak English, so he asked Margaret to translate. The waiter said something back to her.

'What did he say?' I asked.

'He said, "We are in Denmark",' Margaret replied.

After, Margaret and I went out with some of her friends to trawl Copenhagen's achingly trendy bars. I was by now exhausted, frazzled by the day's ride up from Utrecht, my face lumpy and lobster red from windburn. Margaret and her friends weren't that much younger than me, but I felt ancient hanging out with these delicious, shiny, energetic people.

We ended up in the Ideal Bar at 3 a.m., a place pumping out techno and hip hop. My £7 beer grew warm in my hand and my ears felt like they were bleeding. At that moment I would have gladly paid FedEx whatever it was they charged to pick up in Groningen and deliver to Copenhagen.

There was a guy on the other side of the dance floor, making the odd, coy glance in Margaret's direction. I was standing next to her and sensed that she'd picked up on him and was holding his glances.

He was gyrating away, perfect rhythm, gradually sashaying, in small increments, towards where we were standing. He was wearing a white linen shirt, unbuttoned all the way, and underneath he had on a white vest. He looked like a Calvin Klein model, a Capri-driving one at that, and there was something that had been put in motion here that I could not stop as he sidled his way towards us with his peacock feathers unfurled and Margaret pointing her feet in his direction. Then they were together, smiling and bending and synchronising, sniffing each other and wagging their tails.

The guy's friend came over, too, and started talking to me. I believe that this is what is called a wingman, to distract the other guy and do some reconnaissance work to ascertain whether it is all likely to kick off.

And while Margaret was now practically shagging Calvin Klein on the dance floor, the friend, no doubt having passed on the thumbs-up signal, was telling me all about his great passion for dog-fighting.

'Yes, the pitbull is the best,' he was saying. 'If you train it right.'

'I don't know anything about dog-fighting,' I said.

'It is really great,' he replied.

I walked over to Margaret on the dance floor and told her I was shattered and wanted to go back to the apartment.

She fished in her handbag and handed me her only set of keys and said she would text me when she was outside, then I could let her in. I slept through until morning, undisturbed, with the phone next to my ear.

By noon next day there was still no sign of Margaret and her phone was switched off. I wanted to cut short my stay and leave Copenhagen soon. But as I had Margaret's only set of keys, I was stuck. Recalling the scene of them on the dance floor, it might be days before she showed up again.

I left the apartment and went for a walk. Through the Tivoli Gardens, and then past the Sankt Jørgens and Peblinge lakes in the park that runs like a crescent across the north of the city, and then across the Langbro bridge spanning the Inderhaven.

I headed along one of the main shopping streets, where I found a shop that sold industrial protection clothing and a fine selection of earplugs.

Then to the harbourside, and along the waterfront, past the

Gefion Fountain and on to the Little Mermaid, where young Japanese couples waited to have their pictures taken with the statue, queuing as politely as pensioners waiting for a bus.

I found a pavement café and ordered a coffee. Around me, tourists talked in a bewildering variety of tongues. Being a language dolt, I always project huge intellectual powers on to people who can converse in German or Danish, even if they are German or Danish.

I imagine they are discussing whether Camus or Sartre is the true granddaddy of the existentialist movement, or catching up on the latest news from the Cern nuclear test facility in Switzerland.

'I understand they have two linear accelerators generating low-energy particles for injection into the Proton Synchrotron,' said the German sitting with his friend at the table to my left, probably.

'Indeed, that is what I have heard,' said his friend, grabbing a handful of peanuts. 'One of the linear accelerators is for protons and the other for heavy ions. These are known as Linac2 and Linac3 respectively.'

'Fascinating. Fascinating. Another beer, Helmut?'

'No, I think we should go. There is that lecture in the hotel on the reference sequence of the euchromatic human genome this evening, and I wouldn't want to miss the start.'

The Germans left and, shortly after, their table was taken by two middle-aged couples.

'Those leylandii are out of control, George,' said one of the women, in a Brummie accent. 'I know he's your friend, but you're going to have to have a word.'

I imagined the Japanese at the next table were impressed. I finished my coffee and wandered off again.

By 5 p.m. there was still no word from Margaret and her phone was still going to the answering machine. I walked into a pub off Vestergrade and asked the woman behind the bar if I could use the toilet.

'Awright. English are ya?' said a voice to my left, like Liam Gallagher on helium. And Stella. 'I'm from Manchester,' he said, which was not strictly necessary. 'Me name's Dave.'

Dave was on a cruise ship, he explained, stopping overnight in Copenhagen. He was travelling alone and, I would have guessed, in his mid-fifties. He ordered two beers and gave one to me.

He was wearing a white T-shirt, white shorts and white trainers, all topped off with a white floppy hat that sat on white hair. Every item of clothing apart from the trainers carried a St George's cross. This might partly have explained why he was travelling alone.

Every woman who walked past him in the bar got the same greeting: 'Awright, gorgeous, 'ow are ya? Fancy a beer?' And every woman who walked past him in the bar kept on walking. 'Copenhagen's a shithole,' he said to me, taking a long slug of his beer. 'Give me Manchester any day.'

Another tanned, beautiful Amazon walked past. 'Awright, love, 'ow are ya? Wanna join us?'

'I need a slash,' he said to me, after a while. 'If you pull two birds before I get back, don't leave me with t'ugly one, yer bastard.' And with that he slipped off his stool, let fly with a resounding, performance belch and walked towards the toilets doing a one-man conga. From the little of it I'd seen, Dave's life was like one long shame-busting exercise.

A friend of mine had tried some shame-busting himself not too long ago, as part of a confidence-building course that he'd taken, aged 42, after his marriage had fallen apart and his business had followed suit.

One of the exercises meant that he had to stand up on a crowded bus and announce loudly the name of the place it was approaching and the various attractions any disembarkers could find there. If he could affect a silly voice, the better. The idea being that people can stare at you, disapprove of you. But so what? The world will still turn. Nothing really bad will happen. True happiness was connected to letting go of what people thought of you. Crack this, the course leader had said, and the world would be yours.

He had just about managed to stand up and shout 'Oxford Circus, alight here for Liberty's' in his best Joe Pasquale voice before, seeing how startled everybody looked, he'd apologised, stammered that he was not mad but doing an exercise, tripped over a briefcase on the way to the exit and fell on top of an old lady. The old lady had looked shaken, the man whose briefcase he had dented and kicked along the bus was furious, while the rest of the passengers tutted and shook their heads and searched for their flaming torches. He had managed to achieve the hitherto impossible: he had galvanised a London bus into a collective.

The world had stopped turning. Something very bad had happened. That was what he, and, vicariously, me, had learned about shame: it was to be avoided at all costs.

Dave congaed back from the toilet, stopping off to show his Moonwalk to a young couple. We sat there for a while, drinking our beer. I asked him about the other people on the cruise and he reckoned they were all a bit stuck-up.

'Miserable sods,' he said.

'You always this happy?' I asked him.

'Too fucking, right,' he said. 'Don't give a toss, me. What's the point?'

My phone went. It was Margaret. She was waiting outside the apartment. Where was I?

I told Dave that I had to go, that the woman I was staying with needed me to go back to the flat.

'You goin' to shag her, then?' Dave said.

I told him that it was unlikely.

I walked back across Copenhagen, back through Tivoli

Gardens and past the railway station. A woman walked towards me, pushing a pram. She was a typical Dane: tall, athletic, and so unimaginably, beautifully perfect that I felt even sharing a pavement with her was some kind of genetic code violation.

I looked at her as she approached and, just at the time when I would usually have dropped my head and stared at the floor, I kept my eyes fixed firmly on her.

About five yards in front of me, she looked up and straight into my eyes.

'Hello,' I said.

'Hello,' she said back. And, eyes still locked, we both smiled and dipped our chins slightly as we crossed.

I waited for the husband to emerge from somewhere to lamp me, or the gene police to cart me off, but nothing happened. I walked off like Tony Manero.

Margaret was waiting for me on the street by the apartment block's front door. I handed her the keys and followed her up the stairs. Once inside the flat, she rushed around, putting up the ironing board and rummaging through a pile of clothes on the armchair. She asked me what I'd been up to that day, and I told her about the walk and the waterfront and the fact that I'd been to the Little Mermaid.

'Well, you have to, don't you?' I said, and she popped her head around the door from the kitchen and said: 'What? Oh, uh huh.'

Her mobile rang and she answered it, and she spoke in Danish, so I couldn't understand what she was saying, but she started laughing and playing with her hair, before disappearing with the phone into her bedroom.

After half an hour, she re-emerged from her room in a short black dress, holding two pairs of shoes.

'Which ones?' she asked. I pointed to the pair in her left hand. They were black, with three-inch heels. They would be the ones I'd want her to be wearing if she were meeting me in that dress.

'What are you up to this evening?' she asked.

'I've heard Sweden's nice,' I replied.

# 8 Dirk

I rode across the 10-mile-long Oresund bridge/tunnel that links Denmark with Sweden, and then up the east coast, passing little fishing communities, dipping inland every so often to snake through villages of half-timbered thatched-roofed cottages with flower-filled gardens.

I was heading for the next cross, marked about 150 miles away up the coast. The cross didn't appear to be near a town, or even a village, but just scrawled on a section of road as it swept around a small bay.

I was still convinced that following the map was a good idea. It was, after all, my only idea. But my faith that it contained within it the secrets of the universe had been sorely tested. But is that not the nature of faith?

I arrived at what I thought must be the bay. There didn't appear to be anything there but a small grocery store. I parked the bike, walked towards the door and pushed. And pushed. It was stuck fast, so shaking the handle aggressively I pushed and rattled away with considerable force for a few seconds, even kicking the bottom of the door with my boot. Then I pulled. Doors in Scandinavia always open outwards.

Having been alerted to the possibility that somebody was trying to smash her door down, the shop's owner was standing halfway between the till and the door, poised in a highly sprung fight-or-flight stance. Given that she was about

90, I didn't think either action would have been particularly productive.

I walked towards her, like a bow-legged desperado from the day's riding, still wearing my helmet with its darkened visor. For some reason, the old woman still looked terrified. She didn't noticeably relax when I whipped off my helmet to reveal my face covered to the nose in a bandana and started garbling to her in some unfathomable language. As well as being somewhat timorous, she clearly didn't understand English.

I pointed to myself, then I put my palms together and laid them on my cheek. Then I pointed to the jars of pickled fish on the shelves against the wall. I was hoping she would understand that I was looking for somewhere to sleep for the night beyond the wall against which the jars of pickled fish resided. If she concluded that I wanted to sleep with her pickled fish, then I really do believe she might have expired on the spot.

Finally smiling, she made a little upside-down V-shape with her fingertips and prodded towards the wall beyond the jars of pickled fish.

The campsite was stuffed to the gunwales. Every pitch seemed to be taken. The first stratum of campers were in mobile homes and caravans, spread under acres of pine canopy. Within this town on wheels there was some kind of battle of the awnings going on, because as I rode along the track that twisted through them, the awnings just got bigger and more elaborate: from simple lean-tos to great tented structures with arched doorways and fake mullioned windows that would have had Bedouin tribesmen having their photographs taken in front of them.

Surrounding the awnings were little white picket fences and inside were plastic Greek urns full of silk gardenias and busy Lizzies, and Persian rugs and floorlamps in the shape of Roman gods. There were swathes of fabric draped from the ceilings, sofas and even oil paintings on the walls. Ikea once ran an ad campaign exhorting Brits to throw out the chintz. Now I knew why. The Swedes wanted it all to take camping.

Beyond the mobile homes was the area for tents. I had seen tented villages on this scale before, but only on TV news footage of Darfur. I eyed up the one or two spare spaces I could see and tried to visualise whether my tent would squeeze into them.

This might have been an effective planning tool if I had ever actually seen my tent erected. I had purchased it in London a couple of days before departure and brought it along on the trip in much the same spirit as the original frying pan.

In my mind I was the kind of guy that just pulled off the road and camped in the desert, under the stars, a dusky Romany woman under one arm, guitar under the other, strumming some mournful ballad to her as the crackling fire warmed the full English. In my body I was the guy with the dodgy back and right knee, who'd succumbed at the first sight of a Travelodge and the lure of a comfy bed.

Pre-departure, my camping friends had also offered their own sub-genre of Travelling Commandments. The first of these was 'Thou Must Always Putteth Up Thine Tent In Thine Own Garden Before Thou Leaveth', followed by 'Thou Must Always Haveth Thine Tent Up Before It Is Dark'. I probably do not need to point out that, by now, what with all of Sweden having decided to camp in the same field, the sun was rapidly melting into the Baltic.

But lo, a miracle. There, right by the shoreline, under the shade of a pine tree, was an empty pitch. It was just perfect and I laughed to myself how the Swedes, such expert campers, could have missed this.

A small crowd gathered to watch the masterclass in camping incompetence that followed, as poles pinged into my chin and then were inserted though the loops meant for pegs, and the groundsheet somehow wound up on top of the tent, and the fabric was stretched to its limit so that trying to do up the door was akin to zipping Dawn French into a size 6. The Swedes smiled benevolently, as you might do watching a baby trying to feed itself.

The tent was up in a fraction under the hour and the crowds largely went back to their tented car-boot sales.

It now being completely dark, I clambered inside to try and find my headtorch among the jumble and kitchenware that I'd thrown through the flap and which now lay all over the ground.

I groped around for the torch, but found only sharp pine needles sticking through the groundsheet, and the occasional pinecone, whose spiteful form didn't need to be inside the tent to send me flailing and cursing. Outside, I could hear barely suppressed giggling.

I eventually found the headtorch. This was a mixed blessing, because while I was now able to see the fakir's bed sticking through the plastic and the outline of the cones, I could also see the squadrons of mosquitoes perched on the ceiling, who must have abandoned their business at the adjacent shoreline to fly through the unzipped mosquito net of my tent to check out what all the cursing and moaning was about.

So enormous were they that for a second or two I thought they might be some kind of bird. But that theory lasted only as long as it took the first hive to rise on my forearm like a soufflé.

I scrambled out of the tent, leaving the flap open in the hope that my visitors might see themselves out at some stage. I walked over to the camp restaurant. It was full of families, who sat patiently for their food in the little booths. Most of the children would have been been in their mid-teens, I guessed.

Some of the boys wore heavy metal T-shirts and the girls short skirts, eyeing each other up with nascent longing. It made me a little sad to think that this might be their first family holiday that they felt was a chore.

The kitchen was open to the restaurant. I went up to the counter and asked the chef what was good. He recommended the meatballs, which was what I'd hoped he'd say. I asked him where his accent was from, because he sounded like his tongue was too big for his mouth. This opinion I kept to myself, though, having not yet received my food.

'I'm from here, but just returned from working in Cork for 18 months,' he said. He turned to shout at his kitchen workers in Swedish, but when it came to the mandatory chef-swearing sequence, the swear words were in English. We may no longer have an empire, but it's reassuring to think that when the world wants to utter foul oaths, our language has no peers.

I finished the meatballs and went to the bar next door. Along with beer, it sold ice cream and sweets and plastic buckets and spades and other toys for the beach.

Also at the bar were two men in their thirties. After a minute or so, one of them thrust out a hand and said: 'I'm Dirk.' The other one reached over. 'Dennis,' he said.

They explained that they were from the far north of the country, but were currently working seven days a week on a contract at the water treatment plant across the bay.

'Today we dry suck,' Dennis told me. 'Tomorrow we clean the sewers.'

There was nowhere else to go for a beer around here, Dirk said, so they came to this bar.

'But we have not been here for a month,' Dennis added. 'Last time Dirk got a little bit too drunk and … well, the owners banned him. But now everything is cool again.'

Dennis seemed quite reserved. Dirk, a V-shaped slab of a man with a beard like a German porn star, was not. As young girls came up to the counter to buy ice creams or liquorice whirls, he'd look them up and down.

'She is nice, no?' he said to me of one, who looked around 14, and he stared at her and winked, and she held his stare back for a beat longer than she might have done the year before.

'Lovely,' said Dirk, still staring at the girl. 'Just lovely. It's Friday night. We should get some vodka shots down us, no?'

It was 6 a.m. I was lying in my tent. I moved my hand gingerly to stroke my head, which felt like it had been marinated in battery acid and then tenderised with a meat hammer. There was something stuck to my head. It was a chef's hat. There was a low snore. I rolled my head to the right. It was Dennis. He was also wearing a chef's hat. I lifted my head very slightly. Of Dirk there was no sign.

I started the film. There were the vodkas. Then a few more vodkas. Then the tequila. Then there was Dirk, talking to a young girl. Then there was the young girl's father talking to Dirk. Some shouting. Some more vodkas. There was the children's playground. Dirk was on the slide shaped like a dinosaur, with a large vodka bottle in his hand. There was the swimming pool, into which Dirk was urinating. There was the kicking down of a door, and there was a window being smashed. There was the camp security guard shining his torch. And the camp security guard's dog, straining at the leash. There was some running, and a beach, and some swigging of vodka from the bottle. There was the sound of the empty vodka bottle smashing on the rocks. Of the chefs' hats, there was no sign. Of the frames I could remember, I was in every one.

Oh, yes. There was one more thing. Somewhere between the vodkas and the tequilas, there was Dirk telling me about the funniest coincidence, that the last time they'd been in the bar, they'd also met an English biker.

'He was a cool guy,' Dirk had said. 'Funny accent. Could hardly understand a word he said. Oh man, we got so fucked up.'

Two things were very clear to me at that moment. Firstly, I had to pack up and get away from the campsite as quickly as possible. And, secondly, the map had to go.

# 9 Eva

I got back on the coast road heading north. Shortly after, a biker overtook me. On the back of his jacket was embossed: 'If you can read this, my bitch has fallen off.' Then another passed, and another. I looked in my mirrors. All I could see was a great snake of beards.

They turned off into a ferry terminal and, owing to my hangover and my new map-free life, I followed them.

'Where are you guys going?' I asked the nearest Hagar the Horrible.

'We are going to Gotland,' he grunted, cigarillo gripped between his teeth, 'for Scandinavia's biggest biker festival. We get very messed up, ya. You should come.'

Gotland. It sounded Gothic and sinister, like an island shrouded in mist where a princess, guarded by a dragon, lay imprisoned.

I weighed up my options. Arguing most firmly against going to Gotland was the fact that I would have to share it with Hell's Angels from all over Scandinavia. Now, I didn't have anything against Hell's Angels per se. What consenting adults got up to with live chickens was no business of mine. But unless I could somehow hook up with the Quaker chapter, I doubted my liver in its current condition would survive the week.

Arguing most persuasively for going to Gotland was the fact that it was a rock in the middle of the Baltic, some three hours' sailing time away, with only one boat a day. An apoplectic campsite manager, a furious father, two angry chefs and possibly a lovelorn Dennis would surely never think to look for me there. I went to the ticket office.

I sat out on deck. Next to me was a young gap-toothed Julia Roberts lookalike. She was smiling at me. I returned her smile and offered her a cigarette. Sure, she said, why not? Soon she was playing with her hair and touching my leg and laughing at my stories.

Eva was 20, and started telling me a little bit about her life in small-town Sweden.

'I look after old people,' she said.

That's handy, I thought.

She asked me what I was doing. I explained. It was the abridged version. I left out the midlife crisis and divorce bits.

'Don't you ever get lonely?' she asked, with the full, burning compassion of youth.

'Sometimes,' I said.

She picked up my notebook and wrote: Jag er ensam, behaga bli min vän.

'It means I am lonely, please be my friend,' she said, and then smiled sweetly and dipped her head slightly so that she was looking at me from under her fringe.

She went off to the bar and returned with coffee and chocolate for us both. It felt wrong to be flirting with someone so young. But maybe like gambling and salvage laws, being at sea had a separate set of rules. I fought the urge to think about it too much. For the next three hours we sat on the otherwise deserted windswept deck, laughing and joking.

Eventually Gotland floated into view

'Tonight, you sleep with me,' Eva said, taking my hand. I was really beginning to love Sweden.

'Mike, this is Peter, my boyfriend,' Eva was now saying to me, indicating the young man apparently waiting for her on the quayside. This was an unexpected twist. He spoke no English, but chewed a lot of tobacco. He didn't look too happy that Eva had a new friend. He disappointment was nothing compared to mine.

His gorgeous young girlfriend kissed him adoringly. He looked uninterested, sullen. I wanted to shake him, tell him that it wouldn't always be like this.

Peter and Eva jumped on his motorbike and I followed them to the festival, Eva occasionally looking around from the pillion and beaming at me. We paid our entrance fee and made our way through the festival site. Eva smiled her sweet smile again as she pointed out the pitch next to theirs.

'See, you sleep with me, like I say,' she said.

I started to feel ashamed about the thoughts I'd had back on the ferry, and turned away to start unloading my bike. But as I dropped my sunglasses on the floor and straightened after picking them up, I looked across and Eva was still staring right at me.

Tent erected (25 minutes), I walked up a nearby slope. From there, there was a view over the entire campsite.

All I could see for miles was canvas and motorbikes, each bike stationed outside its tent like a guard dog. There must have been a few thousand bikers milling around, stopping to admire the machines and draw on the bottles they produced from their pockets.

Nearly all the bikers were men, mostly corpulent and middle-aged, wearing leather caps and waistcoats, studded wristbands and extraordinary configurations of facial hair. It was like a huge open-air gay bar where everybody had let themselves go a bit – although that was an observation I kept to myself. The air was suffuse with beery breath and the fug of farts.

I took a biker-packed bus with Eva and Peter to a clearing in the forest on the outskirts of town. There the bikers stood around in their various gangs – the Goblins, the Bitches –

looking menacingly at each other, consuming vodka from two-litre bottles like it was Evian. The tension mounted. I spotted an empty bullet casing on the floor by my feet and wondered what kind of violence was about to unfold. Two of the gangs put down their drinks and started to walk, slowly, inexorably, towards each other.

Then, at a given signal, they all lay on their backs and started leg-wrestling.

'This is *rovkrok*,' Eva told me. 'It translates into English as "ass-hook".'

The Goblins' champion had an unusual warm-up technique which involved simultaneously vomiting and urinating up a tree. But it seemed to work for him as he retained his crown and, for his labours, won a bottle of vodka, which was probably the last thing he needed.

Other games followed, including one whose name I didn't catch, which saw two men standing 20 metres apart, each with a rope tied to one ankle, the other end of which resided in the hand of their opponent. This game of great skill and strategy usually lasted for as long as it took the two men to tug on their rope and both fall over.

Finally, there was the blue-ribbon event: the tossing of the caber. This got the beefcake bikers lining up in droves awaiting their turn to be crowned the biggest tosser. Some managed to get the caber upright. Some even managed to propel it forwards. But the majority just bent over, grabbed the end of the tree trunk, farted loudly and put their backs out.

As night fell, we caught the bus back. It was full in the Calcutta sense of the word. Peter and Eva minimised the space they were taking up by locking lips and trying to climb inside each other. Two guys on the seat nearest to me squeezed up and offered me the edge.

The driver, a dead ringer for Jason King, sped around the island's biggest roundabout a dozen times, literally on two wheels, as Swedish rock music blasted out of the bus's stereo.

'This is a very old tradition at the festival,' the guy sitting next to me said. The bikers seemed to love it, this andropausal centrifuge, even the ones throwing up on the floor and those stuck to the windows. Peter and Eva didn't seem to notice.

The bus pulled back into the camp and everybody peeled themselves off it and staggered down the steps.

'What are you up to now?' said the guy I'd been sitting next to.

'I'm not sure.'

'We're off to the party in the main bar. Want to come?'

Time slipped past. It was now 4 a.m. I was on a table dancing, wearing a full-length frock coat the blue and yellow colour of the Swedish flag. I was also wearing a Viking helmet with blond plaits attached. I was singing along to a Swedish folk song, which in reality meant just swaying and saying the words hurdy gurdy. I had a bucket of beer in one hand. The other arm was around the shoulder of Anders, the man from the bus, and my new beshtest mate in the whole wide world.

Originally from Bergen in Norway, he now lived in Stockholm. He was leaving Gotland in three days' time to return home. And so was I. Well, as Anders was my new beshtest mate in the whole wide world, it would be inconceivable for me not to be going with him. Whether Anders had actually invited me or not was uncertain.

Eva walked over. There was no sign of Peter. He'd gone off with his mates earlier to find some dope and she hadn't seen him since, she told me. He was an arsehole. She was tired. Would I walk her home?

We walked across the battlefield, arms linked, not talking, in the half-light. The grass was littered with empty cans and vodka bottles. We stepped carefully over the prostrate bikers, snoring like elephant seals, sleeping where they fell, many wearing Viking helmets.

'Maybe they're dreaming of Valhalla,' I said to Eva.

Just before our tents, Eva slipped her arm from mine and took my hand, now leading slightly. I was confused, partly through the numbness of alcohol, but also because I could still feel the burning shame of earlier, of being so wrong.

We arrived at the tents. Eva turned, and leaned forwards to kiss me gently on the cheek. Then she stood there, waiting, smiling.

The confusion cleared. I didn't want this.

'Eva?' a voice came from inside her tent.

She turned to look at the tent, then returned her eyes to me. She smiled again, this time almost apologetically, shrugged her shoulders and, slowly, released my hand. Then she was gone.

We could have. It was enough. No, it was perfect.

I crawled inside my tent. It never really got dark, or cold, on Gotland at that time of year. It was like trying to sleep inside a 40-watt light bulb. In the distance, the singing and shouting and engine-revving finally started to fade and I entered the world of half-sleep. But then a new, closer, sound rose as Eva started groaning, softly.

# 10 Stockholm

I had been standing in the breakfast queue at my Stockholm hotel for 10 minutes. I was due to be meeting Anders outside the front in half an hour's time. We were planning to ride our motorbikes out through the Stockholm archipelago, a collection of 24,000 islands linked by bridges and ferries where the well-heeled Stockholmites sail their boats or retreat to their red-roofed summer cottages perched on rocky islets.

Anders had said it would be a while before we had lunch, and advised me to have a good breakfast. I had arrived in the grand ballroom where breakfast was served in what I considered plenty of time to have said breakfast. But 10 minutes after arriving, I was still in the shuffling filter lane of the queue waiting to enter the main buffet breakfast arena.

The hotel was a mahogany and brass relic of a bygone age. I had justified the cost of a bit of luxury after four days in a tent had done nothing for my back, and the time spent with the bikers had had wholly predictable consequences for my liver. I might not have had any alcohol for 24 hours, but I was still hung-over.

A pianist in the corner played 'Moon River'. Huge exotic plants filled the room, their fat and furry tongues looking like mine felt. Above, a glass atrium and beyond the blue Stockholm sky. Still the queue was moving forwards with all the speed of a tortoise, on lithium, on his way to the dentist.

I tutted and muttered away to myself out loud. I sounded like a voiceover artist on *Points of View*.

I filled my time as productively as I could by looking down my nose at my fellow queuees. Why, oh why, I wondered, do all modern middle-class, middle-aged international travellers these days have to wear the same outfit, consisting of beige nylon cargo pants, multi-pocketed waistcoat and floppy brimmed hat of the kind previously only ever seen on Magnum war photographers? I believe that a company called Rohan is responsible for this stay-pressed, unstainable, pack-downable beige revolution, if anybody wants to write to Terry Wogan.

The queue inched forwards. We eventually entered the main breakfast arena. I now had a plate in my hand. But the buffet nightmare was far from over. At the head of the buffet, about 10 people ahead of me, I could see an elderly couple, faces still smudged and eyes still flat from sleep, staring blankly at the smoked-fish selection, trying to decide between herring in mustard or salmon in mustard or just mustard in mustard. It was like one of those motorway traffic jams, where it only takes a few people to touch their brakes in Swindon and you've got gridlock stretching back to Bristol.

The couple deliberated for a couple of minutes, pointing and prodding at the fish in mustard, before finally eschewing them completely and moving on to the pickled fish. There the whole thing started again. Then it was the 16 different types of eggs, then the cold cuts and cooked meats, thereafter the EU bread mountain and the 12 types of juice and the 23 varieties of cereal and the 31 types of fruit from all corners of the globe. I know how many choices there were. I had time to count them.

We are not cut out for this when we've just woken up. We are overwhelmed by having to make an infinite series of decisions when maybe just 20 minutes earlier we'd been running away from unspecified menace, or standing in front of our school assembly naked, or, in my case, speeding on a train through a tunnel with a 20-year-old Swedish girl called Eva. And I don't want to get all Stalinist about it, but don't give people Vast Bloody Choices at the Breakfast Buffet. It. Melts. Our. Brains.

And there's a grand style of hotel, of which this was one, that always has a joke section at the end of the table. There you will find the vodka in an ice bucket, and huge mounds of trifle and gateaux, and caviar and truffles, and profiteroles and custard. And there we stand, paralysed again, trying to work out whether the revulsion we feel at the presence of such things at a breakfast table is because we are plebs.

So we load up a side plate with swan, or perhaps larks' tongues, because it is there and is, of course, free, and it wouldn't be there if there wasn't a demand for it from a certain type of person, one almost certainly classier than you. But as you finish your single croissant, eat your egg, drain your orange juice and walk out of the breakfast room, you notice that the joke food has been simply transferred from the buffet table to side plates on the dining tables and left there, untouched, by people now fully awake and heading off on their walking tour of Gamla Stan, or perhaps to capture the moment a napalmed orphan runs through the courtyard of the royal palace.

I felt a nudge in the back. 'Move forwards, please, we are waiting.' It was a nice, silver-haired old lady, pointing out the fact that the queue for the breakfast buffet had all but disappeared.

Anders had been waiting for me on his bike for about 15 minutes. I apologised for being late, and we headed off out of Stockholm. It was a spectacular June day, and the sun streamed through the tall pine trees like shafts through a Venetian blind and bounced off the cobalt lagoons as we made our way towards Vaxholm on the inner islands.

I had liked Anders the minute I'd met him on that busload

of bikers in Gotland. He was with two friends, Joachim and Eric, and the three of them, blond and handsome and clean-cut, looked like a boy band who'd found themselves wrongly booked at a ZZ Top gig.

But there was something special about Anders, something in his eyes that seemed to convey gentleness and compassion. We'd spent a lot of time together on Gotland, riding around the island, going, with Joachim and Eric, whom at 25 and 30 were ten and five years younger than Anders, to the bars and nightclubs of Visby, the capital town. While Joachim and Eric danced and chatted up girls, me and Anders sat in a corner, talking. He'd been very curious about my trip, and I'd told him the reasons for taking it. The unabridged version.

We arrived at Vaxholm and found a waterfront café. With a large glass of Chablis in my hand, and looking around at the Swedes at leisure, promenading in the sunshine, it was possible to imagine this life for myself. Anders and I talked about the ride out and the beautiful women strolling past and about that evening's World Cup football game between England and Sweden. There was a pause.

'I've been thinking about what you were saying back in Gotland,' Anders said. 'About you feeling a bit lost as you hit middle age.'

'Sorry about that. It was the whisky talking.'

'No, no. It was interesting. I'm not old, only 35, but recently I have been feeling a bit like that. It's as if all the things that used to excite me don't any more.'

'Like what?'

'Work, my future, women, you name it. I used to think that all I wanted was to get married, have kids and carry on with my job. But now I'm not sure.'

'What's changed?'

'Sometimes I feel that maybe it's because I don't have a wife or children. I think that if I did, maybe I wouldn't have all this time to be thinking about my life.'

'Do you think that would help?'

'It might. I get home from work and as soon as I close the door, all I've got to think about is me, about where my life is going, about all the things I was going to have done by now but haven't. It's exhausting. At least if there were kids to feed and talk to and a partner to sit and have a glass of wine with, then I wouldn't have time to be so hard on myself.'

'Some of my married friends with kids in London are feeling the same way about themselves. Maybe it's the modern disease. We all seem to be looking for a big life now, think that happiness is some kind of given. That if we're not fulfilled we must be doing something wrong.'

'But wanting to be happy is normal.'

'Of course.'

'What's wrong with looking for it?'

'Nothing.'

'This is a fantastic place to live, I have friends, earn good money, I'm healthy. I'm not unhappy. Just not as happy as I was.'

'There's a line in a Hanif Kureishi novel,' I said, 'where the lead character is having a bit of a midlife meltdown. "It feels like I'm sucking stones," he says. "Things and places that I used to go to and look at for sustenance, I still go there. But there's nothing. I have to find new things. Everything here is arid and dead."'

'I am not having a midlife meltdown.'

'I'm not saying you are. I can only talk about my own experiences of getting stuck, grimly hanging on to some game plan I'd devised for myself way back. Even when it became obvious that the game plan wasn't working out, I kept using it, kept trying to suck at dry stones.'

'You think we should give up everything we've ever aimed for? Accept what's going on? If I'm unhappy at work, I can do something about it. If I'm unhappy with a girlfriend, I dump her. If I want a holiday, I jump on a plane. I am in control. I know what I don't want.'

'That's great.'

'You don't believe me?'

'Maybe we should change the subject.'

'Why?'

'Because I'm not sure what I'm talking about.'

We both picked up our glasses simultaneously and took a sip.

'Ever think you'll have kids?' Anders asked me.

'I don't know,' I said. 'All I ever wanted when I was younger was to have kids at a "normal" age. I couldn't imagine me living my life not having experienced that. That was my game plan. After I got divorced, I went through a phase of being angry when I saw parents pushing a pram down the street. Or angry at other people's functional familes, or angry at others' happiness. I felt like I'd been cheated.'

'There's still time.'

'Oh sure. But that's not really the point any more. That anger is fading. I guess that's what I was trying to say. This isn't what I would have chosen, to be 42 and childless and divorced and going nowhere at work. But it is what it is. I can make choices. But it seems those choices come down to two things: accept where I am, with all my limitations and flaws, or fight it. For a long time I thought that acceptance was the same as giving up, lying down and letting life give you a kicking. But maybe the opposite is true.'

'Still sounds you're giving up,' Anders said.

'Maybe I am.'

The waiter came over and asked if we'd like another glass of wine. Sure, why not, we said.

We sat quietly for a while.

'So when did it all start for you?' he asked.

'What?'

'The dissatisfaction.'

I told him that I thought it was after my marriage had broken down. There was all the agony of that, of course, but there'd also been something else, something that I was still trying to work out.

'It was as if I'd spent my life believing that the contract I'd made with the universe – that if I did the right things and worked hard and behaved properly – then the universe would protect me. But then came a loss of ...'

'A loss of what?'

'Well, it sounds lame, but it felt like I'd lost an innocence, and that the future would be lived grieving for that loss. How about you?'

'What?'

'Well, you said that you were struggling with things a bit.'

'Oh, no problems really. Not when I think about it. Work's okay. Life's okay. My dad's been sick. I've been flying back to Bergen to see him.'

'How is he?'

'Not sure. The doctors keep running tests. It's something to do with his heart. But he'll be fine. He's a strong man.'

# 11 Rain

'Charming', 'picturesque', 'one of Norway's most beautiful cities', the opening paragraph of my Scandinavian Europe guidebook had read, as I reclined on my hotel bed in Stockholm.

'Where it rains for at least 275 days of the year,' said the second, which I had finally got around to reading shivering over breakfast in a Bergen café, staring out into the kind of downpour that has animals lining up in pairs.

Charming and picturesque it might have been, but from the inside of this cloud it was impossible to say.

After a few more glasses of wine on that sunny day in Stockholm, Anders had waxed lyrical about his home town with the kind of misty-eyed zeal only ever witnessed in those that don't actually choose to live in their home towns any more. I am much the same way when talking about Birmingham.

As I'd headed west across Sweden and into Norway, the fact that I had entered a different country was signified by only two things. One, the road signs changed from blue to yellow. Two, I hit a line of traffic that would make your average funeral cortege look like the *Cannonball Run*. The speed limit is 5 mph in Norway, or something like that and, being good law-abiding citizens, nobody breaks it. I sat in line for a while, but riding a motorbike in slow-moving traffic is like going down a red run using the snowplough. I slipped the bike into second, accelerated up to 30 mph and started over-taking. Drivers looked at me in horror as I passed.

After Vang, as much an onomatopoeia as a town, the road became seriously, mind-blowingly scenic. First, through the forests of the Jotunheimen National Park. Then the mountains started to rise around me; initially, low-level folded ridges of black granite with patches of snow that looked like hunkered-down Friesians; then perfect saw-tooth cartoon mountains with steep, plunging lower slopes carpeted with spruce and topped with white bonnets. They were the kind of mountains a child would draw.

Then the tunnels started. On the road to Bergen there were 45 in all, drilled through the mountains. The first one went sharply uphill and then corkscrewed, like a Disney ride, shooting me out high above a fjord with waterfalls tumbling down the massive bluffs and minuscule white cruise ships humbled below. Then, plunging back into another, over 15 miles long, this time the road falling away from me steeply down into a diesel fug, like a descent into hell.

I took in the clutch and (look away Kevin Sanders) let myself roll, bottling it when the speedo glowed 60 mph and I was still accelerating. After an eternity in the gloom, I was fired back blinking into the bright light again and flying, leaning sharply into the bends, buttocks clenched, the tyres slipping slightly. Inside my helmet I was screaming at the top of my lungs. For this was the landscape I had imagined when I first dreamed of hitting the road: majestic and vast, wild and remote.

And whether it was because I'd got a few thousand miles under my belt or something else, I didn't know, but for the first time it was difficult to feel where the bike ended and I began.

I suppose that when I finally arrived in Bergen, I must have had the look in my eyes of an evangelist. As I pulled up outside a hotel on the Vågen waterfront in the Bryggen quarter, with its long, medieval timber buildings, I removed my helmet and just stood there for a while, reliving the epic road.

A woman approached me, as people tend to when your eyes are on fire. American, gorgeous, she asked what I was doing in Bergen. I told her about the trip, that it was supposed to be the ultimate, midlife fantasy, just giving up everything, freedom, hitting the road. And for the first time since leaving home, they were not just words: it was what I felt.

There was a flicker of something in her eyes. Not sadness exactly, but something close, a recognition, and she looked over my bike and moved nearer and asked me more questions.

But then a man was by her side, and she introduced me to her husband and then relayed to him what I was doing. He just replied, 'Cool, man' in a detached way, a way that told me he wasn't happy with me talking to his wife.

'Come on, honey, we gotta go,' he said. And with that, he put his arm around her waist in an extravagant and proprietorial sweep. She smiled, held up her hand and scrunched her fingers like a clam closing. Then they walked away.

The heavens opened and I felt the flames in my eyes being slowly extinguished.

After finishing reading the guidebook's Bergen chapter and my coffee, I took the funicular railway to the top of Mount Fløyen. At the viewing platform, shadows flitted through a mist blown about in swirling eddies by the biting wind off the North Sea. I bought a postcard of the magnificent vista – the city's seven hills and seven fjords – and held it out at arm's length to try and imagine the dramatic landscape. I could barely see the postcard.

Two tall men walked past, smoking fags. They had haircuts and beards the like of which I'd not seen since *Match of the Day* circa 1975 and were wearing florid jute tunics of red and burgundy. Through the fog somewhere I could hear grunting and the clash of steel. I followed the sound and, in a clearing in the mist, found more florid tunics topped by mullets, leaping and pirouetting and banging swords half-heartedly in a display of Viking battle skills that looked like it drew more from *West Side Story* than Woden. After a while, all but one mullet would be laying inert in the hay on the ground and the half a dozen cagoules gathered around would clap. Then the corpses would rise and the whole prancy, shouty thing would start again.

I walked back down Mount Fløyen and returned to my hotel.

I asked the guy on the front desk if it always rained this heavily in Bergen. 'This is not rain,' he replied. 'It is air density.'

We chatted for a while. His name was Henrik. 'Is that your BMW in the garage?' he asked.

He asked what I was doing in Bergen and I went through the spiel and told him about the column I was writing in the *Observer*.

'What is there to do in Bergen when it's raining?' I asked him. Though I could have saved myself the last three words of the sentence.

'Well, there's always the leprosy museum.'

'I'm not that desperate,' I replied.

'A severely affected lepromatus patient can be the carrier of several kilograms of bacteria,' my guide at the leprosy museum was telling me about an hour later. 'In the nineteenth century, Bergen was the European capital of this disease.'

Behind her, housed in cases, were lancets used for blood-letting and saws for amputations. On the walls were diseased feet and death masks so swollen and disfigured as to make John Merrick look like he'd suffered nothing more than a few gnat bites.

The tour took just over an hour. I was the only one on it.

On my way out, I looked at the visitors' book.

'Very moving,' Elizabeth from Cape Town had written.

'Italy 3, Ghana 0,' Massimo from Milan had predicted for that evening's World Cup game, suggesting he had been rather less moved.

'Don't forget this,' the guide called after me. It was the information booklet about leprosy that was included in the admission price.

'Thank you,' I said.

I returned to the quayside. The rain was even heavier now. There was a market of stalls sheltering under tarpaulins selling sweaters of the chunky type once made fashionable by Starsky and Hutch.

Then there were stalls selling burgers. Hval seemed to be a popular meat, and the accompanying picture of a smiley creature with a big water spout coming out of its head meant that I had learned another Norwegian word.

'Whale meat again, huh?' I said to the burger vendor, who was wearing a natty Eddie Shoestring number. But his blank stare back told me that he clearly didn't speak English. Or prat.

There were cod burgers with cheese, gourmet fish burgers with fennel, Mexican fish burgers with chilli, curried fish burgers, haddock burgers, pollock burgers and somewhere, probably, for all I knew, coelacanth burgers.

TV detectives assigned the case of the missing North Sea fish stocks would do well to make Bergen their first stop. Having wrapped up the mystery in double-quick time, they'd have plenty of time to stock up on knitwear.

I took the last place on a low wall under an awning, conger eel burger in hand. I opened the box, then opened my mouth. My mouth remained open as a series of drips turned into a steady flow of rainwater from the hole in the awning directly above my head, finding my conger eel burger and turning it into gloop. I put the box down at my feet and started reading the museum guide.

My mobile rang. It was Henrik.

'Hope you don't mind, but I got your number from the hotel's registration form,' he said.

'No, I don't mind. Is there a problem?'

'No, no problem. I was just wondering if you were busy tonight.'

Erm, let me see. There was the leprosy by candlelight exhibition that I quite fancied. And there was a whaling retrospective at the town hall that had been getting great reviews.

'No, not at all,' I replied.

'Well, me and my mates are holding our Whisky Club party this evening. I went online and read your article in the *Observer*. I think we might all have a lot in common. You're very welcome to come.'

There were about 20 guys at the house in the Bergen suburbs. Most had just turned 40 and had known each other since school. Four times a year they took turns to host their friends. The host was responsible for cooking up a gourmet feast, supplying fine wines and, of course, the eponymous whiskies.

As the food was dispatched and the drinks flowed, the guys started to bombard me with questions. Most of them seemed wide-eyed with my adventure and my reasons for doing it, and I felt like some apostleagram who'd jumped out of a cake. But I noticed that one or two, including Henrik, were becoming more distant from me as the evening wore on, as if I might have some dreadful disease.

They began tell their stories. There were the divorces and the failed businesses and the health scares and the desire to do something different before it was too late, and all the usual midlife-crisis suspects, all relayed with great humour and self-deprecation. If occasionally someone strayed into deeper emotional territory, they were quickly hauled back, amid much back-slapping and tousling of hair. Or, in some cases, bald pates.

'Do you play poker?' asked Karl.

'Of course,' I replied, really quite drunk by then, when the honest answer would have been 'no, I've never played in my life'.

But for a bad biker dude to admit that he'd never played poker would have been unthinkable, like never having had a threesome or not being in the mile-high club, or having had trials for a professional football club; all things that I believe most men haven't done, but that guy rules dictate that we pretend we have.

So Karl dealt the cards and I did my best Lee Van Cleef impersonation, scrutinising my opponents' expressions, and scanning my cards, and very soon I had lost all my money.

Via a cashpoint, a few of us moved on to a Bergen night-club. I went to the bar and ordered a round. I then asked the barmaid if she'd mind waiting while I went back to the cashpoint and, depending on whether or not my card would permit me to withdraw the equivalent of the GDP of China, possibly also to the corner shop with a balaclava, a large sack and a gun. Bar prices in Norway could easily take their place alongside the Great Pyramid of Giza and the Colossus of Rhodes as one of the wonders of the world. Every non-Norwegian complains. It is how you can tell who's foreign.

I returned with the drinks and handed them out. Henrik knocked back his straight double Scotch in one. We stood around talking, but Henrik was still keeping his distance. A few of the guys went off to dance or to the toilet, leaving me and Henrik alone.

He came up and threw his arms around me, then started stroking my face. 'I hope you enjoy your time in the light,' he said. 'I am very happy for you.' Though something in his eyes said that he wasn't.

Time passed. Henrik's eyes grew more glazed. The hugging and stroking resumed, this time with more intensity, until it became pulling and pushing, hovering on the threshold of violence.

'You know fucking nothing about my life, about anything,' he spat, jabbing his finger in my chest.

'What?'

'Well, you stand there all fucking smug and important, like you're some big fucking man.'

'I didn't ...'

'Fuck you. Everybody gets older. What's the problem?'

He launched into, what has to be said, a piss-poor impression of me.

'Oh, poor little me. My wife left. I don't like my job. I don't know what to do with my life.'

Two of the other guys had returned from the dance floor. They started laughing at Henrik's impersonation. Maybe it wasn't so piss poor.

'I've met people like you,' he said, moving so close that, had we been so inclined, we could have rubbed noses. 'They make me sick. You make me sick.'

'Why? What did I say?'

'I thought you a really cool guy, taking a road trip, but you're pathetic.'

Two bouncers arrived. They asked Henrik to calm down.

'Fuck you,' he said. 'Fuck everything.'

And that was the last I saw of the Whisky Club, as Henrik and his mates were escorted out of the door and on to the rain-lashed streets beyond.

I was alone, but not for long, because two young women who'd been standing close by came over.

'What was that about?' said the blonde.

'Probably just the drink,' I said.

'Men are such arseholes,' the blonde said.

She told me her name was Elizabeth.

'You live here?' I asked.

'She goes out with a footballer,' said the brunette, who introduced herself as Maria.

'I'm Bergen's Posh Spice,' Elizabeth said, laughing like a machine gun and then throwing her head back like a snapped dandelion. She had a tan that was not, in all probability, gained under a Bergen sky.

I bought some drinks. The girls asked what I was doing in Bergen. I told them I was just riding around on my bike for a while.

We finished our drinks. Maria and Elizabeth said that they wanted to see my motorcycle. But when we reached the hotel, the prospect of going to the garage suddenly seemed less appealing to the girls than the prospect of going up to my room.

I had seen this type of film, I was thinking, but surely my character would have a six-pack, a ridiculous moustache and a curly perm. I was suddenly nervous, but also excited about the prospect of having one less thing to lie to other guys about.

This laughably optimistic prognosis was dashed as soon as we walked into my room and the girls made straight for the minibar. I realised that they were not there for 'Mike Does Bergen', nor the scintillating lecture about touring on a motorbike.

A bottle of Hooch in one hand and a Toblerone in the other, Elizabeth started giving me her theories on men.

'I can control them,' she said. 'They are all stupid, so easily manipulated.'

'That's not true,' I replied, handing Maria a £25 half-bottle of wine.

'Can I have some cashews?' Maria asked.

Elizabeth started telling me about her boyfriend, how she didn't love him, was only using him for his money.

'He is an arsehole,' she said. 'All men are arseholes.'

'Why don't you leave him?' I asked.

'Why should I? He gives me everything I want.'

'Maybe it's that you're afraid of being alone?'

But it would appear that I had asked the wrong question, as if I had pressed some magic button, because Elizabeth was getting quite angry now, more Scary than Posh, shoulders pulled back.

'Now I can see why you're on your own,' she shouted, pointing her finger at me. 'You know nothing about women, about anything. I could be on my own if I wanted to be. It's no big deal.'

And I looked out from my tenth-floor window, at the rain and the grey dawn. I looked at my watch. It said 5 a.m. I was drunk, and all I could think about was calculating how many hours it would be before I would be sober enough to ride my bike away from Bergen.

The radio clicked into life.

Cher sang the opening line from 'I've Got You Babe.'

I crawled out of bed and walked towards the bathroom as Sonny picked up the next line.

In the bathroom, brushing my teeth, I could hear the end of the song, which was followed by the weather forecast. Why the weather in Norway should be being broadcast in English was a mystery, but it was going to be rain, rain, rain that day in Bergen.

I woke up.

In a café down the street I ordered a double espresso, and then another. I also gave myself a good, hard slap across the face. Whether anybody has ever accelerated the sobering-up process by self-flagellation is debatable. But in that busy café, I did manage to get a whole table to myself.

Through the window, across from the café in the main

pedestrian thoroughfare, I could see a human statue preparing for his day's work. With time to kill, and only Norwegian newspapers for company, I was rapt.

He seemed to be going for the gold Egyptian boy-king look, and I imagined he was going to produce some gold boots from his bag to cover the bottom third of his jeans. But he had either forgotten his boots, or run out of paint, because he clambered up on his milk crate and went about his statuely business. At this point, the children who had been watching the preparation with great interest wandered off.

Hung-over, Mr Grumpy joined me, as I reflected how I'd not felt particularly impoverished by a childhood, adolescence and early adult life completely free of human statues. But now they were ubiquitous. Occasionally, you come across one who is genuinely interesting, like the man in Covent Garden who'd stuffed coat hangers in his jacket and tie and sculptured his hair with Fixadent to make it look like he was in a wind tunnel. But most just wrap themselves in a sheet, or paint themselves with emulsion, and stand on a knackered old box and do things that proper statues would find impossible, like talk to the next statue, or blink, or scratch their arses. And for this we are invited to deposit a few coins in a hat next to their (twitching) feet.

And what would the dinner-table conversation be like?

'Nice day at work, dear?'

'Oh, same old, same old; a lot of standing around. Pigeons are getting worse. Must speak to the council.'

And what about deep-vein thrombosis? Could a human statue actually die on the job and put in the performance of his life?

Or how about future art historians? Will they draw a line from Lascaux to the Renaissance to the Impressionists and end up in the twenty-first century with a bloke on a box in a Tutankhamen mask fashioned from cornflakes boxes?

Oh, it makes me mad, like those kids with their bloody

hoods. What are they? Monks? And Christmas. I mean, it's okay for kids, but why do we have to go through the charade of buying overpriced crap for people who've got everything they want, that'll lie in a cupboard until they pluck up the courage to take it to the shop that'll ensure that, while the Romanian orphans will not have a family, at least they'll have a Clairol foot spa? And bendy buses? Lethal if you're on a bicycle. And those hoodies never pay the fare, just jump on and off through the back doors. If we still had conductors, things might be different. But, oh no, it's all profit over service these days. The trains are the same. And the utility companies. God, things used to be so much better, when everyone was happy all the time, and you didn't have to lock your doors and ...

'More coffee?' said the waitress.

'No, I think I've had enough.'

I gave myself a last slap just to make sure that my blood/alcohol level was below the 0.02 per cent Norwegian legal driving limit.

I returned to my hotel to check out. It was the first time that my minibar bill had come to more than the cost of the room.

'Is Henrik around?' I asked the woman behind the desk.

'He hasn't turned up yet,' she replied, looking at her watch and then shrugging her shoulders.

# 12 Equipment failure

I spent the afternoon navigating the high, snow-covered plateaux and sea-drowned glacial valleys of the western fjords where, high above me, tiny red-roofed farms clung limpet-like to the steep slopes. I hopped on and off the ferries that served as floating roads to cross the immense, brooding tracts of water.

I was enjoying the sunshine. The rain had stopped abruptly about 10 miles outside Bergen. I wasn't sure where I was going. And as long as it wasn't back to Bergen, I didn't care too much.

By late afternoon, I was right on top of a mountain pass overlooking Geiranger, a vast axe wound of a fjord, the UNESCO-listed covergirl of Norwegian tourist brochures that had recently been voted the world's most beautiful holiday destination by *National Geographic*.

But I was in no mood for sightseeing, fixated as I was by the two words flashing hypnotically in red capital letters on my motorbike's console: BRAKE FAILURE.

The only way down was the Trollstigen, an intestinal tract of road with more hairpins than Vidal Sassoon and a precip-itousness best suited to mountain goats and those intent on suicide.

As a motorcycling dilettante, I'd been quite happy to sit astride my beast of a machine outside bars, or at traffic lights, with attitude, for all the world to think: 'Look at that dude/prat.' But now things were Going Very Horribly Wrong indeed, I just wanted my teddy bear.

I dug out the owner's manual from the bottom of my panniers. Engine failure, clutch failure … ah, here we are. 'Always keep the use of the rear brake to a minimum, especially on steep mountain roads,' it said. 'Overuse could cause it to overheat with potentially catastrophic consequences.'

I thought back to all the riding I'd been doing on the steep mountain roads since I'd entered Norway. I guessed that, at a pinch, you might have been able to conclude that I'd been a tad heavy on the rear brakes. No, actually, what you would have been able to conclude without any fear of contradiction was that I had forgotten all of the principles of motorbike braking the minute I'd hit the mountains. Everything that Kevin had taught me: forgotten. Everything that the owner's manual had said: ignored.

I'd been tapping away at the brake pedal like a concert pianist on acid playing the *William Tell Overture*. I gave myself another good, hard slap around the face.

I inched my way down the Trollstigen, walking my motorbike like a hobby horse. If I'd packed some stabilisers, I would have put them on. I still had minimal braking, for now, but I was going so slowly that, once or twice, I actually dipped under the Norwegian speed limit.

At the bottom, I released my fingers one by one from the death grip they'd been holding around the handlebars and asked an aged local where the nearest motorcycle garage might be.

'There will almost certainly be one in Bergen,' he said.

'Anywhere else?' I asked.

He thought for a while until I believed he might have fallen asleep. Then he thrust his finger in the air and loudly exclaimed: 'Ålesund.'

'Pardon me?'

'Ålesund. It is a small town a few miles north of here.'

I found the garage and they agreed to take a look at my bike.

'It is very odd,' said the mechanic. 'The bike is quite new and yet the rear brake is already worn out.'

'That is very odd,' I said.

The BMW would be repaired overnight, and so I took a taxi into the centre of town. Sitting on a finger of granite, Ålesund appeared as if floating like a mirage on the North Sea. It burned to the ground in 1904 and was rebuilt entirely in art nouveau style. It felt like a place that had died and was reborn. There was definitely magic here.

The cab dropped me off at a hotel and, after dinner, I went out for a walk, along the quayside, then through the cobbled streets.

I peered in through the window of a bar in a pastel-painted building. It was only 8 p.m. and, as my bank manager would doubtless have agreed, dangerously early to start drinking.

But it seemed so inviting, what with its little alcoves and cartwheels on the wall and soft music playing from the jukebox and white-bearded locals with denim fishermen's caps laughing and slapping each other on the backs and, what else? Oh, yes. A gorgeous, dark-haired woman serving behind the bar. What the hell. I could always just drink water.

'How much?' I said to the gorgeous dark-haired woman serving behind the bar as she placed a beer in front of me. I was trying not to react so predictably, but it had become almost Pavlovian.

'It's nothing to do with me,' she said. 'Foreigners are all the same. Always complaining about the prices.'

'I'm sorry,' I said.

'I'm used to it,' she replied.

She went off to serve a couple of fishermen's caps, then popped out from behind the bar and cleared away some glasses from the tables. I noticed all the men turn to look at her as she passed their tables. They seemed bewitched. About my age, there was something about her that reminded me of the Juliette Binoche character in the movie *Chocolat*, and not just because of the way she looked. She danced through the room like a woman at the peak of her powers – sexually confident, unselfconscious.

She came back behind the bar and put the glasses in the dishwasher. Then she returned to me.

'Where are you from, then?' she asked.

'London,' I said.

'On holiday?'

'Kind of. I am riding a motorbike around for a while.'

'Ah, an Englishman on a motorbike,' she said, smiling. 'They are two of my favourite things.'

'Really?'

'Yes. But only the ones who don't moan about the price of beer.'

'I'm sorry,' I said again.

'I know,' she replied.

'I'm sorry,' I said again.

She laughed.

'Hanne,' she said, offering her hand.

Another beard at the end of the bar shouted an order at Hanne. She pulled three pints. She carried two of these to the beard. Then she returned and plonked the third in front of me.

'On the house,' she said. 'To stop you complaining.'

'A barmaid who serves free beer,' I said. 'Two of my favourite things.' It was a piss-poor line.

'I am the owner, actually,' Hanne said.

'Sorry,' I said.

'Again,' she replied and once more went off to serve another customer.

'Have you owned this place long?' I asked her.

Hanne told me how she'd only arrived in Ålesund the previous year.

'I got divorced and my two kids had gone off to university, so I thought it was time for a change of scenery.'

'But you had friends here?'

'Didn't know anybody. When I told people that I was leaving to start all over again in a new town, they said: "What, at your age? You will be ruined. Miserable,"' she told me. 'But they are afraid to ever do anything. I reminded them of their own sorry situation, stuck in their ruts. Some laughed at me. Some got angry.'

'You're not from Bergen, are you?' I asked.

'Oslo. I could never live in Bergen, with all that rain.'

By 3 a.m., the locals had all long left and Hanne had locked up. We had been sitting on one of the sofas chatting and drinking for over an hour. Hanne had told me all about her plans for the bar, how she was starting to book live music acts a few times a week, about how she'd found a great chef and, between them, how they'd sharpened up the menu. Bookings were slow at first, but now business was picking up.

'I've never done anything like this before,' she said. 'It was a lot to learn, but I'm happy I took the risk.'

She looked around the empty bar and smiled.

'You seem really happy here,' I said.

'I am. Happier than I've been for a long time.'

'What happened to your marriage?' I asked.

'Oh, you know. It just kind of ran out of steam,' she said. 'When we first met we were very young and he was this great guy.'

She was smiling as she said the words.

'And then, well, like I said, it just ran out of steam. People change. I'm not sure we're designed to spend our whole life with one person. After the kids moved away, it wasn't like there was any great reason to leave, more that there wasn't any great reason to stay.'

'That was tough on him.'

'He kept accusing me of not being the woman he married, of wanting something he couldn't give me. I felt guilty. But I couldn't stay. How could I? Something had changed. I could have chosen to stay, but it was as if I'd spent all that time looking after him and the kids and neglecting myself. He wanted me to carry on looking after him.'

'Spending our lives with one person? It seems impossible.'

'It's the fantasy. We all grow up thinking there's "the one" out there. That it's just a case of finding them and then everything will be fine for ever.'

'It's not such a bad fantasy.'

'It keeps you going for a while,' Hanne said.

'Seeing anybody now?' I asked.

'Been out with a few guys since I came here, but nothing's really happened. Nice guys, but no spark.'

'That's a shame.'

'I'm not that bothered. It's fun flirting in the bar, but I don't want anything from them. For the first time, I feel happy to be on my own. How about you?' she asked.

'Oh, I spent most of my life quite happy to be on my own.'

'And now?'

'I'm not sure.'

'Can I ask you a question,' Hanne said. 'As a man?'

'Is it about the offside rule?'

'No. Stupid.'

'Go ahead, then.'

'Well, most of my girlfriends, when we talk about guys, it seems that they're all really, well, miserable.'

'Your girlfriends?'

'The guys. I saw it a lot back in Oslo. I see it here.'

'All guys?'

'Your age, our age. They just seem to go a bit weird.'

'Weird?'

'Some of the guys I've been out with, it's like they're trying

97

to prove themselves all over again. They do stupid stuff, risky stuff, you know ...'

'Like buying a motorcycle?'

'Exactly,' Hanne said. 'That's why I thought you might be an expert.'

'Or leaving your home town and starting again in a place where you don't know anybody?'

'That's different,' Hanne said.

'How?'

'Well, okay, it was risky, but it felt like I was moving on. The guys I'm talking about, they're dating younger women, or trying to, taking up dangerous sports. As if they're trying to prove something.'

'There are theories about this.'

'Go on.'

'They're really dull. Can't we just drink beer?'

'I'll get you a beer if you tell me.'

'It might take more than one.'

'Just start.'

'Well, as young men we go out into the testosterone-fuelled world and it is like one giant playground. The world dances to our tune. But then something changes. We get older, we can't sustain that energy and at the first signs of waning virility, with younger guys circling the airport waiting to land, we see that our whole identity is under threat. It might help explain the ridiculous displays of virility.'

'Like going off on a motorbike?'

'Yes, yes. Don't go on. According to these theories, women in middle age often move in the opposite direction. They reach their sexual peak. Their confidence soars. They start to worry less about what the world thinks about them. And they stop taking bullshit from us. Just as we are falling apart, you are coming into your own. These are the two points where men and women are furthest apart.'

'What age is that?' asked Hanne.

'For the sake of argument, let's say 42,' I replied.

'What else?' asked Hanne.

'Well, according to Carl Jung, men must let go of much of this identity. It can only bring misery. He split the personality into the animus and the anima. The male and the female. To find peace in middle age, and while women are discovering their animus, men must develop the anima. But, having been lottery winners, it can be tough for guys to let go.'

'That would explain a lot,' Hanne said.

'Quite. A female colleague of mine at the newspaper once wrote that, instead of young boys, it should be middle-aged men we send to war,' I said. 'They love big, loud toys, are as angry as hell, and nobody would miss them.'

Hanne laughed.

'They are just theories,' I said.

And I know what you're thinking, dear reader, that here is a man sitting next to a gorgeous bar-owning, English-motor-cyclist-loving Norwegian in the small hours, who has blown the moment with his pompous and clumsy attempts to quote gender theory and long-dead Swiss psychoanalysts.

But instead of looking at her watch and yawning, Hanne moved closer and started kissing me.

'Tomorrow, my bike will be fixed, and I will be leaving town,' I told her, when we came up for air. Suddenly I was like a grotesque parody of every badly drawn road-movie character.

The bike was fixed the next morning. But the next evening I was still in town, having dinner with Hanne. We were in a Chinese restaurant. The waiter's Norwegian was fantastic, but I didn't comment on it.

'Would you like to come back to my apartment?' she asked over the fortune cookies.

By midnight, we were in bed. The soft, perpetual twilight of the Norwegian night streaming in through the window.

Hanne was on the bed naked, supine. She had perhaps the most beautiful body I had ever seen. Everything was perfect. Except for one thing.

'I'm really sorry. This has never happened before,' I said to her.

It had, of course, but in the past it had been alcohol, or tiredness. This was different. It felt like fear: of what I didn't know.

'I am so sorry,' I said to her. 'It's not you. How could it be?'

She reached up and, cupping my face in her hands, kissed me softly on the cheek.

'Don't worry about it,' she whispered.

# 13 To the sea

I stopped for the night at a campsite about two hours away in a straight line north from Ålesund. I hadn't done many miles, just riding around in circles all day really, but enough to know that I wouldn't be going back. At least not that day. I had felt terrible when, that morning, I'd woken up and told Hanne I would be leaving. But I had to get away.

There was nobody at home at the reception desk, but as all the keys to the cabins were sitting in their respective locks, I helped myself to one down by the lake. The site looked deserted. I dug out the six-pack of beer I'd bought from a store down the road and sat on the little terrace, looking out at the snow-capped peaks beyond the lake. That solitude felt glorious, desolate.

With the beer gone, the hunger arrived, so I headed back to the highway and started walking towards a cluster of roadside buildings about a mile away. I found a café, ordered a pizza and another beer, and took a table in the corner of the otherwise empty room.

The bell over the door tinkled and two men walked in. One went to the counter, the other scanned the empty room, then came over and sat at the seat next to me.

His name was Thomas, he told me, and his friend was called Björn. He indicated the man at the counter.

'I saw you ride into town on your bike,' Thomas said.

'That's a mighty fine machine. I'm thinking about getting me one.'

Thomas was originally from Texas, he told me, but moved to Minnesota in his teens and, after that, to Alaska, where he drove a dogsled team.

'That's where I met my wife. After a while she got homesick and started nagging me about moving back to Norway. So a few years back we did.'

'Seems pretty quiet round here,' I said.

'Hicksville, man. Driving me nuts. Gotta go miles for any action.'

Björn came over with two beers. Thomas said something to him in Norwegian. Björn went back to the bar and returned with another beer, which he set down in front of me.

'Thank you.'

'You're welcome, dude.'

Thomas asked where I was headed. I told him I wasn't sure, that maybe I'd be going to Ålesund, or that maybe I'd head north.

'Fine town, Ålesund,' Thomas said. 'Pretty. Good people.'

'So I hear.'

'If you head north, though, you don't want to be riding your bike through that country,' Thomas said.

'Why's that?'

'It'll get stolen, for sure, dude. They are rednecks up there. Drink methanol and sleep with their sisters. Slit yer throat soon as look at you.'

I wanted to ask Thomas whether he'd heard me correctly, that it was central Norway I was considering riding through, as opposed to, say, central LA. But as he had tombstone teeth and was wearing a baseball cap with a picture of a tractor on it, I figured he must be something of an authority on the subject.

'What's the name of the boat that goes way up to the top?' Thomas asked Björn, who to that point had said not one jot.

Björn took a deep breath, paused, then said 'Hurtigruten', which manifestly, for linguistic authenticity, should be pronounced as if one were simultaneously having an asthma attack and bench-pressing a Ford Fiesta.

'That's one cool boat ride, man,' Thomas said.

'Where's it go from?' I asked.

'Nearest port is Trondheim. That's what I'd do if I were you. Friends of mine been on it. Say it rocks.'

'You'd hope so, what with it being a boat,' I said.

Blank stare. Potato, partarto.

'Anyways, me and Björn are goin' fishing,' Thomas said, and he winked and touched his nose. 'Fancy joining us?'

It was 10 p.m. Outside, Bergen had come to town, the vertical bullets ricocheting off the road.

'Where you going fishing at this time?'

Thomas pointed up into the mountains, where the peaks had disappeared into a pelmet of mist.

Björn opened his large holdall and invited me to look inside. There were two planks of wood and a length of thick rope.

'For fishing,' he said, and winked.

I told them I was tired. They drained their beer and headed off into the rain to do whatever it is two men do in the mountains at night above a small town in Norway armed with two planks of wood and a length of rope.

I finished my beer and scuttled towards the campsite. Once inside the cabin, I went to open my pannier to get the guide-book to see what, if anything, it had to say about the Hurtigruten. I looked at the length of rope lashed around the handles. It was exactly the same thickness and colour blue as the one in Björn's bag.

The next morning, I turned on my mobile phone. I had a text, received way after I had gone to sleep. It was from Hanne. 'I miss you. When are you coming back to Ålesund? Hxx'

I loaded up my bike and rode through the deserted camp-site to the reception area. There was still nobody around. In fact, I'd seen nobody at all since I arrived. I counted out what I thought was a fair price for a night's stay and, spotting a rock on the desk already holding down a note in Norwegian, which possibly said 'we have all been abducted by aliens, please call the police', tucked the money under it and left.

I rode back to the main road. I looked left along the road heading south towards Ålesund, and then right at the road heading north, then left again. Then I turned right, in the direction of Trondheim.

The MS *Nordlys* was waiting by the dockside at dawn the next morning, one of the fleet of ships that trawl the Hurtigruten (literally 'rapid route'). Every day, year round, 11 ships combine to provide one daily service in each direction and the boats stop off at 34 ports along the way. Almost immediately after it commenced in 1893, the Hurtigruten became an icon of the intrepid Norwegian spirit, navigating as it did the then uncharted and treacherous coastal waters, providing a lifeline to remote communities along the mountainous coast-line so inaccessible that it was easier for them to reach Scotland than Oslo.

These days, the roads have reached most, but not all, of those communities, and the Hurtigruten carries as many elderly check-trousered American tourists and emotionally retarded motorcyclists as it does vital supplies.

I rode my bike up the ramp into the cargo hold and strapped it down. Then I clambered up the metal ladder and stood out on deck, watching the workers on the quayside release the giant hawsers. There really is no feeling like leaving a place by boat. It always feels like an adventure. Even on the Woolwich ferry.

With an elegiac blow on the horn, the *Nordlys* slipped away from the dock and pointed her bow north. Once out of the

Trondheim fjord, the ship began to navigate the thousands of rocks and islands that lay off the mainland like a strip of Morse code. Threading through them, the captain steered the immense ship with all the grace and insouciance of a skateboarder weaving through Coke cans. Often, the vertical bluffs towering above the ship were so close that I could have sharpened my penknife on them; the turns so tight that passengers instinctively started leaning into them. Hurtigruten captains must have nerves of titanium. And sphincters to match.

I settled into the gentle pace of life on board. At the breakfast buffet, even I was unflustered by the 15 minutes it took Bob and Vera Komiseroff from Boise, Idaho, to peruse and ultimately reject the fare on offer from the sea of the pickled variety.

After breakfast, there was a lap or two of the deck and a look at some rocks, before queuing up for the buffet lunch and some more pickled fish, and after that there was only time to cram in a quick snooze on a steamer before the queue for the dinner buffet began.

We all followed this strict routine, except for the bird-watchers, who eschewed the food and the snoozing and trained their binoculars out to sea and in to land and everywhere in between. You could have mistaken them for living statues save for the odd extension of an arm, the unfurling of a finger and a cry of '*Fratercula arctica!*' which, I understand, means puffin in old money.

Occasionally, the *Nordlys* would pull a handbrake turn and we'd all rush to the rail to stop it tipping over. Then we'd be in one of the remote settlements, just a cluster of red-painted timber houses around a dock, for whom the Hurtigruten is like a parent bird returning with food. Forklift trucks would scuttle around the quayside like worker ants. The *Nordlys* would duel horns with the buses. The locals would line up on the dock to stare at the ship. The passengers would line up on the ship to stare at the locals. The birdwatchers would stare at a cliff behind the village and say '*Fratercula arctica.*'

Under way again, and as the southbound ships passed, the bridges would have a little chat using the horns and the staff would quixotically line up on the deck and wave their white tablecloths at each other frantically in greeting. Of course, it's possible that they were just shaking off the crumbs from the first dinner setting, but thankfully Sancho was not on board. It was all so romantic, I wished that I could have had somebody there to share it with. Then I remembered Ålesund and thought, one day, hopefully.

At some stage, we crossed the Arctic Circle. There was no dotted line on the water, so I cannot pinpoint precisely when this momentous moment occurred, but Neptune didn't appear with trident in hand to shave my genitals and tar my head. Or was I getting confused?

I reclined on my favourite steamer – at the stern, right next to the door that led to the bar – and, wrapped in a blanket, beer in hand, watched the most glorious sunset of oranges and lemons and pastel candy puffs, mirrored in the smoked-glass sea.

The sun never did set, of course, content just to hover on the horizon, but I was on beer number five before I'd managed to work that one out.

However, towards the end of day two, the *Nordlys* was beginning to feel like a prison ship. As stunning as the scenery was, it was the twisty roads corkscrewing up the distant mountains that started drawing my attention. I kept thinking about my bike, tucked up in the hold, restrained by straps. I wanted to go below and stroke it, a thought I felt best not shared with my fellow passengers.

I wanted to be riding it again. Sure, the boat was moving, but I was a passive partner, a passenger. It was as if I'd acquired some insatiable attention deficit disorder, always wanting to be free, moving, an itch that no amount of scratching could salve. It struck me then that one day I would have to relearn how to be still, overrule the nomad, cultivate a garden. One day, but not yet.

'Settlement for any length of time, in cave or castle, has at best been a sporadic condition in the history of man,' wrote Bruce Chatwin in *Anatomy of Restlessness*. 'Prolonged settlement has a vertical axis of some ten thousand years, a drop in the ocean of evolutionary time. We are travellers from birth. Our mad obsession with technological progress is a response to barriers in the way of our geographical progress.'

Could this be true? Chatwin claimed that movement was the very essence of life. That, deprived of it, restrained, we 'invent artificial enemies, psychosomatic ilnesses, tax-collectors and, worst of all, ourselves.'

After Bodø, the *Nordlys* heaved to port, leaving land behind and ploughing across the open expanse of the Vestfjorden. The birdwatchers were bereft at the meagre pickings, and some actually managed to eat something or lie on the steamers, sulking like petulant teenagers.

After a few hours, the mountains of the Lofoten islands hove into view. For over 100 miles, the islands stretched in a curved wall across the Norwegian Sea, their jagged crocodile teeth snapping at the sky, the peaks rising sharply from the inky depths, attended by constellations of seastacks and skerries like the spires of inundated churches. The birdwatchers did a little jig.

Initially, I feared that the captain of the *Nordlys* may have been overpowered and the helm taken over by ramraiders, heading full-steam as we were for an impenetrable wall of granite. But just at the moment when even a sphincter crafted from titanium would have been feeling the strain, the islands opened their arms and ushered us into their labyrinth of narrow straits, sounds and fjords.

At Svolvær, I collected my bike from the hold and left the

*Nordlys.* I rode for a while along the road that hugs the shore-line, connecting the dots by plunging under the sea through tunnels or flying high over it on bridges like a spooked cat. It felt magnificent to be back in the saddle again.

Down to the tip of Lofoten, to the town of Å, as desperate an attempt to get the first listing in the Thompson Local as I'd ever seen, then back to Nusfjord, a ridiculously pictur-esque gaggle of nineteenth-century red-timbered fishermen's huts jammed into a tight cove. Å might get the listing, but Nusfjord would get the cover shot.

With no clues that it might be evening, I rode late into the night. When I pulled over for a cigarette and looked at my watch, it was 11 p.m. Opposite was a college purged of students for the summer and offering rooms.

I lay on the single bed and imagined the first nights that must have occurred between those narrow walls when the door was finally shut and the noises faded to silence.

At midnight, I walked off campus and into town. I found a packed beer terrace and took a seat. Everybody was wearing sunglasses. People were running around like Duracell bunnies, bumping into things. It reminded me of the moment just after Mike Read had shouted, 'Runaround. Now!' Three women were doing step aerobics using chairs, fags in one hand, Bacardi Breezers in the other. Everybody had a look on their face like they'd just had a sack removed from their head. I asked a passing waitress when the bar closed.

'September,' she said.

On the table in front of me was a discarded tourist booklet advertising the charms of a northern Finnish town called Rovaniemi. The home of Lordi, it exclaimed on the bottom. Ah, Lordi. They were the gothic, prosthetic-wearing monsters of rock who'd won Eurovision that year. In one foul swoop they'd redrawn the Eurovision map and consigned to the dustbin forevermore the folksy ballads of wholesome lederhosen-clad lovelies singing about their lost sheep, and Cliff. I supposed we owed them one for that.

I started to read the booklet. It seemed that Rovaniemi had quite a rock and roll pedigree. It had sired Absoluuttinen Nollapiste, for a start, which if it wasn't the Finnish for completely mullered, really should be. And then there was Beherit, a three-piece comprising Nuclear Holocausto on vocals, Daemon Fornication (guitar) and Sodomatic Slaughter (drums), who'd penned timeless classics such as 'The Oath of Black Blood' and 'Werewolf Semen', a tune which, I was guessing, hadn't accompanied too many newly-weds' first dances.

I read on. Rovaniemi was also home to Santa Claus. And the world's most northerly McDonald's. Could a town have much more going for it?

I looked up and noticed a man staring at me, like he was weighing up whether he knew me or not. He'd removed his sunglasses to focus better but the resulting squinting just made him look like a mole emerged from its hole. He was trying, with only modest success, to prop himself up against a fence post.

He reeled over, walking like a man who had just been hit on the head with an iron bar.

'I am Olaf,' he announced. 'How old are you?'

It was a strange opening gambit, but really no more or less strange than the very strange people in the very strange bar at this very strange latitude.

'I am 42,' I told him.

'I'm 50,' he said.

A pause.

Olaf told me how he'd sailed his replica Viking longboat across the Vestfjorden from Bodø earlier that day. He assured me that he was a very fine sailor. So fine in fact that he told me three more times.

A pause.

'I go back tomorrow. You should come along. Just the two of us, eh? I am a very good sailor.'

When the Hurtigruten had stopped in Bodø, I had caught the start of the week-long Norwegian accordion championships. I told Olaf I was in no hurry to go back.

'How old are you?' Olaf asked, like he was seeing me for the first time.

'I'm 42,' I said.

'I'm 48,' he said.

We both stood there in silence for a while. Olaf seemed to be struggling with something.

'Tell me this,' he said, finally. 'Why is it that the English are so shit at skiing? In Norway, we have only four million people, yet we are the champions of the world.'

To communicate that this was a question of grave importance, one which he had doubtless pondered many times on those long, dark days, Olaf attempted to give me what I took to be his most serious face. In actuality, it looked like Stan Laurel's most supercilious face.

'That would be because we have no mountains and no snow,' I told him.

Olaf now gave me his blank face, as if he were trying to imagine that such a place could really exist.

A pause.

'I am 46,' he said. 'How old are you?'

'I'm 41,' I told him.

'Want a beer?' he asked.

I told Olaf that I was tired and going to go to bed. That I had a long day's ride tomorrow.

'But you should maybe get to the bar quickly,' I said. 'Before you are too young to get served.'

Blank.

'Where are you going?' he asked.

'To bed.'

'No, tomorrow.'

'Finland,' I replied.

'Miserable fucker,' Olaf said.

'Pardon me,' I said.

'Peter,' Olaf said. 'Miserable Finnish fucker. They all are. They take a bit of getting to know, but then they're okay. Not Peter. He's a miserable fucker. Down to his miserable fucking bones.'

'Why's he a friend?'

'Who?' Olaf asked.

'Peter.'

A pause.

'Who's Peter?' Olaf replied.

# 14 Yo, ho, ho

I rode across the bleak, wet wastelands of northern Sweden and over the swirling torrent of the Tornionjoki River that marks the border with Finland. At the end of the bridge, I turned right. Straight into a herd of reindeer stretched across the road.

They were the first I'd seen on the trip, as if they'd been dispatched to the border by the Finnish tourist board. I could imagine them standing around, Gary Larsen fashion, smoking fags or playing quoits with their antlers until, hearing a vehicle approaching from abroad, Rudolph, Prancer, Dancer and the gang would put out their fags, remove the quoits from their antlers and assemble in the middle of the road so that tourists could think: wow, this must be Lapland. Of a fat man in a red suit there was no sign. But it was July. Maybe he was in Benidorm.

After an hour, I stopped at a café, surrounded by nothing for miles in either direction but pine forests and straight highway arrowing into infinity. Like the roads, the café was deserted, save for the proprietor and his wife. While eyeing up his selection of tasty-looking flapjacks through the glass counter, I asked the man how far it was to Rovaniemi.

He looked at me blankly. After Sweden and Norway, where it had been possible to converse with just about everybody, I'd fallen so much into the habit of assuming that every person on the planet spoke English that I had stopped asking.

But at the petrol station a few miles back, and when I had stopped just after the border to ask directions, and then again to ask the same question of a group of young people waiting at a bus stop, I had encountered blank responses. It looked like I was into shouting-loudly-and-charades territory.

Most borders on this trip had seemed like little more than arbitrary lines on a map, the people living on either side largely indistinguishable from each other in manners and appearance. The experience reminded me of one of those paintshop palettes, where you move from red to yellow in such subtle shade changes that you barely notice.

The border with Finland hadn't been like that. It seemed to mark a different world to the one I'd just left. Red and yellow separated by a river. And the language thing wasn't the only difference. After a month of garrulous Danes, Swedes and Norwegians, the Finns I'd encountered seemed more stoic and reticent, watchful and doleful, like characters in a Russian novel. Even the landscape seemed melancholic. Perhaps something in Olaf's brain had been working after all.

I thought about the months that lay ahead: Eastern Europe, Turkey, the Balkans. Maybe it would be a long time before I would able to speak to people so easily and freely again. The thought made me feel quite down.

I pointed to one of the flapjacks, then to the coffee pot and I raised my hand to my mouth and did that little twisty thing with my wrist. Then I went and sat down. The owner and his wife both sighed, then propped their elbows on the counter to watch me, as glum as if they'd just been told that Nuclear Holocausto were moving in next door. The clock on the wall ticked loudly.

I took a bite of the flapjack. It was made from soggy rice and tasted of methylated spirits. That is not what you want in a flapjack. Unless you are Finnish. I put it to one side and, to cheer myself up, picked up the local newspaper.

Reading newspapers in a language one cannot understand

is an exercise in optimism. Most of the photographs are of happy-looking groups of people shaking hands, or cutting ribbons, or getting married. And although the caption accompanying a picture of a smiling family might inform you it was taken the very second before a Sputnik fell on their heads, you never find out. Ditto the story about the murder in the next town or the economy being just about to go tits up. No, you inhabit a deliciously ignorant little bubble filled with double vowels, umlauts and fluffy children and the world seems a benign place.

I opened the paper. On page three was a picture of an unsmiling couple standing outside a church, surrounded by their unsmiling families and friends. They looked like they were all about to commit suicide.

I went to the counter to pay up. The owner produced a visitors' book and insisted that I sign it. It was empty. I wrote something about the fine food and convivial hosts and slipped it back across the counter. Then the owner popped through the back door, re-emerged with a camera and indicated that he would like a photograph of me and him standing next to my motorbike.

Having taken the picture, the wife disappeared inside and came out holding the remnants of my flapjack which she was busily wrapping up in tissue paper for me to take away, perhaps imagining that I'd been enjoying the ambrosial morsel so much that I wanted to savour it slowly.

The guilt I was feeling right then about the comment in the visitors' book was as to nothing when the owner then refused to take any money from me. At least, I thought that was what he was suggesting. Perhaps the next day's paper carried a story about an English motorcyclist doing a runner from a café near the border, complete with picture of a grim-faced owner and the thumbs-up, grinning suspect.

*

I don't know whether it's possible to osmotically assume the character of a country, but on the way to the home of Finnish rock and roll, I got the blues pretty bad. Perhaps it had started with an anticipation of the language isolation I thought I'd now be facing through the long miles ahead. Perhaps the events in Ålesund had kicked up a lot of dust. My mood was certainly not helped by the flat, grey, gloomy landscape and the cold. I knew I felt quite tired. But maybe it was just one of those days; those days where you bump into everyone coming towards you on the high street, as opposed to dancing around them.

Sitting on a motorcycle, your head wedged tightly inside a helmet, is not the best place to be on such days. The sense of aloneness is immense. As the negative thoughts and self-doubts presented themselves in front of me, there was nowhere to hide. Trapped behind a visor, and with no distractions like a radio or someone to talk to or a phone to pick up, it was like being in Room 101.

Unbidden, the tape of my marriage failure cranked itself into life and refused to stop until it was done. All I could do was sit there and watch. Before long, the cloak of melancholia was wrapping itself tightly around me.

I'd always believed that it was good to talk about painful experiences, that the only way to release that anger was to get it all out into the open, not to suppress it. Think it all through for as long as it took and it would eventually wither and die. It had to. An entire profession of psychotherapists and self-help authors surely couldn't be wrong.

But recently I'd started to look at it from the other direction. It sounds glib, but I noticed that the only thing that happened when I started thinking shit thoughts was that they would beget another shit thought, then another, until the whole thing was unravelling like a snagged cardie. When we let the mind take control, when we are its slave, it's easy to get dragged back into the past and flung far off into the future. Two places we inhabit at our peril.

Might we actually actually become what we think about? Might our lives be a physical manifestation of our thoughts; a constant series of self-fulfilling prophecies? Demand a traffic jam when you're late and it'll usually show up. Imagine hard enough that you will fail a test, or screw something up, create the failure almost by an act of will, and you are generally not disappointed.

What if life really was that simple? Think it and it is?

Riding along, I thought about my dad after he'd left us. He'd lived alone and never shared his life with anybody and eventually hit the bottle pretty hard. I tried to get closer to him, and sometimes it seemed like I might, but there was usually a savage strike from the depths and the walls would come up again and I would retreat. I tried, and tried again, but each time the walls came up, they got thicker. Eventually, I conceded defeat. Most people would.

That was 30 years ago. When he was my age. He still lives alone, still behind the wall, still finds something too painful to deal with without the Teacher's; it can make his eyes so sad, so far away. Sometimes there's a glimmer, and recently I saw his eyes grow rheumy at a sad memory we shared. A solitary tear slipped down his cheek. That had been a first. But I'm not sure what he was grieving for.

I thought back to London, and saw myself sitting in my flat drinking alone in the evening. It was wine, for now, most nights, as it had once been for my dad. Sometimes I can open a second bottle. And a third.

But what came next? In 20 years' time, would I be living in a borrowed flat on a sink estate, where heroin users shot up in the stairwell? In 30 years' time, would my sister get a phone call from a hospital saying I'd set fire to my flat after falling into a drunken coma?

Was this the inevitability of my life? Is this what happens when men float off, drifting along on the currents and the winds? Or could it be target fixation? Stare at the tree on the bend, and you will hit it. Look ahead up the road, and that's where you will go. Think it and it is …

As I say, dangerous places, motorcycle helmets.

I arrived in Rovaniemi and checked into the Hotel Santa Claus. It hadn't really gone overboard on the Father Christmas theme, in that there wasn't anything to distinguish it from any other hotel: no ho-ho-hoing receptionist, no elves to carry my bags, no 'Jingle Bells' in the lifts. Nothing.

I dumped my stuff in the room. Not even a sleigh bed. I went straight back out for a walk. I didn't want to start on the minibar.

On the main street, market stalls sold black T-shirts decorated with hangmen's nooses and skulls and heavy metal pumped out of every shop. Death-metal muzak was piping through the PA system in the mall and, seemingly out of every open window and manhole, came the crunching chords of electric guitar, the crash of drums and the tones of a man screaming as if on fire. Rovaniemi rocked. Literally.

I wandered over to a caravan plastered with posters and picked up a flyer for a gig that evening. The band was called Shit On Your Face, or something like that, and the photograph showed a four-piece who looked like they might certainly do just that given half a chance. For a second, I was tempted, but concluded that an evening of werewolf's semen and getting flobbed on was probably going to do nothing to lift my spirits. All the same, it felt like being in Seville and not going to the flamenco.

I went to the world's most northerly McDonald's – well, I wouldn't not want to have that on my CV. I perused the menu. There was no McRudolph.

The guy at the counter could speak some English, fortunately. Unfortunately, the words he knew included being able to tell me that I looked like Morrissey.

I think this might only partly have been because the

helmet monologues had given me a face like a smacked arse. I looked at my reflection in the window. Having not had a cut since London, that day's helmet hair had produced a quiff of Tin Tin proportions.

I took my burger and fries and found an empty bench opposite the caravan. A song, I'm assuming by Shit On Your Face, was now playing in English whose lyrics seemed to involve nuns with chainsaws slaughtering a few cardinals before jumping off a cliff.

A man sat down on the bench. For a while, we both sat there listening to the music.

He asked me something in Finnish. I turned to explain, and saw that he was pointing to an unlit cigarette in his mouth.

'You are English?' he asked.

He was in his sixties, with long straggly grey hair sitting under a homburg, and wearing a battered old leather jacket. He looked not unlike Willy Nelson.

Yamos was a merchant seaman, he told me, originally from Rovaniemi. His current ship had just returned to Helsinki from Argentina and he was up here on leave for a week. The ship was then sailing with timber to Spain and then on to the US.

He slipped a small silver flask out of his pocket and offered it to me.

'Thanks,' I said, and took a swig. It tasted like Finnish flap-jack. I blinked my eyes hard. Yamos laughed.

'You don't like?'

'It's strong.'

'A man's drink.'

'You like this music?' I asked him, pointing to the caravan.

'That is not music,' he said. 'That is noise.'

'What do you like?'

'I don't like music,' he said.

'Fancy a chip?'

'No, thank you.'

'They taste no different,' I said.

'From what?'

'From any other McDonald's.'

'Why should they?'

'Well, Guinness tastes better in Ireland. London gin is supposed to be the best. I thought being the world's most northerly McDonald's, the food might taste, erm ... I dunno really.'

'That is the world's most northern McDonald's?'

'I believe so.'

'I did not know that.'

Yamos leaned over and took a chip.

'You married?' I asked him.

'Used to be.'

The music from the caravan stopped abruptly. We both sat there, braced, waiting for the next song. Nothing. Silence. Gradually other noises filled the space, children shouting, a truck reversing, the sound of heels clicking along the pavement.

'To a woman from here?'

'Yes.'

'Still in touch?'

'We have kids.'

I took out two cigarettes and offered one to Yamos.

'Thank you.'

'Must be hard, being away at sea.'

'I've been doing it 30 years. I'm used to it.'

Yamos took another slug from the flask and offered it to me again.

'No thanks,' I said.

'How old are your kids?'

'My son is 35. My girl is 30.'

'Grandchildren?'

'My son has twins, a girl and a boy.'

'Your daughter?'

'Married an arsehole.'

'Oh.'

'Divorcing him.'

Yamos took another slug. Then he sat there silently, staring at his cigarette, which had burned itself out at the stub.

I offered him another. He took it.

'Ever think about moving back here,' I asked, 'once you've finished with the sea?'

'Sometimes,' he said.

By next morning, the storm had passed. And, as I began the shuffle around the breakfast buffet table, Rovaniemi had saved a special rock-and-roll treat for me. For there, surveying the bread rolls and the pickled fish and the anteater giblets, were Shit On Your Face, complete with stripy spandex trousers, sleeveless T-shirts – each had a different Horseman of the Apocalypse on it, nice touch – and Spinal Tap hair. I recognised them immediately from the posters, though I suspected a good ten years had elapsed since then.

They still wore the remnants of their stage make-up that, a few hours earlier, from 100 yards, through dry ice and smoke and fireworks, had probably looked great, but that at 8 o'clock on a Sunday morning made them look like a quartet of portly, middle-aged transvestites who'd been caught out in the rain.

I would imagine that the cluster of young women who tottered behind them in heels and miniskirts and crisp tour T-shirts still freshly creased from the packaging had probably, high on the music and the drink and whatever else, thought that the guys had looked pretty hot stuff on stage too. Now the girls just looked shellshocked.

# 15 Haircut

The Helsinki hairdresser was asking me how much I wanted cut.

'Oh, just a trim,' I told her. 'But please leave a bit on the top so I can do that gel thing.' And I scrunched up my fingers to demonstrate.

Evidently her little Finnish ears heard something quite different, because 20 minutes later, there I was outside the salon looking like a Nazi stormtrooper and old ladies were crossing to the other side of the street.

I entered a pub by the main railway station and the bouncers gave me the hard-man look of affinity. I found a stool at the bar.

Sitting next to me were a couple, her on his lap. I could sense him giving me the onceover, and after I had asked the barman for a beer, his attentions seemed to intensify.

'You are English,' he said.

He introduced himself as Andreas.

'This is Ingrid,' he said, pointing to the woman on his lap. His other arm disappeared up the back of her jumper, ventriloquist-style.

Andreas took a long drink from his beer bottle, looked slowly at my shaved head and then stared into my sunburned face.

'Inter-City Firm ... Headhunters ...' he said.

'Eh?'

'Zulu Warriors ... Bushwackers ...'

'What ...?'

'The best.'

'What are?'

'Your hooligans.'

'Oh.'

'Here in Finland, the hooligans are rubbish, but yours are the best in the world. I have them all on DVD. Millwall v Birmingham, play-offs, 2002. That is my favourite. Those guys were fucking animals. And the horse police on the run. Man, it was war. I watch that DVD many times, don't I, Ingrid?'

Ingrid nodded.

'I'm from Birmingham,' I said. I don't know why.

'You are a Zulu?'

'No.'

Andreas looked disappointed.

'But I had a run-in with them once,' I said.

Andreas's eyes widened.

'I was working in a sports shop in New Street. They came in and stole all the tracksuits.'

'Ah. I have heard of this. Steaming it is called, yes. They are fucking cool guys, no?'

'I was working on commission. Didn't get paid.'

'Ha, ha.'

'One of the gang came back the next day. Wanted to exchange his Fila trackie bottoms. Said they didn't fit.'

'What did you do?'

'Called the manager.'

'Why?'

'Dunno. I was only 16.'

'What happened?'

'Guy pulled out a knife. The manager swapped his trackie bottoms.'

'Great story, man. What's your team?'

'West Bromwich Albion.'

'Ah, the Baggies.'

'You know a lot about English football.'

'What's your crew, man?'

'Erm. Not sure there is one any more.'

'No crew? What happens at games?'

'Everyone jumps up and down and sings boing, boing.'

Andreas looked at me, a disappointment spreading across his face.

'It makes me sad.'

'It's quite funny, really.'

'No, now I am 40, I realise I will never fulfil my dream of becoming a hooligan in England. If I had my time all over again, that is what I'd do.'

'Things have changed,' I said. 'Prawn sandwiches and all that.'

'Ah, Roy Keane. A real man. That tackle on Håland, man. He fucked his knee up so bad. Fucked him up then called him a cunt when he was on the floor. I have that on DVD as well, don't I?'

Ingrid nodded.

'Vinny Jones, Tommy Smith, Norman Hunter. All on there. Psycho as well. Real men. Where are they now, huh? Where are the hard men today?'

'I don't know.'

'Wearing your missus's knickers. Makes me fucking sick.'

'I know.'

We drank our beer.

'This your local?'

'Slags.'

'Who?'

'Pop stars, titty models.'

'What?'

'Them,' Andreas said, pointing to the giant TV screen on the wall. It was showing a group of English Wags at the

World Cup, walking down the street glammed up, pursued by photographers.

'There's money in the game now,' I said.

'Slags.'

'It's changed.'

'Stupid bitches. Who gives a fuck?'

When I got back to my hotel, I asked the woman behind the desk about ferries to Estonia. She ferreted around and handed me a leaflet for Viking Line. She looked concerned.

'You have good insurance for your motorcycle?' she asked me.

'Why?' I said.

'Because Estonians are thieves.'

She wasn't the first Finn who'd questioned me on the merits of travelling in Estonia. I'd been asked many times about where I was heading next, and when I said eastern Europe, the reaction was invariably the same.

In my mind, I'd constructed a lawless, Wild West of dilapidated infrastructure and dilapidated morality, where swarthy ne'er-do-wells with cut-throat razors hung around on street corners, and danger lurked everywhere.

I asked the woman behind the desk what dreadful things had happened to her in Estonia, but she hadn't been there personally, had just heard all kinds of things from people who had.

I already had mixed feelings about visiting the former Soviet Union. And here, I have a terrible, dirty secret to confess: my name is Mike and I was raised a communist. There, done.

Both my parents had been in the party, my father a full-time official for a long time. For a while, I was a member too.

I'm lapsed now, of course, in these days of there being only one gig in town. But sometimes, when the talk is of house prices and the *X Factor*, of million-pound City bonuses and failing state schools, of body-dysmorphic teenagers and page after page of cosmetic surgery ads, I find myself coming over all sentimental for the world I was brought up to imagine I'd be living in by now. Oh, I'm so confused.

For clarification, when I say communism, what I mean is socialism: free, decent health care, pensions and education for all, redistributive taxation policies, nationalised industries running not-for-profit services, internationalism, nuclear disarmament, etc, etc.

What I don't mean is gulags, death squads, despotic and paranoid leaders with large Swiss bank accounts, huge nuclear stockpiles, shit weather, uniformly crap cars and all the other things that would have found their way on to *Grumpy Old Menski* circa 1950 if there had been a free media and the writers hadn't been chained to a post in Siberia.

In my fluffy, naive world, we would be allowed to live in peace and, our basic needs taken care of by the state and paid for by equitable taxation, we might even be permitted to smile occasionally. We would still be allowed to make bundles of cash if we desired. It's just that, what with the gulf between rich and poor having narrowed, people might just start looking elsewhere for their status kicks.

That's how it seems to work in Scandinavia. That's why they always win World's Strongest Man: you get no kudos for flashing the moolah, but boy, if you can drag a truck 100 yards with your teeth, you'll be fighting 'em off with a stick.

But I know my views are naive. I know that if we all stopped buying stuff we don't need our economy would collapse so quickly that we'd all be back in caves by midnight. Besides, these days everybody seems happy enough to tell me I have flawed thinking.

'Socialism? Ah, bless,' they say at parties. 'People just aren't like that, darling. Human beings can only function when motivated by self-interest. It's Darwinian, in our genes. That's why capitalism triumphed. Have you met Roger here? He's a flat-earthist. Now that is an interesting theory.'

And now that I feel like I've come out, I'll say no more about it.

A man approached the hotel reception desk. He had been sitting on one of the sofas quietly when I came in and, dressed in a suit and tie and reading the newspaper, looked like he might be a businessman waiting to meet a client.

'When are you going to sort this out?' he shouted at the woman.

The embarrassed smile she flashed back at him suggested that this wasn't the first communication she'd had with him, and she turned back to me to continue our conversation about the impending throat-cutting awaiting me across the Gulf of Finland.

The man stood there for a while.

'Stupid bitches,' he spat.

I looked at him a little more closely, seeing things I'd missed before: the worn, dirty shoes, the trouser hems hovering around the ankles, the stain on the tie, the bruises on the hands. Standing so close to him, I could now smell the sour alcohol on his breath.

I told him to watch his language or else he'd have to leave.

'Fuck you,' he said.

We were toe to toe. Before my eyes I saw his courage drain away and him shrink further. I could sense everyone else in the lobby tuning in to the situation.

Who knows what had happened to him, what had unravelled in his life to make him so angry, to bring him to that lobby, or the dozens of other lobbies that he doubtless found himself in?

The right thing to do would have been for me to hover around in the background and ensure the guy didn't get violent, while the receptionist would call the police and they'd do what they're paid to do by clearing up the mess and taking it out of sight. Order would be restored and we could tut and speak about the slipping standards in society and go back to our sorted lives.

But I didn't. I grabbed his wrist and he capitulated limply, as I'd suspected he would, and his arm twisted easily behind his back like a familiar formation dance move and we started to walk towards the door, him leading me.

When the electric doors swooshed open and we were outside, I let go of his wrist and expected him to turn around and give me a mouthful of abuse, or swing a punch. But he didn't. He just walked away from me without once turning back.

I went back into the lobby and was fussed over, and the manager came out of his office and offered me free dinner in the restaurant, and the receptionist said she'd book my ferry for me, and they told me how brave I'd been.

I wasn't feeling heroic.

'Thank you,' the manager said. 'If only more people would do that.'

'He was harmless,' I replied. 'It was nothing.'

Next day, I was heading across the Baltic towards Tallinn. When I'd checked in at the port, the woman at the desk had repeated the concerns of the hotel receptionist about the dubious character of Estonians and Eastern Europeans in general and the racing certainty that very soon my motorcycle and I would be saying farewell.

I stood on the deck and watched Helsinki disappear. I felt a wave of apprehension, like Marlow heading for the Belgian Congo.

Finns use the service much as many Brits do when they pop across the Channel on day trips: to stock up on cheap booze. They whiled away the crossing by drinking prodigious amounts of vodka and dancing to summer anthems piped through like ship's PA system. Even though the Baltic was without a ripple, they moved like people dancing on a pitching ship.

Pieter appeared by my side. I'd met him earlier at the quayside in Helsinki when, despite being on a bicycle and eligible to walk it to the front of the long line of vehicles, he'd resolutely queued alongside me and my motorcycle for over an hour.

Pieter had revealed himself to be an Estonian, which immediately made me think he was up to no good. Was he the plant, sent by the crime lords to scope out potential hits, to be whacked and disembowelled the minute they disembarked?

Even his cover story was plausible. He'd supposedly been on holiday, riding his bicycle around Finland for three weeks. From my downwind position, it smelled like it could be true. Moving to the rail on the other side of him, I asked him why most people in Finland seemed to think that Estonians were all criminals.

'It is bad that people have this opinion,' he said. 'But it is just ignorance. You will see for yourself that Estonians are kind people. It is the Russians you should watch out for. They would murder you just like that.' He clicked his fingers.

I asked Pieter what he could recommend in Estonia.

'Saaremaa is beautiful,' he said. 'It is an island, very peaceful. Estonians go there to escape the city.'

'Volare' was pumping out of the sound system. It was cut off abruptly and replaced by a message telling us that we would shortly be arriving in Estonia.

I looked over the railings and there indeed was Tallinn coming into view. Pieter and I made our way to the car deck, where he had tethered his bicycle to my motorbike. We rode down the oily, slippery ramp together.

At the gates to the port, I looked around for large men in

fur coats driving Wartburgs with blacked-out windows, to whom Pieter would be making covert hand signals, but there were none.

Pieter repeated his warnings about Russians, hugged me farewell and then wobbled off, hopefully to have a shower.

I rode into the centre of Tallinn. But what was this? Somebody had stolen the Eastern Europe of mine and Finland's imagination, because all the belching Trabants, food queues and grim factories were gone, and everybody seemed to be sitting outside chrome and glass-fronted cafés, wearing Prada while supping cappuccinos and tapping away at their laptops.

Or else they were driving past in their Porsches, or BMWs, or rollerblading down the street with poodles trailing behind on a lead like a Bodyform ad. It could have been Knightsbridge on a July afternoon.

Where were the babushkas, the soldiers high-stepping their way around the eternal flame, the grey, nicotine sky? Dammit, even the sun was shining. It made my apprehensive departure from Helsinki look ridiculous. Tracking down Kurtz here would not be difficult. He'd be in Comme des Garçons.

I found a hotel near the centre and went for a walk around the city's Old Town. Set behind honeystone medieval walls, it was a warren of narrow cobbled streets and dusty courtyards, fourteenth-century merchants' houses, Gothic town halls and looming spires; the kind of place travellers fantasise about stumbling across, a timeless scene more like a museum diorama than a real-life city.

But a walk into Raekoja Plats, the main square, quickly shattered such fantasy. There was a vast Molly Malone's Irish pub, advertising a giant screen showing English football, pizza shops, designer boutiques, the Maharaja Indian restaurant and Ye Olde Estonia, where comely wenches dressed in peasant costumes served the tourists.

After 50 years of Soviet austerity, and three years into EU membership, Tallinn seemed gripped by conspicuous consumption, evolving so quickly you could almost see it, like watching one of those accelerated time-lapse sequences of a flower unfolding.

But watching the stag and hen groups perusing the prices outside the myriad lapdancing and strip clubs, and the bars offering free shots and foam parties, and the stretched limos ferrying their pissed-up charges around, with one always poked through the sunroof with arms akimbo like a homecoming hero, and the tourists travelling so far from home for a pint of Carlsberg and a chicken tikka masala, I felt like I could be in Doncaster.

I wondered what my dad would have made of it all. He hadn't been back to Eastern Europe since the fall of the Berlin Wall. To me, it all looked like a victory parade as triumphalist as any witnessed in Red Square.

I went into a bar just off Raekoja Plats and ordered a pint of Guinness.

'You are from Britain?' the barmaid asked. She put my pint on the counter. There was a perfect shamrock in the creamy head. 'Why do men from your country like to get drunk and remove their clothes?'

I told her that not all British men liked to remove their clothes.

The big screen was showing great misses from football games. Kanu was putting the ball over the Middlesbrough bar for West Brom from two yards. The miss was shown from four camera angles. The clip was accompanied by Bono singing 'Stuck in a Moment - You Can't Get Out Of.'

I went to the toilet. As I stood at the urinal, at eye level, a video screen was advertising a nearby boutique. With such a captive audience, was this the most depressing, desperate and cynical delivery method yet devised by the stuff-pushers?

A young, beautiful man sashayed his young, beautiful hips, in front of his young, beautiful friends. Then the film of the boutique ended and was replaced by one advertising a lapdancing joint. It was very explicit, lots of writhing around naked on poles, and soon I had a problem that was growing by the second. I'd finished what I'd come to do, but I had to stand there for a while longer, thinking about my nan on the bog. It was halfway through the next ad, a gruesome but no less explicit one for a plastic surgery clinic, before I was in any position to return to my bar stool and another minute before I could sit down comfortably again.

A girl came up to me and said hello. Her name was Karin, she said, and would I like to join her and her friend, Clara, for a drink? Clara and Karin were on a weekend break from Stockholm, Clara explained, and Karin loved Englishmen.

At Clara and Karin's table, we were chatting away when the sky darkened for a second and, unbidden, Rubeus Hagrid joined us. He said nothing as he sat down with no drink in front of him. He seemed content to just stare at me, as if we were playing the who-can-blink-the-last competition.

I smiled at him. He stared back at me. He looked as angry, and as mad, as the Helsinki hotel lobby guy.

It dawned on me what this might be about. Some men, when they see a guy sitting with two girls, take it as a personal affront when they are sitting with none. It was meant to be a challenge to me; tens of thousands of years ago, he would have been pissing up against my cave. It's great being a guy sometimes.

Hagrid leaned forward towards me some more and, in case the subtleties of the situation were lost on me, he clenched both his fists. He started to speak, slowly and softly. It was in Russian, and somehow when a man who should really be in a circus is speaking in Russian, it always seems like he is saying: 'I vant to kill you.'

'What's he saying?' I asked Karin who, luckily, spoke Russian.

'He says that he wants to kill you,' Karin told me, no longer smiling, and I was suddenly thinking that Karin's ability to speak Russian was perhaps not such a lucky thing.

Hagrid pointed to my Helsinki haircut and banged his fist on the table, getting more angry by the second.

'What's he saying?' I asked Karin.

'He says that he knows you are in the Russian Special Forces,' she said. 'He has been in the army. Says you are all scum. That is why he wants to fight you.'

I asked Karin to propose to Hagrid that it was most unlikely that the Russian Special Forces would find a fertile recruiting ground among middle-aged, non-Russian-speaking sub-editors from England, irrespective of their hairstyle. But Hagrid was in no mood to be appeased.

I laughed, but it was one of those empty laughs, just a noise really. I felt my heart quicken and my head get lighter as the flight or fight mechanism kicked in and the blood rushed to the arms and the legs, getting ready for action.

Behind Hagrid, Kanu was lifting the ball over the bar again.

There was a part of me that wanted to get angry. Not with Kanu, I'd got over that. But with this ogre, take him on, not just for humiliating me, which he was certainly doing and which was the whole point, but because he'd made me realise just how much I cared about being humiliated. I had nowhere to go. A question had been asked. An answer would have to be given. We were spiralling down into feral territory.

Decision time. We'd reached that point when men fight or surrender, when final calculations are made by sniffing each other for fear and checking out your opponent for weakness, looking for them to glance away, or listening for their voice to change pitch, or seeing them swallow hard. And while I did all of these things, Hagrid did none.

I leaped to my feet and Hagrid did the same and chairs and

glasses went flying. I remembered those sad Helsinki eyes as I, followed by Karin and Clara, turned around and fled out of the bar and ran, first breathlessly and then laughing like children, through Tallinn's cobbled streets.

# 16 The Idiot

Pieter had been right about Saaremaa. Straight away off the ferry it was clear why the island held such a special place in Estonian hearts. Carpeted in thick spruce forest and juniper groves, fringed by white-sand beaches and flecked with dusty, ancient villages, it had a magical feel.

I rode past old windmills and lighthouses as slender as Doric columns and along the Sõrve Peninsula, where convex cliffs reared up like great waves frozen from the Baltic Sea.

Along the peninsula were dotted the abandoned detritus of occupation: the immense former collective farms, overgrown and forlorn; the spindly watchtowers and the flyblown barracks covered in Russian graffiti. I sat on top of a missile silo for a smoke, attended by a few curious sheep and, looking out to sea, imagined how, just a few years previously, it would have been armed and aimed at me.

I rode into Kuressaare, the island's small capital, past the fourteenth-century dolomite castle. With its moat and draw-bridges and red-tiled conical turrets, it was a Gothic fantasy the like of which I thought only existed through a Disney animator's pen.

The citizens of Kuressaare seemed to be dealing with the pace of change a little more sedately than the people of Tallinn. Cafés and craft shops lined the main thoroughfare. Extended families sat around the leafy square, taking refuge from the fierce sun under the canopy bestowed by a crescent of plane trees.

I found a hotel in the shadow of the castle. The receptionist's name was Anna, according to her badge. She was also beautiful, according to her genes. She was blonde, in her early twenties, with big mournful eyes of such startling intensity that it was an act of will not to stare continually into them.

She asked me where I'd come from and what had brought me to Saaremaa. I told her a little bit about my trip. The semi-abridged version.

'Ah,' she said. 'The midlife crazies.'

The phone rang, and she answered it. I took it as my cue to pick up my panniers and head to the room. But she gestured for me to stay as she started talking into the receiver.

As she spoke, I found myself staring at her again; looking at those eyes. On the Tube sometimes, if I was feeling dislocated, I'd find myself looking at my fellow passengers, especially the middle-aged, grey and stressed-looking ones, and try to peel back the years, imagine what they'd looked like as a child. When it worked, it was magical.

Lately, I'd found myself doing the reverse: looking at young people and adding a few lines and a few pounds, with a couple of life's reversals chucked in for good measure, to try and imagine what they'd look like 20 or 30 years down the road, rather like one of those age-accelerated police posters seeking a long-missing person or, indeed, a trawl through your own photo albums. This never felt magical. It felt like I was trying to rob them.

I did it with Anna, wondering what she'd look like if those eyes were dimmed with time.

She put the receiver back in its cradle.

'So,' she said. 'Have you found any answers?'

It was a big question, no doubt, the kind that usually comes up after the second cork is popped, or the third. And as it was a big question, and as I am a tosser, I quoted Kierkegaard's assertion that life can only be understood backwards, but must be lived forwards.

I told her that it sometimes felt that the constant moving was creating a never-ending desire to be somewhere else, and threw in Chatwin's theory that, although it's the antithesis of modern, civilised societies, movement is our natural state, that only through it can we be fully alive. I was rocking.

'But what was it that Pascal thought?' she said, as the phone started ringing again and she reached over to pick it up. 'That all human misery is caused by man's inability to sit quietly by himself in a room.'

'Ding, dong,' said the Idiot in my head in the voice of Leslie Phillips. Ah, the Idiot, the priapic ghost in the machine. He'd not put in an appearance since, well, since three minutes earlier when I'd seen those two women walking out of the hotel as I was walking in.

One minute, I'd been happy playing Philosopher Top Trumps with Anna, and now all I wanted to do was rip her clothes off. Socrates had called it his Lunatic; Kingsley Amis had declared finally losing his libido in old age to be one of his finest moments 'after being chained to this idiot for 50 years'. My dad had recently told me he'd experienced the same. Although I can't remember what he'd called his.

As I waited for Anna to finish on the phone, I thought about all the things that man could spare himself without the Idiot: the wars, the infidelities, the Porsches. But I also started to think about the other stuff: the discoveries, the engineering, the sport.

On and on, I pondered the concept of male genitalia in human development. Until I caught myself. Was it normal to think about these things while you're waiting for somebody to finish a telephone conversation in a hotel lobby? What about that man over there? Was he thinking about how we'd have never made it to the moon without the XY chromosome? Or was he just thinking about what he was going to have for his supper?

The man looked over at Anna. He was definitely not thinking about what he was going to have for his supper.

Anna finished the call. She returned to our previous conversation, asking me about the restlessness. I didn't have too much to say on the subject now, content as I was just to stand there dribbling, grinning like a big eejit.

'Can I buy you a drink after work?' the Idiot asked her.

'No,' she said.

The Idiot was on great form that night at dinner, too. I hadn't invited him, but sure enough, after I'd ordered a steak and a bottle of wine from the waiter, I'd scanned the room and seen two women chatting at a table and the Idiot had squeaked up and said hello.

I busied myself with the solo diner's props of notebook, pen and guidebook, writing not too much really, obsessed as I was rapidly becoming with how I could make my move. I glanced over. One of the women was looking at me. She turned back to her friend and they giggled.

The stakes were high-risk, no doubt. A crowded restaurant, two women together – always a tricky dynamic to invade unbidden – the real possibility that they didn't speak any English, the lack of any exit strategy on rejection, apart from scuttling back to my table and pretending to write insouciantly into my book with the eyes of the restaurant burning into me.

I did a quick risk-assessment. No, there was no way I was going to put myself through that. The Idiot had other ideas. Don't bore him with risk-assessment. Would a matador pull out of a fight because his muleta had faded in the wash?

I glanced up again. The woman was looking over in my direction once more, smiling, stroking her cheek. The Idiot was now taking complete control, putting on his cape, the master of my destiny.

I'd been encountering major problems with the Idiot since hitting middle age. Where women were concerned, while I'd reverted to being a tongue-tied adolescent, he remained a stud-muffin at the peak of his powers. No, actually his stud-muffinness had, if anything, grown in inverse proportion to reality.

While all the same insecurities I'd felt in my teenage years had resurfaced, the Idiot couldn't see what all the fuss was about. Surely you should have mastered all this by now, he would say. What's wrong with you?

But it appeared that the man sitting at the next table with his friend had brought his idiot along, too, because he got up and started walking in the women's direction.

Ah, so they'd been looking at him all along, I thought.

You blew it, was the Idiot's take.

The man bent over and whispered something into the smiley woman's ear, and she laughed for a second and played with her hair. Then she shook her head. The man whispered something else, and again the woman laughed, and then again she shook her head, a little more forcibly this time.

The man shrugged his shoulders and returned towards his friend with a walk of mock indifference. They drained their glasses in unison and, shortly after, without a glance towards the two women, left the restaurant. Smart work, fella. Pluck up the courage only after the bill had been paid and the exit strategy worked out. A true pro.

Having witnessed another man's humiliation, I should have been content to sit there and finish my steak. But the Idiot cares nothing about humiliation or shame. That isn't his department. But he is a cunning sod. Soon he was telling me that the reason the other guy got rejected was because it was really me that the woman had wanted to go over.

Sensing my reluctance to embrace this hypothesis, the Idiot started reminding me of my encounter with Dave in the bar in Copenhagen. I thought you'd learned a valuable lesson that day, he said, that nothing very bad can really happen. So what if you get knocked back?

What have you got to lose?

After five more minutes of the Idiot's hectoring and sophistry, I found myself walking in the footsteps of the recently departed and, with my heart in my mouth, bent over at the women's table and asked if I could buy them a drink.

The smiley woman laughed and twiddled her hair. I held my breath, my little adolescent heart going like a gerbil's. Shortly after, she shook her head. I bent down and asked her if she was sure. She nodded her head. Quite sure, she said.

I turned around and scuttled back to my table, where my half-eaten steak stared back at me. It felt like something very bad had happened. The Idiot was nowhere to be seen. Gone.

'Why didn't you come over and join us?' said a female voice.

I looked up from my steak. It was the friend of the smiley woman.

'I just asked you if you wanted a drink, and you said no,' I replied, my poor little adolescent brain growing more addled by the second.

'Here in Estonia, if a man buys you a drink, he thinks it entitles him to sleep with you,' she said. 'They are all just idiots.'

I smiled at the comment. She smiled back.

'Come over,' she said. 'It would be nice to talk to you. My friend thinks you look nice.'

It felt like something very good had happened.

The next day I rode my bike out of Kuressaare looking for Kaarma. Not so much to top an account that, on balance, was probably still just in the red on this trip, but a tiny hamlet of that name buried somewhere deep in the pine forests and juniper groves.

After going over to the women's table the previous evening, Isabel, she of the smile, had told me about a friend of hers, an Englishman, who was living in the woods nearby, in Kaarma. Still being vaguely of the opinion that my journey was being driven by cosmic ciphers and an idiot, I thought that here was one signpost I would be wise to follow.

An hour later and I was utterly lost. The rutted dirt tracks that wound through the trees all looked alike and, obviously, the trees did nothing to distinguish themselves apart from stand in a row and look the same. The cosmic signposting might have been present, but their really useful terrestrial cousins, the metal boards with writing and directional arrows on, were sadly not.

I smelled a pig farm long before I saw it and pulled over to ask for help. I knocked on the door of the house and was invited in by a Central Casting Russian peasant woman in a headscarf and the advanced stages of dental decay. She spoke no English, so she went off to find another woman. She also spoke no English, but seemed to have all of her teeth. After a while, they both disappeared, and returned with two men for whom neither English nor teeth played any part in their lives.

For a while we stood there, the silence punctuated only by the odd grunt from the other side of the window.

I fished out my guidebook, whose conversations and essentials section furnished me with the Estonian for 'I am in a lot of pain, where is the nearest hospital?', but sadly not how to ask the whereabouts of an Englishman living in the forest.

I adopted the pose of a jolly jack tar looking out to sea, pointed to myself enthusiastically (which I hoped was going to convey the fact that I was looking for an Englishman and not just some random fat bloke), and chanted the word Kaarma, at first quietly and then with increasing volume until I was shouting it so loudly that surely even a foreigner would be able to understand.

It seemed to do the trick, as the woman with all the teeth turned to the one with few teeth and said, 'Kaarma! Kaarma! Da, da.' 'Ah, Kaarma! Kaarma!' she replied. 'Kaarma!' said one of the men. There was a lot of Kaarma going around.

The one with the teeth started to give me directions in Estonian. But then, realising the folly of it, grabbed a piece of scrap paper and began drawing a map. The map, when it was finished, consisted of the farm, a road going off to the right, then a tree, after which an arrow indicated I was to turn left, then shortly after another tree, where I was to turn right. Doubtless this would have been a very useful map in the Serengeti but, I feared, rather less practical in the middle of a pine forest.

Perhaps sensing my lack of confidence in her map, she beckoned me to follow her outside, whereupon she jumped in a decrepit blue Lada and sped off, leaving in her wake a comet's tail of flying dust and debris, through which I blindly steered the bike, the stones pinging off my helmet, the trees either side my only guide to the straight and narrow.

The woman abruptly stopped. My bike, not the happiest of campers on loose dirt, did not, skidding and juddering into the place at the back of the Lada where the rear bumper had once sat. I hit the floor, the bike and the gravel combining to make a noise that put me in mind of Shit On Your Face.

It seemed like I was unhurt, which on one level was a pity as I'd just learned the Estonian for that situation, but on another was for the best, as doubled-up in agony I'd have missed her arm sticking out of the window and pointing up a dirt track before she careered off.

I picked up the bike and, at the end of a track, came to a clearing in the trees. In the middle of it stood an immaculate timber-framed thatched cottage that, in any self-respecting nursery story, would have contained a wizened old crone or a graduated trio of bears scratching their heads and pointing to the porridge.

A young couple emerged from the cottage.

'We've been expecting you,' said the man. 'Isabel called to say she'd met an Englishman on a motorbike. Did you find us easily?'

I told him about the pig farmers.

'Yes, we are remote here,' he said. 'We don't get many visitors.'

He introduced himself as Steve and the woman by his side as Ea, his Estonian wife.

They made me a cup of tea and we sat in the garden. Steve told me that he and Ea had been travelling around doing a variety of jobs in Britain and the US. In 2004, after Estonia had joined the EU, they had decided to give it a go in Ea's homeland.

They'd bought a piece of pine forest, cleared it and built the house. Then they'd built up a cottage industry making organic soap in their kitchen and then selling it mail order. The name of the company? Good Kaarma, of course.

'That must guarantee success,' I said to Steve.

'You'd have thought so,' he laughed, then the smile trailed off. 'But these first two years of trading have been very, very tough. It's not easy to compete with the big companies.'

Steve gave me a tour of the house. He showed me where they heated the fats and essential oils, where the blocks are left to cool, and where they were eventually cut and boxed up. On the shelves, soap with marbled swirls of organic chocolate were labelled 'Dance of the Dakini'. Another, with flecks of vanilla, was called 'Kaarma Sutra'.

'That one's a good seller,' said Steve.

'I can imagine.'

We returned to the garden and drank some more tea. Looking at Steve and Ea, sitting in their own little Walden, I had a pang of jealousy.

'I envy you two,' I said to Steve.

'Why?' he asked.

'It takes guts to live life in the way you do, travelling, taking risks,' I told him. 'I envy you probably because I would never have the courage to do what you've done here.'

'Giving everything up and taking off into the unknown on a motorbike takes a fair bit of guts,' Steve said.

'That's different,' I said.

'In what way?'

'Oh, I don't know. Possibly because there's no investment in what I'm doing. No permanence. It often feels like a kind of thumb-twiddling, a limbo. Albeit with great scenery.'

'There have been plenty of times over the past couple of years when we would have loved to just run away from all this,' Ea said.

'Did you go to Tallinn?' Steve asked.

'I only spent a day there.'

'What did you think?'

'It's beautiful,' I said.

'You should have spent longer there,' said Ea.

'I would have. But … I found it a bit …'

'A bit what?'

'A bit … depressing.'

I immediately regretted saying it.

'Why depressing?'

'It's nothing.'

'Come on.'

'I guess I have naive views about politics,' I said. 'That's all.'

'What does that mean?'

I told her about my dad.

'I grew up with an idea that there was a different way to live.'

'And I grew up with it,' said Ea.

'That's why I should keep my mouth shut.'

'You think it was better when we were not free to travel, had no food in the shops, could not learn about history, were not allowed to go to church, speak our own language?'

'No, I don't think that at all.'

'You think we should be denied these things?'

'I don't. Of course I don't. It's just that …'

'What?'

'I don't see a lot of happiness in Britain. I see broken communities, rising divorce rates, people popping anti-depressants, getting into debt. Exploding prison populations. Everything is aggressive, fractured. We're always in competition with each other, fighting over resources. It's exhausting just trying to stay still, trying to survive. People are constantly restless. We now live in a culture that demands we are constantly restless, dissatisfied with our lives, always wanting to be someone else, somewhere else, anything but our dreary selves, buying stuff to fill the hole. Maybe the state should be powerful; maybe we need protecting from ourselves.'

'If you had lived under Communism, that is not an argument you'd be supporting.'

'I'm not a communist.'

'Every generation thinks that the past was better. Communism, capitalism, it's all the same thing in the end.'

'I don't believe that. Anyway, I'm not a communist.'

'Some older people in Estonia are beginning to get sentimental about life under the Soviets. They forget.'

'One view of the world. That's what we end up with. One idea about how we should live. The only party in town, spread the word. Is that the end: 2,500 years of civilisation and we declare ourselves the winners, surely there's got to be something else?'

'Communism is not the answer.'

'I am not a communist.'

Waiting for the ferry back to the mainland that afternoon were two other bikers, their Harleys heavily customised, muscular and low-slung, naked women lacquered on their petrol tanks. On their heads, they wore German helmets. The bikers, not the women.

The ferry docked, threw down its ramp and the two Harleys growled into life, prompting other passengers to check the heavens for storm clouds. I pressed the start button on my bike. It suddenly sounded quite camp.

Once the bikes were secured, I introduced myself. The two guys, Arnie and John, were from Kirkenes on the northern tip of Norway and were spending two weeks riding around the Baltics. I could have roughly guessed their latitudinal origins, wearing as they did a just-escaped-from-a-coal-bunker look on their faces.

Arnie pulled three beers out of his worn, leather holdall and handed one each to John and me.

'How was Saaremaa?' I asked John.

'Brilliant. How about you?'

'Great. Did you ride out to the peninsula?' I asked. 'Through the juniper groves, past all those lovely windmills?'

'Didn't see jack-shit,' John said. 'Spent the whole time fucking whores in the brothel.'

'Oh ...'

'Man, they were animals.'

'I didn't know there was a brothel on Saaremaa.'

'Should have done your homework,' said John. 'Bet you've fucked plenty of whores on your trip.'

I nodded. What else could I do?

I looked down at their battered luggage held on to the bikes with string, and at their leathers, with the skull motifs, and the women on the tanks and the cowboy boots on their feet. These were bad boys and no mistake. Then I looked down at my Gore-tex all-weather riding suit and my sturdy aluminium panniers and my sensible boots. I felt like the swot at school who was just about to fall in with the wrong crowd.

We rode off the ferry and into a monsoon. I should have felt all snug and smug in my riding suit, but instead looked up the road with puppy-dog admiration at Arnie and John battling heroically through the rain.

We stopped in a café to take shelter and ordered some

coffees. Arnie pulled out a flask and poured something into his. Then he offered it to me.

'No, I'm cool, man,' I said. 'Just spent three days getting wasted on Saaremaa. Got a mate lives in the woods there. Brews his own stuff.'

I thought about the mugs of camomile tea I'd downed with Steve and Ea.

'Where you heading?' Arnie asked me.

I told him that I didn't do no crazy shit like make plans.

They looked impressed.

'Come with us to Pärnu,' Arnie said. 'It's the party capital of the Baltics. Full of pussy. We're gonna rip it up.'

I lit a cigarette, inhaled deeply, rocked the chair back on two legs and then released the smoke, slowly.

'Sure,' I said.

We found a campsite with wooden cabins in Pärnu and transferred our gear from the bikes to the room. In the Norwegians' case this was achieved in a few minutes. In mine, considerably longer.

John pulled a two-litre plastic bottle of vodka out of his holdall. Either his holdall was the Tardis of motorcycle luggage, or it was now empty.

'You guys known each other long?' I asked.

'About 20 years,' said Arnie. 'We met in the army.'

They'd been in the special forces. They had the quiet aura of the truly hard.

They talked about their army adventures and previous road trips. And they talked about their numerous encounters with prostitutes and the most recent adventures in the brothel on Saaremaa.

'Those women were like models,' Arnie said. He described in detail his philosophy towards paying for sex in a way that made it sound so uncomplicated, so perfect for all concerned.

'The girls get paid well,' said Arnie. 'We get laid, don't have to deal with all the normal shit.'

John nodded. 'They enjoy it,' he said.

'Sometimes a massage is enough,' Arnie said.

We drank some more.

'How come you're riding alone?' Arnie said.

'Oh, prefer it that way,' I said. 'Free to do what I want.'

'Married?' John said.

'Divorced.'

'Amen to that,' said Arnie.

'You guys married?'

'Not now,' John said.

'We tried that, eh buddy?' said Arnie. He reached over, grabbed the bottle and filled our glasses.

'To the road,' he said, holding up his vodka.

'To the road,' we replied.

There must have been a thousand women in the Sunset Beach club that night. And every single one of them would have been the prom queen or the small-town beauty heading for Hollywood.

Arnie, John and me leaned against the bar watching them walk past, tall, lithe, athletic, wearing pelmets for skirts and very little else. Because men are such horribly shallow creatures, we felt like pigs in the proverbial.

But if a man's heart breaks every time he sees a woman that he knows he will never have, that night ours were shattered. The Idiot was going nuts.

'The girls are stunning,' I said to the barman.

He nodded, casually.

'Estonian women are the most beautiful in the world,' he said. 'But because they are all beautiful, they cannot afford to have the attitude. So, being an Estonian man is also the best thing in the world. It is a man heaven, no? They will talk to any man. Maybe even you.'

He didn't get a tip.

I returned to Arnie and John with the drinks.

147

'We should go and talk to some girls,' I said to them.

They both looked at me as if I'd suggested we remove our clothes and conga through the club or, worse, swap motorbikes. This surprised me. They were good-looking guys.

'Later,' Arnie said.

'Come on,' I said. 'What's the worst that could happen?'

'We're cool,' John said. 'You go.'

I spotted a brunette and a blonde standing at the end of the bar. Next stop, Oxford Circus, change here for Liberty's.

I walked up to them with as much confidence as I could muster. The vodka had helped, but not much.

'Hello,' I said to the dark-haired one, who may have been Cindy Crawford. She didn't look me up and down, or have that slightly panicked look of a cornered animal, but smiled sweetly and said hello.

The blonde, who was possibly Claudia Schiffer, leaned over and kissed me on both cheeks. She asked me why I was travelling in Estonia and, really, you're on a motorbike, I love men on motorbikes, and how did I like the country and what was my name and did I have a girlfriend. This is what it must be like to be George Clooney.

Stumbling over my words less, I asked Cindy how it was that Estonian women were so gorgeous. Thinking about it now, from the world's biggest cabinet of truly awful lines, that was from the top drawer.

'It is our genes,' she replied.

'And we also like to be good wives,' said Claudia. 'Perfect women, don't you think?' And she cradled an invisible bowl in her left arm and made a whisking motion with her right.

The unreconstructed chauvinist pig in me agreed completely. As did the Idiot, who was on the verge of dribbling. The feminist-raised, liberal, *Guardian*-reader naturally did not, he wanted to upbraid these women for their lack of ambition. So I sent him home early and told him not to wait up.

'Can I buy you a drink?' I asked the girls.

'No,' they replied in unison.

I felt my stomach sink and my cheeks start to redden, anticipating the walk of shame back to the guys.

Then I remembered what Isabel had told me about women in Estonia not accepting drinks off guys. Here was just your run-of-the-mill cultural misunderstanding. Of course, it didn't mean they wanted me to bugger off. Pillock. Why hadn't I asked her to dance?

'Do you want to dance?' I asked Cindy.

'No,' she said.

A pause. Silence. I was marooned in no-man's-land. I looked at Cindy and then I looked at Claudia. As the numbness in me rose they seemed to get even more beautiful. What was I thinking, imagining either of these stunning women would be remotely interested in me? The thoughts started to unravel, one after the other. I glanced over at Arnie and John. They were watching.

I felt a hand grab mine. It was Claudia.

'I'd love to dance,' she said. 'If you'd ever ask me.'

Cindy touched her on the arm and whispered something in her ear. Then she led me on to the dance floor.

'What did your friend say?' I asked Claudia.

'Oh, that we shouldn't be long,' she replied. 'I'm staying at her house and we promised her husband we wouldn't be home too late. Anyway, we've both got to be up for work in the morning.'

The Idiot groaned. I felt elated. We danced for the first song and, when it was finished, I gave her a little bow and gestured with my arm towards where Cindy was standing.

Claudia looked over. Cindy pointed to her watch. Then Claudia grabbed my hand and started dancing again. Over her right shoulder I looked at Arnie and John. They were still frozen to the bar.

# 17 Karina

The wind whistled along Riga's Daugava River. To my right was the old Akmens Bridge, where ancient rattling trams more in keeping with my Eastern Europe fantasies clanked towards the art nouveau toytown skyline beyond. Behind the bridge was a Flash Gordon skyrocket of a Soviet communications tower. To my left, the Vansu Bridge, a modern goliath of a suspension bridge, bringing traffic from the international airport over the Daugava to the new steel and glass hotels, office blocks and conference centres that encircled the old town.

I'd read somewhere that UNESCO has warned Riga it may withdraw its protected status if the voracious programme of building remains unchecked. There were tower cranes everywhere I looked. The Vansu Bridge sang in the wind.

With 6,000 miles on the clock since leaving London, I had come to Riga to get the BMW serviced. I had not anticipated staying in town long. The only other Baltic capital I had visited was Tallinn, and the combination of vomiting stags and homicidal Russians had not encouraged me to repeat the experience.

Not being much of a planning ahead kind of guy, I had pitched up unannounced at the garage and asked if they could sort out my bike. Being a planning ahead kind of organisation, they had said yes, they could indeed service my bike when they had their next available slot. In four days' time.

So, if I was to be in Riga for four days, I decided I would do it in style. I asked the guy at the garage where the king would stay if he'd pitched up unexpectedly in Riga on a weekend mini-break. This wasn't an actual king, you understand, one who might require from the hotel a butler to dispense his toothpaste, or access to nearby deer-hunting grounds, or the level of discretion needed in order to secrete burlesque actresses into his room without bringing down the state. No, my king was a notional figure. A man used to the finer things in life. I might have easily used as my theoretical figure a Premiership footballer, but I don't think I could have afforded it.

That's how I came to be standing outside a hotel by the Daugava River, listening to a singing bridge. It was not the singing that was keeping me outside, though. It was the President of Kazakhstan. He had doubtless asked the same questions as me regarding his accommodation, because he was pulling up in a convoy of large armour-plated cars, attended by a coterie of machine-gun-wielding men with the kind of joy and animation in their faces I hadn't seen since Easter Island.

The President was clearly not a man who enjoyed sharing hotel lobbies, or indeed streets, with the great unwashed, a conclusion I reached when one of the aforementioned statues shooed me away from the entrance and along the road like a tiresome street urchin.

From a distance, I counted enough personnel to have easily included a toothpaste-squeezer and several young women who looked like they could be burlesque actresses. My garage guy had been bang on the money. I was clearly in the right place.

With four days to kill in Riga, and a WiFi connection in my room, I decided to join that great human tide who live their lives convinced that there will be a tomorrow, and even a next week. I fired up my laptop, got on to the Internet and joined a couple of websites.

The first was called Horizons Unlimited, a site specifically created for motorcycle travellers. John and Arnie had told me about it. On it there was a communities section, divided by country, where you can send messages to members world-wide, telling them you're going to be passing through their town and asking if they'd like to meet up, or even put you up.

I fired off dozens of emails to motorbike clubs throughout Eastern Europe and Turkey and Greece and the Balkans and everywhere else I imagined I might end up over the coming months, putting my mobile number on the bottom.

It felt like a bit of an infidelity to providence. But then again, so was using canaries down a mine shaft, or researching which mushrooms might kill you, or googling a fledgling partner and discovering they'd changed their name by deed poll from Lorena Bobbitt. That's what I told myself, anyway.

Straight away, I had a text. 'Mike. It is Boris. You come to Zagreb and we get plenty fucked up, yes?'

Minutes later, I got a message from Istanbul. And then one from Cluj-Napoca in Transylvania. It was miraculous. A few minutes previously, I'd been feeling totally alone, and now I was acquiring new friends faster than, well, faster than the last and only time I had used the Internet to meet people.

That had been a while after I'd separated from my ex. A very attractive, very lovely female friend of mine had met a guy on a dating website. I met him. He seemed normal. Better than normal. He was smart, funny, handsome. They eventually got married. 'You should try it,' she said to me one night, when I'd been moaning about the lack of women I was meeting. 'Everybody's doing it. There's no stigma any more.'

Back at home that night, I'd had a look at some of the female profiles on the site she'd been on. I soon discovered all sorts of things about women that had hitherto been unknown to me.

For starters, all of them professed an inability to describe themselves, so they'd asked a friend to do it for them. Every single woman in the cyberverse liked nothing better than a long walk in the countryside followed by a long lunch in a rustic pub.

That said, however, they would be just as happy to be curled up on a sofa at home watching a DVD in front of a roaring fire with a glass of red wine. Always red.

Nobody smoked. When asked about drinking habits, all had ticked the 'occasional' box. When asked the question who would you like to have been in a former life, they all said Audrey Hepburn. Favourite food? Spaghetti alla vongole. Everybody. How weird was that?

Looks in the man they were seeking were not as important as the twinkle in his eye and the ability to make them laugh. If he had the brooding passion of Maximus twinned with the sensitive soul of Rilke, all the better. The single most important thing, though, seemed to be that he shouldn't take himself too seriously.

Here was the blueprint for becoming the perfect catch. All I had to do was post a picture of me in a clown outfit, order pasta with clams for them on the first date, then ask them if they'd like to come back to mine to watch *Breakfast at Tiffany's* in front of my roaring log fire while working, with moderation, through my collection of fine clarets. I'd be fighting them off.

But pictures are just pictures, and words are just words. For a while, the Idiot thought Internet dating was the best invention ever, but then he was never there when those awkward third-date conversations took place, between me and them, or between them and me, that although we'd had a good time, there would be no more of them.

Somehow, the women I met in the flesh never matched the chimeric fantasy females I'd constructed in my mind. If I thought back to all my significant relationships, would I have picked any of them from an Internet site based on their profiles? The answer, in most cases, was no. Maybe I took it all too seriously. I am a man, after all. My romantic adventures in cyberspace came to an end.

But time can do strange things to us. And so, maybe, can having four days to kill on your own in Riga. I googled around and discovered an international dating site that seemed to fit the bill. For the price of a couple of beers in Norway, I could join for three months and write ahead of time to single women in towns I might be visiting. Hand on heart, I honestly believed that, along with the Horizons site, it might be a good way to meet people for friendship. Honestly. It is possible that the Idiot had his own agenda.

I sat down to compose my message. It read: 'Guy, 36, divorced, on a solo motorcycle road trip, riding through (insert name of town here) for one, possibly two nights. Would like to meet a woman to show me around in exchange for dinner and red wine.'

Messages sent over the coming months: 37. Replies received over the same period: 0. Women, huh? Never understand them.

Emails dispatched, and with only three and three-quarter days left, I went out for a walk. There was a casino just down the road from the hotel.

I bought a few chips and won a few hands of blackjack, then took my pile of plastic counters to the roulette table, put them all on red and doubled my stash.

I looked around at the other players. I recognised a few of the President's men, faces still like granite, tossing down chips and staring at the spinning wheel like they were waiting for their doctor to read them the results of a biopsy.

I won some more and now had about a hundred quid riding on black. It was the largest bet I'd ever had on anything and thought that, now the amount was significant, I'd maybe finally understand the buzz of gambling. But as the ball whirred around and clicked into red, all I felt was indifferent. I drained my complimentary Scotch and walked out of the casino and back to the hotel.

I logged on to the Internet again. It had been over 45 minutes since I'd last checked. There were dozens of messages from the motorbike site inviting me to come and stay in countries on my route. This only confirmed my growing conviction that motorcyclists, along with gardeners, are the nicest people on earth. Put motorcycling gardener on your CV and I guarantee St Peter will have you down on the VIP list.

One Aussie couple, Joe and Sue, emailed me to say they were riding around Europe and were currently heading for Poland. After that, they'd be going to Romania and Bulgaria and Turkey. If our paths crossed, they said, it would be great to tour around together for a few weeks. I emailed them back.

'Would love to,' I wrote. 'Hopefully see you in a few days.'

There was, sadly, no response from bikers in Riga. It was hard to understand, but ever since sending out the emails, I'd felt a wave of loneliness descend. Like I was part of a community, but estranged from it. In my mind, I had the image of all those people staring into lifeless mobile phones on trains and buses as if willing them to ring.

Now there were people out there I could be spending time with, instead of wandering around alone. Before, I'd been mostly okay with the solitude, but now it threatened to crush me. All I could think about were my friends back home; what they'd be doing; how good it would be to have a beer with my mates, talking shite.

My phone beeped again. Another text. 'You are welcome at my house in Bar, Montenegro. Gasho.' I looked at the map. If I set off now, I could be in Montenegro in four days or so. But then I remembered I didn't have a motorbike. It was in a garage somewhere on the outskirts of Riga. I felt trapped.

I went down to the bar and ordered a large drink. On the bar stools next to me, a couple. He looked to be late middle-aged; she maybe early twenties. He touched her leg in a manner suggesting he was not her father; she gave him a thin smile, her eyes flat. I looked around the bar. Dotted in corners were four, maybe five, other such pairings.

I walked out of the hotel again and along the Daugava River, thinking about what I'd seen in the bar, and also back in Tallinn and other hotels on the road. The bridge was still singing, the wind whistling through its cables.

It felt like the barometer was falling, quickly. I thought about Arnie and John. I thought about my ex-wife. I thought about Hanne, and about the girls in the Pärnu nightclub, and Anna and Isabel. I thought about my dad and the clump around the head. I thought about Arnie and John again. My mind was racing. I walked under the Vansu Bridge and sat on a concrete bollard for a cigarette. Then another. I breathed deeply, slowly. The barometer stopped its slide. I walked back to the hotel.

'I will bring a couple to your room and you will tell me which one you like,' said Lucian, the concierge.

But Lucian was not talking about a tie or a jacket I would have to borrow for dinner, or a choice of the hotel library's guidebooks.

'What you like? Very young? Blonde, dark? One of each? You tell me,' he was now saying. I could feel a bead of sweat running down my back.

I'd walked back into the lobby and, as I suspected he would, Lucian had asked me how I was, and I'd told him I was feeling so, so, and then, with a wink, Lucian had suggested, as I also knew he would, that a little company might be just the thing.

So instead of saying, 'No thanks, I'm not that kind of guy. I think prostitution is an evil trade that exploits the vulnerable', as I'd done all the times before on this trip, I'd said 'splendid idea' as I also knew I would the minute I'd put out the second cigarette. There'd been a tree on the bend, and I had stared right at it.

I told Lucian to bring along just one girl, any girl, that I wouldn't have the heart to choose one and reject the others in front of them. Lucian looked at me as if I was a bit strange. 'The only thing I'd ask would be that she could speak English,' I said. Lucian was now looking at me as if I was some kind of pervert.

'And please,' I'd said to him sotto voce, 'don't tell anybody.' I've no idea what I meant by that.

Lucian just said: 'Don't worry, this will be our, how you say, little mystery.'

Nine-thirty was the appointed time, and at nine I was having a shower and then I ironed a shirt and put on some aftershave, all things made difficult by my shaking hands.

I was more nervous than before any first date. I opened iTunes on my laptop, and scrolled down for something suit-able to be playing when the girl arrived. It was tough. Romantic? Upbeat? Middle-of-the-road? But then I thought, is this really what a man does before inviting a prostitute into his room? I attacked the minibar.

At 9.30 exactly, there was a gentle knock on the door. I double-clicked on Rodrigo's *Concierto de Aranjuez*. My heart was thumping in my ears as I opened the door and tried to look oh-so casual, albeit with the pallor of a man just about to suffer a huge coronary.

Lucian was standing there in his concierge's uniform. Beside him was a girl around 20, blonde, Slavonic, gorgeous. He stated the price, as if he were about to sell me a rug, and said that he required the money upfront.

I counted out the cash in front of them both and handed it to Lucian. He stood there for a few seconds, counting the money then recounting it, before slipping it into his breast pocket, stepping backwards, still smiling, closing the door as he left.

Then it was just me and the girl standing in front of the full-length mirror by the door. I was the middle-aged, fat guy in the hotel bar.

I asked her what her name was.

'Karina,' she said.

'Nice to meet you,' I said, and reached out to shake her hand. She looked a bit unnerved. 'I'm … John.'

I ushered her into the room.

'You look nice,' I said, meaning the pink, knee-length skirt and crop top she was wearing. But the words, when they hung in the air, sounded sinister, corrupt, like I was grooming a child.

I asked her if she would like a drink.

'Orange juice, please,' she replied.

I went to the minibar and poured it, hands still trembling, and tossed the bottle into the bin where it clinked against the pile of empty miniatures.

I gave the orange juice to Karina. We sat down, some distance apart, on the edge of the bed. *Concierto de Aranjuez* was playing out its final, soft, notes.

'This is the first time I've ever done anything like this,' I said to her.

We both jumped. Shaggy was in the room. The laptop was on shuffle.

'What you want is some boombastic romantic fantastic lover.' Shaggy.

I leaped up and raced across the room.

'Mr Lover lover, Mr Lover lover, girl Mr Lover lover.'

I fumbled with the laptop, trying to hit mute but only succeeding in increasing the volume.

'She call me Mr Boombastic say me fantastic touch me in the back, she say I'm Mr Ro … mantic.'

I found mute.

'Sorry,' I said.

'I like that song,' she said.

Karina then told me the rules. They were precise, clinical. Certainly not first-date smalltalk.

'No anal. You will wear a condom. No kissing.'

'No kissing? How could we have sex without me kissing you?' I asked.

Now Karina looked at me as if I were weird.

'They are the rules,' she said.

I'd booked an hour, like you might a squash court, but I had no idea what to do next. I suppose I should have served. But how?

We just sat in silence for a while.

Karina stood up, lifted up her skirt and pulled her thong to one side, showing me her shaved, childlike vagina.

'What do you think?' she said.

'Looks like a neat job,' I said. 'Isn't it painful?'

'What?'

'Having that done.'

'I meant … doesn't matter.'

She let her skirt drop and sat back down. More silence.

'Are you from Riga?' I asked her.

'I'm only here during the week. I'm from Kaunas, in Lithuania, about 100 miles away. I go back at weekends.'

Silence.

'Do you have family there?'

A pause.

'I have a girl, four years old,' she said. 'My mother looks after her while I'm away.'

'Don't you miss her?'

'Like a hole in my heart,' she replied. 'I call every evening before she goes to sleep. I have her picture by my bed, so I see her at night and in the morning. She wants to be a pop star.'

'How's her singing?'

'Like an angel's.'

'What do you say to her, about why you leave?'

'We tell her mommy has to go work in a pizza restaurant in another town,' she said.

A pause.

'Have you got a picture of her on you?' I asked.

'No,' she said.

More silence. I looked around the room, There were framed prints on the wall, of Notre Dame, of St Paul's, of the Duomo.

'What about the girl's father?' I asked.

'You ask many questions.'

'I'm sorry. Just interested.'

'You want me to tell you how terrible my life is?'

'No.'

'Would that make you feel better?'

'That's not ...'

'He disappeared soon after the birth,' she said.

'I'm sorry.'

'He was no good. A drunk. Left us with big money problems.'

'So you had to do this?'

'Don't judge me.'

'I'm not. Sorry.'

'I do what I have to do. For now, it is this.'

'The money's pretty good, for Latvia,' I said.

She laughed.

'How much did you give Lucian?' she asked.

'One hundred and sixty euros.'

She laughed again.

'Know how much I get? About 20 euros.'

'Shit.'

'Don't tell Lucian I told you,' she whispered. 'He would have me beaten.'

I said it would be our little mystery.

With about 15 minutes to go, Karina pointed to her watch and said that we should get on with it, time was running out.

'Sex without kissing,' I said. 'Can't imagine it.'

'It is not allowed,' she replied.

'I know, I remember you saying.' I smiled at her.

Silence.

'Fancy some music?'

'Sure.'

I got up from the bed, walked across the room. Scrolled down. Found Shaggy.

I sat down again. Karina was tapping her foot.

I slipped my hand across the bed. Rested it on top of hers.

'This is really your first time, isn't it?'

'I told you.'

'How old are you?'

'Forty-two.'

'That's crazy. And you wasted your money.'

'Not all men use prostitutes.'

I looked across at her.

'They do in my world.'

Bang on 10.30, there was a gentle knock on the door and I opened it to see Lucian standing there, a smiling Sgt Pepper, ready to take Karina off to her next appointment.

'Bye, John,' she said.

'Bye, Karina,' I said, and kissed her on the cheek.

She glided out soundlessly.

'Okay?' Lucian asked, looking puzzled.

'Fine, thank you,' I replied, and closed the door.

I looked at myself in the full-length mirror, closed my eyes and breathed deeply. The room was full of Karina's sweet fragrance, like jasmine.

# 18 Kaunas, Lithuania

**8**.30 a.m. My first electric shock of the day from the hotel's elevator call button. The lift looked like it could be a remnant of Soviet days. As did the surly staff who, upon hearing my complaints, did not seem to think that electrocuting the guests was a big deal.

8.35 a.m. Breakfast. I had potato stuffed with sour milk and thin gelatinous strips of meat. I asked the waitress what it was. 'That is pig, how you say ...' and she grabbed her right ear.

9 a.m. Managed to avoid an electric shock by pulling up my T-shirt and using it to press the elevator button, exposing my stomach. The staff on the front desk looked on, unmoved.

9.30 a.m. Went to the Internet café to pick up my emails. There was one from Joe and Sue. They were heading for Katowice in Poland to stay at a Horizons' member's house. They would be there in three days' time. I emailed them back, saying I'd meet them there.

10 a.m. I visited a museum celebrating the history of Lithuanian pharmacies. The curator, slumbering in his chair, awoke and looked slightly shocked to see me. He regarded me with what can only be described as suspicion. He took me around and told me a little of the history of Lithuanian pharmacies. I am assuming that this is what he was telling me, because he didn't speak English.

11 a.m. I called into a museum celebrating the role of the

devil in Lithuanian folklore. Set over three floors, there were over 2,000 statues of Satan in his various guises. I learned that the devil created alcohol from she-goat's urine and that tobacco first grew from the grave of the devil's mother.

12.30 p.m. Lunch. I sat at a table outside a restaurant and had *cepelinai* – translation: Zeppelin – a Lithuanian peasant dish that consisted of a rugby ball of potato dough stuffed with meat. It was created to keep out the cold during the long, harsh, Lithuanian winters. It was not necessarily the best choice when it was 90 degrees Fahrenheit. My phone beeped. It was a text message. 'When are you coming to Zagreb. We get fucked up. Boris.'

1.30 p.m. Still sitting at the table, unable to move.

2.30 p.m. Staring at an enormous naked man in the main square. It was a statue, though the bronze budget obviously hadn't stretched to a fig leaf. A big boy. My guidebook told me that its erection had caused outrage to the good folk of Kaunas.

3 p.m. I visited the tourist office to try and discover where the museum was that celebrated fumbling around in the pitch black, feeling stuff. The woman behind the desk said that she'd call them to see whether they were open, but the phone just rang and rang and she eventually replaced the receiver and told me that she thought it might be closed.

'Maybe there is somebody new working there,' I said to her, 'and they're fumbling around in the dark trying to find the phone.'

I laughed at my clever joke.

'No, they are closed,' the tourist woman replied.

3.15 p.m. Bought new underwear to replace the binbag of dirty laundry I accidentally left behind in Riga, which at that very moment was probably being examined with a cattle prod by a man in a white boiler suit and a face mask. Also bought a new T-shirt. It read: 'I ♥ Lithuania (but where is it?)'

4 p.m. Visited the museum celebrating the history of

Lithuanian taxidermy. In Pavlovian fashion, I lifted up my T-shirt to call the lift to get to the start of the exhibition on the third floor, once again exposing my stomach. The woman waiting alongside me with her two young children decided to take the stairs. There were 13,000 creatures on display, from snow leopards to Siberian tigers, crocodiles to walrus, butterflies to zebra. Discovered what an aardvark looks like.

6 p.m. Went back to the hotel. Forgot to use my T-shirt. The people on the front desk were the same as in the morning. They laughed. Got to my room and ran a bath. There was no plug. I rummaged around in my washbag to find my universal travel plug. It fits every plughole in the world. Except this one. I used one of my new socks. The bath filled up. The water was the colour of cognac.

8.30 p.m. A restaurant on the main drag and a dinner of chicken in champagne, served with tinned peaches and a mushroom sauce. There appeared to be grass growing from the ceiling. A medley of pan pipe music was playing over the PA, including 'I Will Survive'. This was followed by 'We Are The Winners (of Eurovision)', Lithuania's 2006 Song Contest entry, though thankfully not on the pan pipes.

10 p.m. Go back to the Internet café to pick up emails again. There was one from a guy called Wayne. He had been reading my newspaper columns and had felt compelled to write to me. 'You are a pathetic and pointless waste of space,' he'd said, 'a whiny, middle-class git poncing around Europe while the Middle East burns.' But quite how the two things were connected he didn't explain.

10.30 p.m. Lying on the bed in my hotel room, thinking about Wayne. He'd got under my skin. He'd have been delighted. Waynes love the Internet. As much, if not more so, as the Idiot. What could be more fun than spreading your bile via the anonymity of your send button?

I started composing an email in my mind.

Dear Wayne,

Thank you for your email. While I agree with you that the situation in the Middle East etc, etc, is indeed grave, I cannot see that I can do much about it. Maybe if I spent my life doing worthwhile things, then you might have more respect for me ...

I paused, thinking it all through for a while. Outside, a truck was reversing, its beeps pulsing in the night.

... actually, fuck you. I don't really care what you think.

I never did send the email.

# 19 Osas

On arrival at the border between Lithuania and Poland, it was the same old routine. Rummaged around for passport. Found passport. Then found unused bundle of banknotes from country I was leaving. Apologised to border guard, got passport back, turned around and headed for the nearest place to spend aforementioned wedge. This nearly always turned out to be a garage. But there is only so much petrol and vodka and cigarettes you can buy and, of course, car air-fresheners and fluffy dice are not the most useful thing on a motorcycle.

In this part of the world, many garages doubled up as hunting stores, but how many decoy ducks, gutting knives and whistles that simulate the mating cry of the moose can a guy need? Departing countries with pockets full of soon-to-be-useless currency is something we all become arch at avoiding when we're returning from our holidays, tipping the taxi driver to the airport generously, or splurging on an inflatable travel cushion.

There'd been the Swedish krona and the Norwegian kroner (although it is absurd to imagine that one might ever leave Norway with any money. They actually have insolvency specialists at the borders). Then there'd been, briefly again, Swedish krona, then Finnish euros and Estonian kroons and Latvian lats and Lithuanian litas. Now there was the Polish zloty. Honestly, somebody ought to invent a Europe-wide currency. It would save a lot of hassle.

The planners, the people who'd have sat down and mapped out a route and the must-see sights, and worked out where they would sleep, and returned home with tales of amazing discoveries, would never end up having to buy decoy ducks at a sleepy border post. But, then again, they would probably never have spent an afternoon at a taxidermy museum, so who's the fool? What's an aardvark look like, huh?

Riding through the Baltic states, I'd been wondering where all the trucks had gone. I found out: they are all in Poland. It seemed like the entire contents of Poland were being carried from one part of the country to the other, and then moved back again.

On the single-lane 'motorways', the tarmac was warped from wear and cold and heat, and the ruts trapped my wheels from time to time like tram tracks and took them off towards the oncoming juggernauts. Target fixation's not an issue in Poland. It's perfect midlife crisis territory. You just get in a rut and see where it takes you.

Leapfrogging a truck at a time was the only way to progress – escaping the fug of exhaust, a brief face-off with a wall of metal speeding my way, a sonorous blast of a horn, and a return to a warm lungful of diesel. It was like a perpetual game of chicken.

I got off the murderous main roads and on to the yellow country lanes, past watering holes in rivers where families of Poles laid towels out on the grassy banks and children did backflips from each other's shoulders and dive-bombed from ancient wooden bridges. Older men gathered under trees to smoke and talk in grand councils.

In Poland, nearly every telegraph pole by the side of the road had a pair of storks nesting on top of it. Big beasts, storks, and ordinarily a telegraph pole would be about as useful to it as a home as it would be to me or you. So kindly farmers fix a wooden cartwheel across the top, upon which the birds build their nests and return year after year.

The arrangement suits all parties. The storks get a free home close to good transport links, and the farmers get their crops blessed by the good fortune the storks bring.

I stopped to take a picture of a nesting pair, parking the bike some way away so as not to alarm them. As I approached, first one head then another popped up like periscopes. As I got closer, the storks got to their feet and stretched to perhaps a metre in height to get a better view of the strange creature in a helmet.

Another stork stood up. Also an adult. I wasn't sure what was going on in that nest, but I felt I shouldn't be photographing it.

I rode through one of Europe's last primeval forests in Bialowieża, and as I emerged an acute pain shot up my left leg. At first I thought I might be having a stroke, but then it occurred to me that it was possibly even worse: there was a wasp in my boot.

Ignoring the sensible action of pulling over and removing my boot, I started to smash myself in the left foot while riding one-handed through the traffic. This only seemed to encourage the wasp to intensify his attack.

It also encouraged the attention of the local police who'd been sitting in their squad car in a lay-by and, in this most Catholic of countries, probably concluded that here was some kind of self-flagellating tour of penitence.

They drove behind me and gave their siren a quick toot. I pulled over, dismounted Frankie Dettori style and hopped around in circles, simultaneously punching myself in the foot while trying to get my boot off, shouting 'wasp! wasp!', which, in all probability, was not the Polish for wasp. The two policemen looked confused, unsure of what the appropriate action was to take.

The stings kept coming. Finally they stopped. I removed

my boot and a battered wasp fell out. Can wasps smile? This one looked pretty happy. The policemen looked pretty happy, too.

'Wasp, wasp,' I said, pointing to the lifeless stripy corpse.

'Osa, osa,' they said together.

To compose myself, I popped into the adjacent café. A group of hunters in plaid, armed with rifles like a militia, drank plastic tumblers of vodka. On the television in the corner was a Bollywood film with Polish subtitles.

'Nescafé,' I said to the girl behind the counter. This was an important distinction. I'd already learned that if you say 'coffee' in Poland, you get given a thick, gloopy brown sludge with metal filings in it. I believe it is also available in Britain. We call it tarmac.

After a while, a young man sat down next to me and introduced himself as Christoph. After visiting his family in the south, he was returning to his army posting nearby where he was completing his national service.

'I saw you punching yourself over there,' he said.

'Osa,' I replied.

'You speak Polish,' he said. 'Very good.' His eyes blazed with curiosity, intelligence.

Noticing that my cup was empty, he offered to buy me another coffee. That would be very kind of you, I'd said. He was already at the bar before I remembered.

'Where are you from?' I asked him, feeling the enamel peeling off my teeth.

'Zamość,' he said. 'It is very beautiful. You should try and visit it.'

I said that I might.

Christoph asked me about my trip. I listed the countries I'd travelled through, and some of the things I'd seen along the way.

'Sounds like a great journey,' he said.

'It's been interesting,' I said.

I asked him what he planned to do when he'd finished his national service. Presumably move back to Zamość, I'd said, 'meet a nice girl, get married?'

'There is nothing for me in Zamość, in Poland,' he said. 'I am an engineering graduate. There is no work.'

He told me that he intended to move to Britain. London, maybe, or Cardiff. All of his friends were doing the same.

'There's a lot of Poles in Britain now,' I said.

'That is a problem?'

'The economy has been strong. It might not always be that way.'

'Poles are good workers,' Christoph said.

'Sure. But immigration's a big issue at home right now. Bigger than I can ever remember. I can't imagine things are going to get easier any time soon. When times are good, everybody's happy enough, that's all I'm saying.'

I sounded like Enoch Powell.

'We are all in the EU now,' said Christoph.

'In 2004, nearly a million people came to work in Britain. That's got to have some impact. Good and bad. The scale of it is hard to comprehend ...'

'We have no choice but to go. It will be many years before we have the same opportunities here that exist in Britain.'

'And Poland loses all its youngest and brightest people.'

'It is not my job to improve the economy here.'

'How can that ever happen if people like you are making wealthy EU states even wealthier?'

'What is a country? A lump of rock. I will always go where the opportunities are. Where I live is not important.'

'Wouldn't you want to come back and live in Poland one day?'

'I don't have that dream,' he said. 'Maybe my father and his father's generation did, but not me. This is the world now.'

I told him that the world as described by him seemed quite a depressing place, rootless people wandering the globe.

'You sound like my father,' Christoph laughed. 'If I did what he wanted me to do, I would be stuck here. His generation brought down the communists. They lived in their time. We live in ours.'

'But weren't your father's generation fighting for something beyond money?'

'Of course. We are free, thanks to them. There is nothing left to fight.'

I drained my coffee and wiped my teeth with my fingers.

'Another?' Christoph asked.

'I think I've had enough.'

'You don't like Polish coffee?' he asked, looking mock-offended.

'Possibly it's an acquired taste,' I said to him.

The hunters finished their vodka and made their way towards two pick-up trucks. The Bollywood movie had ended, replaced by a wildlife film. Lions were feasting on a wildebeest.

I got up to leave. Then turned to Christoph.

'Won't you miss your coffee in Britain?' I said.

It had passed my lips before I realised just what a stupid question it was.

Tucked away in south-east Poland on the Ukrainian border, Zamość is far from the tourist trail. I rode into the cobbled Rynek Wielki, a stunning Italianate Renaissance square lined by colourful arcaded burghers' houses and dominated by a vast pink, onion-domed town hall, its magnificent steps straight out of a Busby Berkeley musical.

Christoph had told me a little about the town's history, about how, during the Second World War, Hitler had imported German colonists to the town to create what he hoped would be one of the Third Reich's eastern bulwarks. Poles had been expelled from the town and 5,000 Jews, nearly half the population, had been exterminated. Because of Hitler's plans for Zamość, the old town had escaped destruction.

I parked the bike. The square was rammed. In the corner was a large stage, on which troupes of Polish dancers in traditional costumes whirled and whooped to accordion music.

I walked among the dense crowd dancing and laughing in the early evening sunshine. Young people eyed each other up self-consciously. Teenage girls pouted. Little boys chased each other and wrestled in playfights on the cobbles.

On another stage, folk singers were crooning a soft ballad, so mellifluous and sad that it broke my heart even though I hadn't the faintest idea what they were singing about.

In front of me, an old couple danced. Their grandchildren darted around them, ruffling the old lady's skirt. The children's parents held hands and swayed softly together, to the music.

I hadn't known that this festival was going on. It was magical. For once, I was in the right place at the right time, exactly where I should have been, the experience all the more delicious for its unexpectedness.

Christoph had been right about Zamość. I felt sad that he would not be coming back.

# 20 The tennis coach

Everywhere I'd ridden through Poland, I'd seen railway tracks. Every few miles I'd crossed over a set, usually just a single line, often rusty and grassed over, sometimes disappearing into dark, thick, impenetrable forest. But I saw few trains.

There was a terrible, almost unbearable, sadness about these tracks: two strips of steel, leading off into the distance, always going to the place that they go.

I stopped by one of these lines and stepped over a rail to stand on a crumbling wooden sleeper. There was a set of points, taking a siding off to the right where, some few hundred metres further on, through a brick archway under a tower, the track would come to an end. It seemed to me that all railway lines in Poland ended up here.

A short while later, Helena was taking me through the various rooms. There were glass cabinets containing papers and records, postcards written home on the trains, rooms full of mattresses coarsely stuffed with horsehair on the cold, stone floor.

On the walls were grainy, mug-shot photographs, taken in the early days before the cost of film and processing were calculated to be too expensive and tattooing was introduced as a cheaper option. Each individual was staring straight ahead, frozen, gaunt, like death masks. Except one young girl, hauntingly beautiful, whose glassy faraway eyes were looking downwards.

'She had given up already, what chance did she have?' Helena said. 'Look at the dates. She was dead within a week.'

There appeared to be a sliding scale of horror to the tour, because each room eclipsed the last with the tales of barbarity it contained. And the statistics were so immense and the cruelty so ingenious and surreal that it got to the stage where I could not really take it in any more, where my mind stopped even trying to understand, and I could feel, perhaps in self-preservation, my compassion and empathy ebb to be replaced with a cold detachment.

We entered a room containing baby clothes and Helena began to tell me about the medical experiments carried out on children. On children. In that room. I let out a loud laugh. I was mortified by what I'd done, but Helena said that I shouldn't be embarrassed, that it was a common reaction.

On and on, room after room: artificial limbs, spectacles, suitcases with the names of the owners written on the side. But by now I was simply looking at the piles of artificial limbs, spectacles and suitcases, thinking about how they looked like items mislaid on the bus, waiting for their owners to come and collect them. I could cope, thinking like that, that there were no people there, in the room.

But a moment or so later, and I was swallowing hard, great globs of brine running down my face and gathering in small pools at my feet. I could hardly breathe. I was looking at the shoes.

'It is always the shoes,' said Helena.

There were tens of thousands of them, cascading down like some immense penny falls. There were smart women's shoes with little silk gerberas sewn on to the toe, and tiny blue children's shoes with a tiny anchor motif, and men's brogues that had been lovingly repaired at some stage – I could see the patched-up sole. And these shoes had all carried these people to this place. The wave of grief I felt just then was unlike anything I had ever felt before.

We stepped outside, into the heat and the flies.

'This is the execution wall, where the firing squad operated,' Helena said. I looked across. There were people standing against it having their photographs taken. Some put their thumbs up and smiled. Others flung open their arms and tilted their heads in that pose that communicates only: look where I am. Others still raised fingers gently to rheumy eyes.

We padded between the barracks, treading gently on the gravel. Around us, large groups of Israeli youths wandered through the camp, bedsheet-sized Israeli flags draped around their shoulders, like football fans. It seemed aggressive, proprietorial. Helena saw me looking at them.

'This is increasing every year,' she said. 'We don't like it. This is a place of remembrance for everybody who suffered here. It is a shrine commemorating a crime against humanity, first and foremost. There should be no display of nationalism. It is inappropriate; ironic, even. We have tried to stop it, but then we get complaints.'

We walked on in silence for a while.

'It's hard to articulate, because it sounds wrong whichever way you come at it,' I said. 'But seeing those young people swaddled in their flags makes me feel like I am at the wake of a stranger, a voyeur intruding on private grief.'

'You are not the first person to describe it like that,' Helena said.

Along the tracks and through the arch. I had never been to that arch before, but every detail of it was familiar to me. We stopped besides a large black and white photograph of an SS guard gently cajoling a newly arrived old man to hurry up, the guard's finger pointing out the group of women and children just ahead of him. The old man, recently relieved of his suitcase, seemed to be shrugging his shoulders, as if to say:

'What's all this about, then, eh?' But the look on his face was not one of alarm as he jauntily lifted one foot in front of the other and headed off towards the block where, he had just been told, he would take a shower.

'Look at the gates in the background of the picture,' Helena said. 'This is the exact same spot. Just over 60 years on.'

We started walking in the same direction as the old man and the women and children in the photograph. Suddenly, I urgently needed to ask Helena about her life away from here.

She told me about how Poland was changing since it joined the EU, about all the young people leaving and her fears for the future. She told me about the child she was carrying and how she wanted the child to become a tennis player when she grew up, just like the baby's father. She'd met him when she was having lessons.

'You got off with your tennis coach?' I asked.

The sun was shining and the birds were singing

'You seduced your tennis coach!' I said again, teasing her, as we walked past the barracks and towards the concrete blocks.

'I know, I know,' Helena replied, laughing, holding her hand over her eyes, shaking her head.

# 21 The Aussies

'**S**o what's a bloody Pommie doing travelling on his own, then?' asked Sue, which, I believed, is Australian for 'haven't you got any friends?'

'Ah, you know,' I told her. 'Got divorced. Hit the road to work a few things out.'

'Is that right?' Sue said, which, I believed, is Australian for 'wanker'.

We were sitting in a Chinese restaurant in the town of Tarnowskie Góry, just outside the vast industrial city of Katowice. I had parked my bike in the main square next to a Yamaha SuperTenere loaded with luggage and, as arranged, met up with Doroata and Jarek, the Polish Horizons host couple, who were sitting there with their young son Piotr, and Joe and Sue, the travelling Aussie bikers.

'You are welcome to stay in our house for as long as you want,' Doroata said. 'It is small, but you are welcome.'

'Very kind,' I replied. 'Had many bikers passing through?'

'Actually you are the first,' Jarek said. 'We put our message on the website last week and a day later Joe and Sue contacted us. Then you. We didn't expect quite so many people straight away.'

Doroata and Jarek and Piotr looked at the three of us, sitting there in all our motorbike gear. They seemed a little shellshocked.

Sue introduced me to Joe. He was very handsome, not

unlike Bob Hope, complete with magnificent jawline and sandy hair running to silver. He looked a little older than her.

'G'day mate,' he said in a Canadian accent. 'Nice to meet ya.'

Doroata called over the waiter and asked for the bill. The waiter said something back to her.

'The waiter's Polish is good,' I whispered to Sue.

She looked at me like I was a complete tosser.

'It was a joke,' I said.

Sue looked at me like I was still a complete tosser.

We went outside and pulled on our helmets. Sue's had a pair of bright red devil's horns glued to it.

Then we rode the short distance back to Doroata and Jarek's house. I was directed towards my couch in the living room and dumped all my gear on the floor. Sue and Joe took their stuff to the spare room upstairs. Doroata, Jarek and Piotr stood there, in the small hallway, watching the invasion, still looking shellshocked.

We all went out into the garden. We were joined there presently by a cloud of mosquitoes.

Sue sat down next to me, pulled out a map and laid it on the table. I started slapping myself on the arms and face.

'The Horizons site is fantastic, isn't it?' Sue said. She wasn't slapping herself on the arms and face. 'We've met some great people through it.'

I confessed I hadn't used it before.

'Why not?'

'I only found out about it recently,' I said. 'But even then, using it felt a bit like cheating. I wanted to be this heroic loner figure on the road.'

'And how was it?'

'Miserable, sometimes.'

She laughed.

'Blokes are weird. Pommies are weird,' she said. 'What chance have you got if you're a Pommie bloke? You're screwed.'

A wasp the size of a hummingbird started hovering around my top lip. I tried to swat it away with both hands, only to miss the wasp but catch the end of a spoon, flicking it in gambols across the table until it met Jarek's forehead with a thunk. I jumped up and ran to the other side of the garden like a big girl.

'You're like Mister bloody Bean,' Sue said.

'Sorry everybody,' I said. 'Got a thing about wasps. Bad experience recently.'

'Is that right?' Sue said.

I returned from my exile by the geraniums after Sue had given me an assurance that the wasp was not going to eat me.

'How have you survived on the road so far?' she said.

'It's only wasps I have a problem with,' I said.

'And Chinese people speaking Polish,' she replied.

'That was a joke.'

'How's that work, then?'

'Well, it's kinda funny, isn't it?'

'Funny? Like Chinese people speaking English?'

'No. Not like that. You have *Porridge* in Australia, right?'

'For breakfast.'

'No, Ronnie Barker, you know ...'

'Sure.'

'Well, remember the episode where the black guy climbs on the roof and Fletcher goes up to rescure him?'

'Vaguely.'

'Well, the black guy's name was McLaren. And he had a really thick Glasgow accent.'

'So?'

'Well, that was funny. Looking at him, you wouldn't expect him to talk like that.'

'That was in the seventies, wasn't it?'

'It was.'

'Done much travelling?'

'She's winding you up, mate.' It was Joe. 'You know what they're like. Gave me heaps when I first moved to Oz. But especially with you guys. Like bloody siblings, bickering.'

'It's too easy,' said Sue.

'I knew,' I said.

'Is that right?' said Sue.

We looked at the map on the table.

'Where to next?' I asked.

'We're not big on planning,' Joe said. 'But we're probably going to ride through southern Poland, then into Slovakia and Hungary, and after to Romania and Bulgaria and then western Turkey. We want to store the bike somewhere in Greece for the winter and fly home.'

'How about you?' said Sue.

I told them that their route was similar to mine, although I was also thinking about Ukraine and right across Turkey as far as Mount Ararat.

'Don't you need a visa for Ukraine?' asked Joe.

'Not since they hosted the Eurovision song contest,' I said. Joe looked a little confused.

'We could travel together,' Sue said. 'It would be fun.'

I hesitated for a second. I'd been really, really looking forward to hooking up with English-speaking people. I'd missed the nuanced conversation, the banter.

But maybe I'd also grown accustomed to not being challenged; breezing in and out of places; always the novelty act; gone the second the opening dance had come to an end. If constant movement by myself had created the hope of daily reinventions, would the constant of Joe and Sue mean I was stuck with me?

'That could be great,' I said.

'It'll be fantastic to have you along,' said Joe.

I imagined he was thinking about how my effervescent personality and sparkling wit would hugely enhance their road trip.

'If anybody wants to nick one of the bikes, they'll take your BMW over our old Yahama any day,' he said.

The next morning we said goodbye to our Polish hosts. They stood on the doorstep to wave us off, still looking shell-shocked.

Then Joe, Sue and I set off through our own little road-movie montage. We headed across southern Poland, then up the steep slopes and through the summer-mothballed ski resorts of the Tatras Mountains. Then into Slovakia, past brooding castles on hilltops, and through Roma villages where children pumped water from wells in the square and everybody waved at us with broad grins, as if we were flying through on magic carpets. You'd have thought they'd never seen the devil on a motorbike before.

We pulled over at a roadside market. Joe and Sue were of the opinion that what my bum really needed, if it was to survive the heat of the Anatolian desert, was to be sitting on a dead sheep.

'It'll keep you cool,' Joe said. 'Those plastic seats can get uncomfortable in the desert.'

'We've got one. It's great,' said Sue.

I looked at their Yamaha. Its saddle was indeed covered in some kind of animal fur; a nice, clipped, neat affair that I hadn't really noticed until they'd pointed it out to me.

'Back in a minute,' Joe said.

He disappeared and came back with a sheepskin so startlingly white and so startling fluffy that it looked like Don King had shoved his head in a tumble dryer. It also put me in mind of those spirit-level bubbles and the tins of elbow grease.

'You got anything we can use to attach it to the saddle with?' Joe asked.

'Well, I've got this,' I said, pointing to the old rope lashed to my pannier box.

'Perfect,' said Joe. 'We could strip it down and use the strands as ties.'

He set to work unravelling the rope and then threading it through the slits he'd cut in the skin, then on to the frame of the bike under the saddle.

'Why are you carrying round that tatty bit of rope anyway?' Sue asked, as we watched Joe work.

'In case I need a tow,' I said to Sue, 'obviously.' Though I left out the word obviously. Didn't want to embarrass her.

'D'ya hear that, Joe?' Sue said. 'He's got that rope in case he needs a tow.'

'A tow?'

'That's what he reckons.'

They both smiled.

'A tow, huh?' Sue said.

Ten minutes later my bike was transformed into the kind of machine the Marlboro Man might ride at a Pride parade if he'd suddenly developed a horse allergy.

'Don't want to seem ungrateful,' I said, 'but doesn't it look a bit ...'

'A bit what?'

'Well, a bit gay?'

'Gay? Na, mate,' Joe said. 'It looks heroic.'

'Got a problem with pooftahs as well, have ya?' said Sue.

So after they'd taken a few pictures of me looking 'heroic' next to my Bavarian steed, we remounted and continued as before, my bum sliding all over the place on its new hairy perch, which burst out from under me in all directions, small children no longer waving, but pointing and laughing.

We stopped for the night at a small town called Levoća in eastern Slovakia and parked up in the stunning Renaissance central square. After a few more photographs, Sue went off to inspect the various pensions and guesthouses, to haggle over prices and suss out the best options.

Joe and I found a bar, ordered a couple of beers and took them to a table outside.

I removed my boots and socks to give my toes some air.

'Jeezus, mate,' Joe said. 'I've seen better-looking feet on a camel.'

I put my socks back on.

'You've got a good one there,' I said, pointing to Sue, emerging from one doorway and quickly disappearing into another.

'I know it,' he said.

I thought about how easily and gratefully men abdicate responsibility for decision-making and slip happily into the role of being looked after. And how easily and gratefully some women adopt their roles, too. It felt glorious for the first time in ages to relinquish my decision-making duties.

'Been married long?' I asked.

'About seven years.'

'Kids?'

'Not together. I've got three from my previous marriage.'

'And Sue?'

'What?'

'Has Sue got kids?'

'No. You?'

'No.'

'Want to, one day?'

'Maybe. Never really saw myself as an old dad, though.'

'How old are you?'

'Forty-two.'

'Same as Sue,' Joe said. 'That's not old.'

'Did you ever discuss having kids?' I asked.

'For a while. Sue was in her mid-thirties, the pressure was on, you know.'

'Sure.'

'I left the choice to her, really. We sat down and talked it through. Either we started a new family, or we spent the rest of our life taking off on adventures. Just the two of us.'

'Big call.'

'Yeah, big call.'

'How old are you?' I asked.

'Fifty-six this year.'

'Looking good on it,' I said.

'Fine living,' he laughed. 'And a good wife.'

We took a drink of beer. In the square, Sue had collared an old man with her map and was gesticulating wildly with her arms.

'Anybody special, back home?' Joe asked.

'Not at the moment.'

'Sure.'

'I mean, I'd like to meet somebody one day. I think. It's hard work being on your own. Exhausting, really. I think I'm much happier if I'm part of something. Maybe some people are hard-wired to cope with solitude better than others.'

'I've got a lot of mates back home who'd give their right arm for what you've got right now.'

'Same here.'

'Hacked off with their jobs and their lives.'

'I know. But how many of them, given the chance, actually take it? I mean, it's not that difficult is it?'

'Maybe not for you.'

'I'm only here by default, really.'

'Took me a long time,' said Joe. 'It's not so easy when you've got responsibilities.'

'Everybody's got responsibilities.'

'You haven't.'

'What, just because I haven't got kids?'

'They change everything. You have to take yourself out of centre frame. Put your own needs on hold. You wouldn't understand.'

'I've got friends at home who've just had kids. Overnight

they become superior beings. As if anything I've got to say about anything is somehow less valid.'

'It's what we're here for.'

'There are other things in life. If I had kids, I wouldn't be sitting here now.'

'No, you probably wouldn't.'

'Would be stuck at home ...'

'Sounds like you're a bit jealous.'

'I'm not jealous. All that worry ...'

'You wouldn't understand.'

'There are too many people on the planet as it is.'

'You wouldn't say that if you had a child. Can't imagine your dad thinking that.'

'Didn't stop him.'

'What?'

'You say how having kids changes everything, forces you to put your own needs on hold.'

'Yeah.'

'Well, didn't happen to my dad. Walked away when I was a kid. Started insisting that we called him Pete, not dad.'

'Pisses me off.'

'The name thing?'

'No, men who walk out on their families.'

'You don't know him.'

'A man should slug it out. Doesn't matter what's going on. At least until his kids are grown-up.'

'Maybe he couldn't any more.'

'There's no excuse.'

'He was my age.'

'What's that got to do with anything?'

'There's me, fucked off with my life in London, job going nowhere, getting older, the daily grind, angry about everything, blah, blah, blah, panicking about this being as good as it gets.'

'And?'

'Well, are you telling me that if you have kids you are somehow immune to all that?'

'Not immune.'

'That kids are a magic insurance policy against the fear of getting older?'

'I'm saying that parents should do the right thing.'

'I've only started to look at this recently. My dad's mum died when he was a teenager. His father was an alcoholic. He had to look after his five siblings. What's the "right thing" for him? He had a shitty time of it.'

'We've all got problems.'

'I'm not defending him. I've spent most of my life having a go at him for the decisions he's made. But he's getting old. I've been waiting for the phone call. Will I have to summon up some great mechanical display of grief? Or will there be something else? You know? Will there be this regret that I never really knew Pete? Wouldn't allow him to be Pete?'

'He's your dad,' said Joe.

'That's what he says when he leaves a message on the answerphone these days,' I said.

'What are you bludgers talking about, then?' It was Sue, back from the hotel recce.

'Oh, just putting the world to rights,' said Joe.

'Without me?' said Sue.


That evening we had dinner in a restaurant in the shadow of a stunning, floodlit baroque town hall. Sue sat studying the guidebook, reading out places we might visit the next day, asking us what we thought.

We ordered pig knuckles, which came with succulent crackling the size of a boxing glove. We drank good red wine and talked.

There was a dynamic to travelling with others that utterly changed the experience. There was the framework of consensus, an external validity to your journey somehow, no more solo breakfasts and dinners and, perhaps most importantly, someone to tell you when you're starting to smell.

Since meeting them, I'd seen things that would exist permanently in a way many of the experiences to which I'd been a sole witness never could.

Sue asked if she could look at my digital camera pictures from my trip.

'What pictures?' I said.

'You've been on the road over two months, you must have a whole stack of photos?'

That day, Sue had been taking photographs of me from the Yamaha's pillion seat while we rode along. Sue took photographs of everything. Every time we pulled over, there'd be pictures. Me and her. Joe and Sue. Me and Joe. Joe, Sue and me caught in the corner of the frame by some shoddy self-timer set-up work. It was a snapping frenzy, and it had become infectious. I had been taking pictures like a man possessed, too, and my memory card was rapidly filling up. But they'd been some of the first pictures I'd taken since leaving London.

I thought about my photo albums at home. They were like a version of the 7-Up documentary series: a staccato life in pictures. There was an abundance of photographs of me as a kid, but there seemed to be a big gap after my early teens where there were just occasional pictures. At university, I'd filled dozens of albums. Then, as far as my life in pictures was concerned, there was not much until my ex-wife appeared ten years later when, again, every single event seemed to be documented.

Since we broke up, my camera had lain idle. Could it be that we take pictures only during the happy cycles of our lives? An attempt at emotional censorship? Or that maybe a photograph is only worth something when you have someone to share the memory with?

'I'm afraid I hadn't really taken any, until I met you guys,'

I said to Sue. 'Do you think that maybe people only take photographs when they're happy?'

'Jeez, Joe,' she said, tucking into her crackling. 'He's off again.'

It was after six pints, and talking to a stranger in a pub in London, that I'd learned that Ukraine had relaxed its visa restrictions.

'Nah, mate, definitely don't need one,' he'd said. 'When they hosted Eurovision, it was so complicated trying to issue visas to everybody, that they did away with them.'

It had all seemed very feasible at the time but now, standing on the Ukraine border, it occurred to me that perhaps I should have checked, because the heavily armed *Homo sovietus* was waving his big stick perilously close to my head and telling me, in no uncertain terms, to clear off back to Hungary.

'But everything's cool since Eurovision,' I said to him, as he swatted me away like a gadfly with his stick. In context, it was perhaps the most surreal thing I had ever said.

'Visa no problem,' he barked. 'Photocopy of motorbike registration is problem. You need original.'

'But this is the original,' I said, waving my photocopy at him and thinking about the crisp, original, filed neatly away at home in the drawer, where another Pub Guy on another night had said it would be safest kept.

'Niet,' he said and, judging by the veins on his temples swelling before my eyes, he was clearly getting a little excited. I wasn't sure whether heavily armed Ukrainian border guards were yet on-message to the choice-driven, customer-oriented free-market model. So, I concluded that this was what happened in Ukraine, because Pub Guy had said that too, that all I had to do was slip him a few dollars, or a pair of Levi's, and doors, or in this case barriers, would open.

But directly behind *Homo sovietus* was a big sign in myriad

languages, including English, warning of the dire consequences of trying to bribe an official. And although Pub
Guy would doubtless have surreptitiously slipped over the
money, tucked in his photocopied registration document,
and glided through, he was almost certainly still in a pub in
London and not risking an interminable spell in a Ukrainian
jail cell.

The commotion from the next booth told me that Joe and
Sue were also experiencing some difficulty convincing their
*Homo sovietus* of their suitability to enter the Ukraine. Shortly
afterwards, we were huddled forlornly around our bikes,
holding a post-mortem.

'They're tough on the bike documents,' I said.

'Our documents were fine,' Joe replied. 'But we needed a
visa.'

At that point it occurred to me that Australia doesn't do
Eurovision.

So we turned our bikes around and headed past the queues
of cars and lorries we'd so confidently ridden past a few
minutes earlier, back across the river on the bridge of shame,
eyes burning into us. I was transported back to being a
16-year-old in Birmingham, and Boogies nightclub, when the
bouncers had said my shoes were the wrong colour, or my
moustache was too ridiculous, or something, and it's funny
how any rejection triggers the same emotions, even if it's the
delights of Chernobyl, and not grab-a-granny night, that
you're missing out on.

The heavens opened. We sheltered in a barn and discussed
what we fancied next. Serbia? Croatia? Slovenia? I've had
similar conversations before, but they have usually been
about what country's cuisine to order from the takeaway, or
else accompanied by holiday brochures and pros and cons
regarding flights and hotels and, ooh, that spa looks nice.

In the end we plumped for Romania, a decision based not
on anything much other than the fact it was just down the

road. And it was raining again. As if Romanian rain might be less wet than Hungarian rain.

Joe peered through the door and put his hand out with his palm upturned. This wasn't necessary. From where Sue and I were sitting, it looked like Joe was standing behind a waterfall.

'He doesn't like riding in the rain,' Sue said.

A pause.

'I want to talk to you about something personal,' she said.

Uh, oh.

'It's about your underpants.'

'Beg your pardon.'

'Underpants.'

'What about them?'

'How often are you changing yours?'

It was a day of surreal conversations.

'Why?'

'It's important.'

'Every day,' I lied.

'Every day! That's crazy. On the road, you should only change them every other day,' she said, giving me the same look she'd done earlier with the tow rope. 'Or else you'll just spend half your time cleaning 'em.'

I told her I would change my regime.

'I'll be checking,' she said. She didn't say how.

Joe came back over.

'Let's wait here a while to see if it clears up,' he said. 'I don't much like riding in the rain.'

'Sue told me.'

'Has she asked you about your pants yet?' he asked.

'Just now.'

'She'll check, you know.' He didn't say how.

Sue pulled out the remains of the pig knuckle dinner from the night before and divided it into three portions, which she placed in kitchen roll and handed one each to Joe and me.

We ate in near silence, the only sound was of the rain lashing against the felt roof.

After lunch, Joe lay down supine on a bale of straw. Sue rummaged through her bag, produced some scissors and, after cradling Joe's head in her lap, started cutting his hair. He looked like a sultan. A sultan with riches beyond imagination.

'We've got to find you a good woman,' Sue said. 'I know a few lovely ones back in Cairns. You should come visit us one day soon. Before you're past it.'

'I thought that, according to you, men get better with age,' I said.

'It can go either way,' Sue said. 'Not sure about you yet.'

'If I moved to Cairns, would you adopt me?' I said.

'I already have,' she replied.

Joe laughed.

'Your real mum might have something to say about it, though,' Sue said.

'I'm sorry,' Sue said.

'It was a long time ago. Twenty years, next June.'

'You must have been quite young.'

'Fourteen when she first got ill.'

'Jeez, that's tough.'

'Two radiation treatments, two chemos. Kept going away. Kept coming back. Eight years.'

'Shit.'

'Sorry about the conversation earlier,' Joe said.

'That's okay. You didn't know.'

'It must have all started just after your dad left,' he said.

'The following year.'

The rain eased. We mounted up and headed for the Romanian border. I went first through the checkpoint and, just after, pulled over to wait for Joe and Sue. They presented their passport to the guard, who flicked through it and shook his head. Joe said something else to him, but again he just shook his head.

I got off my bike and walked back to the barrier.

'What's going on?'

'We didn't realise, but apparently we need a visa for Romania. We're going to have to go all the way to Budapest to the Australian embassy to get one.'

'Shit.'

'Come with us, then we can come back to Romania together,' said Joe.

I thought about it. Travelling with Joe and Sue had been so easy on the one hand but, paradoxically, spending so much time with them had also been tough. Losing my invisibility should have been great, and in many ways it had been, but weirdly I'd also felt the most exposed since leaving London. It could have been jealousy at what Joe and Sue had got. It could have been that getting close to people meant all I could think about was leaving them. I didn't know. I was like a push-me-pull-you creature at that border post.

'I'm going to carry on on my own,' I said. 'Ride out to Mount Ararat, check it out round there. We could meet up again in western Turkey in a month's time or so.'

'You sure?' said Joe.

'Pretty much,' I replied.

'That's a plan, Stan,' said Sue, smiling.

We hugged goodbye.

They climbed aboard the Yamaha.

'Don't forget about your pants,' Sue said. And with that they were off to Budapest. I watched and listened to them fade to nothing.

Then I walked back to my bike and rode off alone into the rain.

# 22 What am I doing here?

'**V**elcome to Transylvania. I vant to drink your blood,' the receptionist said as I checked into a hotel in Cluj-Napoca. Actually, she didn't, but this was somewhat surprising as the entire population of northern Romania seemed to be working for Dracula Plc. Every town boasted an impossibly sinister Gothic castle high on a hill. Each one claimed that Vlad Tepes had lived there, or carried out a spot of impaling there, or purchased his fags there, with the attendant souvenir businesses selling mugs and T-shirts though, disappointingly, no glow-in-the-dark false fangs. They'd be a big seller.

Thus in Bran, there was Dracula's castle, although it transpires that he never actually went there. Then in Sighisoara there's, erm, Dracula's castle, though, fair enough, he did appear to have been born there, in a house quite close by that's now the Casa Dracula themed restaurant, natch.

Then in Snagov, there's Vlad's tomb, though in 1931 it was opened up and found to be empty. Bearing in mind that Bram Stoker never actually visited Romania, and the whole thing starts to look like a farrago on the same scale as Charles Dickens's London where, if every blue plaque on a pub is to be believed, Dickens's greatest expectations revolved around necking as much grog as possible.

I unpacked my boxes in the room and headed out to find an Internet café. I was trying to hook up with Alex, a fortysomething motorcycling resident of the city, who had responded to my email sent via the Horizons website back in Riga.

'Just send me an email if you're close by,' he'd said. 'And we'll meet up. I'll show you around town, there's lots to see.'

This I'd done the night before, from an Internet café in a city just over the border when, having spent all of an hour away from Joe and Sue, I'd been seized with the need for human contact again.

There was indeed a reply from Alex, but he'd sent it from Constanta, a Romanian resort on the Black Sea some 300 miles away. He explained that he had been unavoidably detained in the resort and would be unable to meet me. He then directed me towards an attachment, which, he said, would explain everything.

I opened it. It contained two photographs of his motorcycle. In the first, a large-breasted woman was draped over the handlebars wearing only a pink thong. In the second, with marginally smaller breasts, a different woman was lying naked, reclining on the saddle. I emailed Alex to say that I wouldn't be expecting him back any time soon.

I walked around the streets of Cluj-Napoca. Back at the border, I had had another 'Heart of Darkness' moment. I had been to Romania once before, about five years earlier, and I remember walking out of the airport in Bucharest and feeling that I could be robbed at any time; as is usually the case when you sit in a metal tube for a few hours and the door opens and you are somewhere completely new, where people look different and the smells are all unfamiliar and the noises are strange.

As the taxi driver put my bags in the car, I'd watched him like a hawk, heaping my prejudices on to him and the people milling around who, I was convinced, were trying to steal from me. Romania was a dangerous place, of that I was sure, the end of civilisation, where dark forces operated (and not just after sunset).

After a week I had re-entered my metal tube and flown away, my prejudices intact, the fact that nothing bad had happened to me being down to vigilance and simple good luck.

But now, walking around the streets, after having been on the road for 10 weeks with nothing bad happening to me, and crossing countries not at 36,000 feet, but about 3 feet, I could finally see Romania. I felt deeply ashamed of the thoughts I'd held.

Cluj-Napoca could have been London, or Rome, or Tallinn. Glamorous people sat at pavement cafés and supped espressos and were decked out in the trendiest of clothes, supplied by the designer shops that lined the avenues. Most people spoke English and the bookshops stocked the great English writers: Thackeray, Trollope, Austin, Archer. The streets were clean and people smiled and said hello, and each time they did, I burned with shame a little more.

I stopped at a newsagent's and looked at the postcards on sale. This was a trick I had picked up on the trip. If you want to know what the main sights of a city are, look at a postcard rack. All the postcards of Cluj showed a big statue of a man on a horse. Dozens of the same man sitting on the same horse from every conceivable angle and from every conceivable time of day and night. On one or two, he had a pigeon on his hat. Actually, London or Rome might have been pushing it. Perhaps more like Nuneaton.

With Alex detained trying to scrape girls off his bike at the seaside, and not wanting to see all the sight in one go, I headed to a local restaurant for a bite to eat. It was jam-packed and appeared to be fancy dress night. I was betting that the revellers were regretting not consulting each other beforehand, because nearly everyone had come in traditional Romanian peasant costume. Elvis or the Pink Panther would have stormed it.

I took a seat. I felt a bit underdressed in my jeans and T-shirt, and occasionally I attracted a glance from my fellow diners, but I reflected back on what I'd been learning regarding shame-busting and returned their disapproving looks with a smile and a wave.

Shortly after the waiter came over and poured me a glass of champagne. I fished in my pocket and tried to give him some money, but he was having none of it. This only convinced me further that here was the most civilised of countries.

An accordion band played in the corner. I finished my champagne and, before I knew it, the waiter was back, topping me up. Again he refused my offer of money. I was loving Romania.

'Why are you here?' asked a man sitting down next to me, who had come as a cossack.

I told him a bit about my story, about the divorce and turning 40 ...

'No. Why are you here?' And he pointed to the floor.

'Aah, why am I here?' I said, and I also pointed to the floor. 'Well ... what's your name?'

'Michael.'

'Well, Michael ... that's my name too. Spooky, huh? Anyway I was with some friends, but they got turned back at the border because they didn't have a visa. I'd been trying to follow providence, see, always going where my instincts lead me ... but then I had this crisis about wanting to be on my own again, which was ridiculous because I'd been having a great time with them, but I'd been connecting it all with the death of my mum, I think, and maybe about not wanting to turn into my father and be alone for the rest of my life. That's universal, no? Do you ever think about that, Michael? Whether we are genetically predetermined to repeat the patterns of our parents, or whether we have a choice?'

He was staring back at me with rapt fascination. I was

clearly unlocking some of the great secrets of the universe for him. I felt it my duty to continue.

'Anyway, after me and the cosmos had conspired to get my friends refused at the border, I was a bit lost. So yesterday I remembered that I had a contact here in Cluj-Napoca, and I emailed him to say I would be passing through, and thought that it was providence pulling its little funny twists and turns again ... But then I got an email back saying he was in Constanta, and he'd attached a couple of pictures of naked girls to explain why ...' I nudged Michael and winked.

'So then I saw this packed restaurant and, well you know what they say about always eating where the locals eat, so I came in and now you've come over and started talking to me so maybe I have a message for you, or you've got one for me, or something. Maybe that's why I'm here.' And I raised my eyebrows and pointed to the floor again.

The accordion band struck up a rousing number and everyone stood up. A woman in a big white dress and a tiara accompanied by a man also dressed as a cossack walked in to the room through a cloud of confetti and the whole place burst into applause.

I put down my half-finished champagne and slipped out of the door.

After having a good, long look at a statue of a man on a horse, I found a bar called Diesel and ordered a Long Island iced tea. What with the suspended glass staircase and the Corbusieresque furniture, it felt like the kind of place in which one should drink cocktails.

I started chatting to the barman, whose name was Ion.

'Why are you here?' Ion asked.

'It's not a wedding, is it?' I said.

'No,' he said, looking a little taken aback. 'Why are you in Cluj-Napoca?'

'Oh, just passing through,' I said.

I asked him whether he worked at the bar full-time.

'No, I am a student at the university,' he said. 'But I have to work long hours here because the wages in Romania are very bad. It doesn't leave me a lot of time for my studies.'

'I guess you'll be leaving when Romania joins the EU?' I asked him. Almost every young person I'd asked so far in Eastern Europe was planning to leave their country soon.

'Of course,' he said. 'I'm going to go to Ireland after I graduate. After next year we will be free to work and travel everywhere in Europe.'

I reminded him about the restrictions some EU countries were going to place on Romanian immigration after accession.

'That drives me crazy,' Ion said. 'Foreigners will be able to come and work here, buy homes here more easily, buy cheap Romanian manufacturing. But not the other way around. That wouldn't happen to you if you wanted to move to France or in Germany, would it?'

'No, it wouldn't.'

'People in Europe think we Romanians are all thieves and beggars.'

'Those views are just held by the ignorant few,' I told him, looking away as I said it.

'Where are you going to after Romania?' Ion asked.

I told him I was going to ride through Bulgaria and then on to Turkey.

'Bulgarians are worse than the Roma!' he said. 'They really are all thieves.'

A succession of limousines were dropping off a succession of stunning women at the door, where they sashayed up the steps in their pelmets, through the bar and then disappeared through a doorway at the back.

'The money might be bad, but the jobs has its perks,' Ion said. 'Romanian women are the most beautiful in the world. And the most beautiful Romanian women live in Cluj-Napoca. And the most beautiful women in Cluj-Napoca come to Diesel and walk past my eyes every day.'

I asked him what was through the door at the back.

'That is the nightclub downstairs,' Ion told me. 'I think if you would go down there, we would not see you again until the morning.'

'I have no desire to go to any more nightclubs on this trip,' I said. 'I'll have another Long Island iced tea, though.'

The barman's name in the nightclub was Demitri. His iced teas were not a patch on Ion's. He asked me what I was doing there.

'Ion upstairs told me I'd regret it if I didn't check it out,' I shouted back. I was regretting it. My brain was being sautéed in techno.

A male Aussie voice besides me yelled: 'Hello, Michael. How are you?'

It was a hair-standing-up-on-your-neck moment. I didn't know anybody in the country. Besides, nobody had called me Michael since school. And even then, it was only teachers using the two-syllable-beats-one-to-communicate-displeasure technique.

I turned to see a man in his twenties, smiling.

'How do you know my name?' I yelled back at him.

He pointed to my wallet open on the bar, displaying my driving licence.

'I'm a detective, mate,' he yelled, 'from Sydney.'

He looked very pleased with himself for this remarkable bit of detection work, and seemed to be suggesting that it would have been beyond his colleagues from, say, Melbourne or Adelaide.

He and his friend were touring the Eastern European capitals on holiday. 'So far we've been to Riga and Sofia and Tallinn. The girls are amazing. That's why we're here,' he shouted. 'You see some of the beauties we've bagged. Makes Aussie birds look like a dingo's arsehole. All you've got to do is wave a few bucks around and they're all over you.'

'Is that right?' I shouted at him.

'Damn right,' he shouted back.

A pause.

'What you doing here?' he yelled.

It was the sixth time I'd been asked the question in as many hours.

'Oh, I've been travelling with two Aussie mates in Hungary,' I shouted, 'but they've gone back to Budapest.'

'Arrww, mate, I've heard the birds there are stunning. I bet your buddies are up to their nuts in it.'

'Probably not,' I yelled.

We both took a swig of our beers. Another ear-splitting techno track came on. I was getting quite nostalgic for Shit On Your Face. It felt like I had the Rank gong man on either side of me hitting my temples with his mallet.

My detective friend pointed out his mate, on the dance floor, trying to rub his groin against the rump of a girl, who in turn seemed to be doing her to best to throw him off, like an angry steer. Finally, she turned round and gave him the universal finger.

'Man, they love it,' the detective yelled in my ear.

I looked around the club. There were plenty of beautiful young people there, for sure, but the more I scanned the room, the more I could see plenty of men, about my age, standing alone in corners, or propping up the bar, taking long draughts of their beer, watching the young, seething mass.

I recalled the middle-aged guys who used to sit at the bar of the nightclub I worked at as a young man in Birmingham, night after night, and the contempt I used to feel for them, the sad old losers, wondering what had gone wrong with their lives. I smiled.

'What?' I said to the detective. He'd asked me a question that I hadn't quite heard above the woodpecker that was now making its way through my cerebral cortex.

'I said that you never did tell me what you were doing here.'

I paused. I was thinking about Budapest.

'I don't know,' I told him.

From Cluj-Napoca I travelled south to Sighisoara, the afore-mentioned dreamy town with a perfectly preserved medieval citadel at its core and a neat and varied line in 'Vlad Tepes woz here' memorabilia. I rode up the steep cobbled ramp and through the gateway into the main square. It was packed with tour parties following guides with umbrellas and stalls selling Dracula masks and T-shirts.

I parked the bike and walked around for a while, down cobbled alleyways flanked by sixteenth-century burgher houses, past the massive clock tower, with its pageant of slowly revolving figurines, and up to an ancient church up on the hill, reached via an old stone staircase with a wooden roof along its entire span.

It was one of the most stunning towns I had ever seen. Sue and Joe would have loved it here, and I would have loved it there more had Sue and Joe been there.

I strolled back to the bike and sat astride it for a while, smoking, thinking, feeling a bit dislocated. The guy who looked after the car park walked over and said hello. He'd been admiring my bike, he said, rode one himself, and told me how he dreamed of hitting the road one day.

His name was Marc. He'd signed up for the Romanian secret service after leaving college 'thinking I'd be tracking people down on my motorbike', but he'd been put in an office in a suit where he typed up reports all day until he could stand it no longer and quit. Now he was looking after this car park until something came up and he could afford to take his road trip.

'But with the money I earn here, maybe this is something I never get to do,' he said, and held his shoulders in a shrug and turned his palms towards the sky. 'But I dream about it all the time. You are living my dreams. You are a very lucky man.'

Thirty-odd miles down the road from Sighisoara, I turned off the main road and followed a rutted, twisting track through a dense forest. My conversation with Marc had been a timely bucket of cold water. What I really wanted tonight was not another bar or nightclub, nor a swish hotel with all the amenities, nor the company of other travellers, nor a Dracula-themed restaurant, nor Aussie detectives shagging their way around the former Soviet bloc.

I wanted to take a dirt track, any dirt track, find a patch of ground, pitch my tent and, accompanied only by the bottle of vodka, the bread and the garlic sausage (it pays to be careful in these parts) I'd bought back in Sighisoara, gaze up at the stars and listen to the forest nightshift go about its work.

It had begun to rain again, with the odd low growl of thunder thrown in for the requisite Transylvanian ambience. Just as I was about to pull over and make camp, the forest ended and I emerged somewhere in the sixteenth century.

The main street of the Roma village – just hardened clay really, turning swiftly to mud – was full of horses, and oxen, pulling carts piled high with straw, the drivers in pork pie hats, ancient bolt-action rifles slung over their shoulders.

Wizened old Roma women in headscarves carried their grandchildren on their backs in slings fashioned from rugs. There was a hand pump in the street from which villagers were drawing water. People sat out on their steps to watch this strange creature pass, and scruffy, shoeless urchins chased after me.

I felt a tad vulnerable, uncomfortable. Five years earlier, I had been in Romania's most cosmopolitan city imagining I was in mortal danger. Now I was in the middle of the forest, in the middle of nowhere and darkness closing in, and I was drawing a crowd, many of whom were armed. It's not easy to be inconspicuous riding a 1,200cc motorcycle through a Brueghal painting.

I stopped and asked a man smoking a pipe if there was anywhere to stay in town. But he didn't speak English, so I made the palms together on the side of the head gesture and made a circular motion with my arm.

He shook his head with a perplexed look on his face, then beamed and said 'Da, da', and beckoned me into his house which had not looked like a bed and breakfast from the outside. For good reason, it would seem, for the next minute he was pointing to his sofa and then making the palms together on the side of the head gesture.

Before I knew what was happening, a succession of small boys were carrying my luggage into the room. Shortly after, the entire village came round to see the stranger. There was lots of giggling and nudging and I poured my vodka into small glass tumblers and chipped mugs and then I cut my sausage into slices with my Leatherman and offered it around.

But they weren't too keen on the sausage and instead the old woman of the house produced a steaming tureen of sour soup with pork and beans, and we slurped it and ate heavy, dark bread, and drank more vodka. They spoke Romanian and I spoke English and we seemed to get along just fine. Vodka makes polyglots of us all.

I went through my guidebook's conversations and essentials section and tried to ask my host in Romanian what his name was, but I don't think I pronounced it correctly as he kept pointing to his hat.

After dinner, I walked back on to the main street. The boys who had earlier carried my luggage were playing football in the moonlight. They invited me to join in and they raced around me, screaming.

The smallest boy fired a shot into the top left-hand corner

of the barn door, only for it to be ruled offside by a consensus of boys whose chief arbitration qualifications seemed to revolve around the fact that they were the biggest. Arguments ensued, and pushing and shoving, and I produced a scrap of paper from my pocket and flourished it at the chief rabble-rouser, who theatrically gesticulated with his arms and pulled his 'who, me?' face, and grabbed his shirt at chest height before looking to the heavens as if seeking divine arbitration.

I showed off my best moves, sending long balls down the line with the outside of my foot, selling dummies to ten-year-olds with relish and trying to organise our midfield into a diamond formation, like grown-ups do who've forgotten the sheer joy of just chasing a ball. But the diamond thing never really took hold and I ended up just running aimlessly after the ball. For a magical few minutes, I actually forgot I wasn't 10 years old.

I turned like Ronaldo and then, like Ronaldo, fell flat on my face. It would have been a cynical foul, if anybody had been near me. The ball forgotten, the boys raced over to me en masse and bodily picked me up, 20 pairs of little hands patting me down like I was a man on fire, with gentle care and concern in their faces. Whether it was the dust, or the pain, or something else, I couldn't say, but after the free kick had been awarded, and I stepped aside to put my knees back in their sockets, I had the smallest of tears in my eye.

From Transylvania, I headed south on the Transfagarasan road, for bikers a legendary ribbon of tarmac crossing the high Fagaras Mountains, laid across the landscape as if by a giant hand drizzling black syrup from a giant spoon. It was built in the early seventies by Ceaucescu, as part of his fanatical, megalomanic zeal to conquer nature. Of course, in the fine tradition of dictators, old Nicolae wasn't actually there getting his hands dirty. No, the thing with megalomanic zeal is that it tends to keep a man tied up in the office.

The Transfagarasan started gently enough, flopping through rolling uplands of sheep-flecked meadows, past haystacks on sticks like upturned candyfloss. The greatest hazard was still the horse-drawn carts that outnumbered cars in the villages and, weirdly, Romanian geese that, unlike any other geese I'd encountered on the trip, seemed to have a personal issue with the engine pitch of a BMW R1200GS.

Some distance off I'd spot them pricking up their ears, or whatever it is that geese prick up, and start to spread their wings in an avian version of 'you wanna piece of me, huh?' By the time I drew alongside them, they would be in a right old flap, squawking and hissing and chasing me down the road. Once at a safe distance, I would pull over and watch other people on motorbikes pass by. Not a peep. Bizarre.

After about eight miles, the road began to sharply rise, and the turns grew more and more angular as I plunged through dense spruce forest. As I climbed, the trees started to first shrink and then disappear completely as I emerged at what felt like the roof of the world, with steep bluffs and foaming waterfalls and, even in midsummer, a white carpet of crisp snow. I had to keep flipping up my helmet to squeeze my nose and pop my ears, and eventually pulled over to dig out my fleece and thick riding gloves.

Through a mile-long tunnel blasted out of the rock and then more breathtaking views, a bleak granite moonscape, clouds bubbling rapidly over the incisor peaks above, the slenderest of margins at the side of the black strip separating the road from the abyss falling vertically away. There were few guard rails. Perhaps Nicolae considered them a bit effete.

There were plenty of shrines, though, and denuded clumps of flowers sitting next to weather-worn photographs of people who presumably were so taken with the views that they forgot to turn the wheel.

But the large number of traffic accidents might also have had something to do with the road surface, which was, to use the technical term, shit. The potholes were so numerous that at times the road resembled a Yorkshire pudding tray, some of them so large that they had people fishing in them. Polish people should come to Romania. They'd soon be feeling much better about their own roads.

I pulled over once again to drink it all in. Shadows from the clouds scudded down the valley. There was nothing save a deep, sonorous silence. A giant golden eagle soared high on the thermals.

I looked at my guidebook to see what it had to say about the Transfagarasan. Ahead of me, apparently, lay another 15 miles of clenched buttocks and white knuckles. There was also Lake Bâlea, which promised to 'hover like a mirror among the rocks' and, surprise, at Poienari, a castle that was regarded as the real-deal, no-doubt-about it, accept no imitations, you've-tried-the-rest-now-try-the-best, roll-up-and-get-your-T-shirt, Dracula's castle. Who was this Vlad character? George Wimpey in a cloak?

The road plunged down the other side of the mountain in a sweep of hairpins the profile of a Jeffrey Archer lie detector test.

With 11 weeks and 9,000 miles of motorcycling under my tyres, I decided it was time to test my skills to the limit. I gunned towards the turns, at 40, 50, 60 miles per hour, my heart in my mouth. I picked the racing line, whatever that was, touched ever so gently on my front brake, shifted my bum to the inside of the saddle, and leaned in.

I remembered Kevin Sanders telling me about an advanced turning technique, where you push the handlebars in the opposite direction to the turn, just like a speedway rider, and the bike gyroscopically tries to fall to the floor.

Perhaps on top of a mountain, on a road full of potholes, with no guard rails, sheer drops and a long ambulance ride to the nearest A&E, this wasn't the wisest place to practise being Valentino Rossi. But it worked beautifully as I became one with the BMW, and with the road, flying round the hairpins, the experience akin to dancing with a supremely gifted partner. I felt my boot catch the road as I banked into a turn, and the wheels slip ever so slightly, and I imagined my rapidly disappearing chicken strips – the worn/unworn edge of the tyre that's a telltale of your hardcore/wimp style as a rider – affording me plenty of kudos with the very baddest biker dudes.

I was riding to the limit of my ability, one tiny error of judgement could have brought catastrophe and the ensuing sickening crunching noise followed by the silence and the stillness before the pain would start to rise and rise. But these thoughts only made me want to ride faster, hooked on the sensation of being on the edge, a delicious glimpse of utter freedom, total peace.

I approached a bend. Fast. I couldn't see the exit. It was tight, and as I leaned into it, it got tighter and tighter. I couldn't touch the brakes. On a road like this, with loose shale on the surface, and potholes everywhere, it could have been fatal, my wheels falling away from under me. This is one of the most common causes of death on a motorbike: misjudging your speed coming into a bend.

I started to drift across the road, unable to keep in my lane. The bend showed no signs of opening up, smoothing out. On the far side of the road were spruce trees. I looked at them. There was one in particular, thicker than the rest. I stared at it. The bike started to straighten, move upright. I headed for the tree. I went to hit the brakes. I was going to crash, no doubt, but any reduction in speed might make all the difference. The whole thing had taken perhaps less than a couple of seconds, but somehow time was stretched.

I remembered Kevin's words. Have faith. Look where you want to go. The bike will follow. It has to.

I ripped my eyes from the spruce tree. It was an act of will. And I turned my head to look at the bend once more. The bike dipped again, leaned in. I think I left the road at one stage, crossing the line on the far side, riding over needles and cones, trees flashing past. But I couldn't be sure, because all I was looking at was the road ahead, the bend opening up, my right hand twisting back the throttle, me whooping like a lunatic.

'The fine will be eight million lei,' the police officer was saying to me.

'But that's ... that's about 200 euros,' I replied, which a quick calculation told me was roughly the average Romanian wage for a month. I could feel my bottom lip trembling.

'You should not go so fast. This road very dangerous,' he said.

'I'm sorry.'

'No good. You under arrest. You get in car and we go to bank to pay.'

I felt like the victim of a cashpoint mugging.

He ordered me to leave my bike by the side of the road and get into the passenger seat of the police car. Then we drove away heading for God knows where. After about 10 minutes, down a quiet country lane, the officer pulled over into a lay-by. Unless there was an ATM in one of the adjacent oak trees, which I was pretty certain there was not, I was guessing that this wasn't the end of the journey.

The officer switched off the ignition, slowly, deliberately, and turned to me, his gun nestling against his thigh.

'Okay. For you, for lei cash, there is 20 per cent discount,' he said.

'Discount?'

'Yes. Consider it gesture of goodwill from the kind Romanian people.'

As he was talking, he was fishing around in his wallet. He pulled out some photographs. My prejudices started to resurface. I imagined they might be of bloodstained cells, or show corpses lying face down besides a lay-by, this lay-by ...

'This my sister, she live London,' he said, showing me a picture of a smiling woman toasting the camera with a large glass of red wine.

'You married?'

'No.'

'I give you her address. She is very nice. Make good wife.'

'I'm not looking for a wife,' I said to him.

'You no like my sister?' he said.

'It's not that, it's ...'

'How about this one?' He'd pulled another picture out. 'She live Coventry.'

'She seems very nice, too ... Look, I'm flattered you think I might be good enough for your sisters, but I'm not interested ...'

'Thirty per cent?'

'What?'

'Discount. Thirty per cent, as goodwill and because you think my sisters very nice.'

I laughed.

'What would the discount be if I married one of your sisters?' I said.

The policeman suddenly looked at me solemnly, gravely.

'Mister. You try bribe Romanian police officer? Is very serious offence.'

At that point I remembered something someone had told me before I left England, about the police in Romania. Possibly Pub Guy, with his PhD in Ukrainian Visa Regulations. Whoever it was had told me about the dodgy Romanian police, about the last vestiges of the once-endemic corruption and how it was being clamped down on as the country moved towards EU membership and how, if you get pulled over, you should always insist on going to the police station and getting a receipt.

'I think we should go to the police station,' I said. 'I will need a receipt for the ticket.'

For a second, a melancholy filled the policeman's eyes, as if recalling a lost, glorious age, a time when he'd been king.

Then he put away the photographs and we drove off, slowly, in silence, to the police station, where I got a receipt for the 30-euro fine.

# 23 The stripper

The road into Istanbul was insane; a seething mass of humanity and animals and belching trucks and buses that followed no discernible rules and roadworks and chaos and horns going off. The city sounded like a vast orchestra tuning up.

The air was so cloying with the heat and the dust that I wanted to constantly swipe it away from my face. The traffic signs were almost non-existent. Not that signs would have helped me particularly. All I could remember from 20 years earlier was that I had stayed in Paksim, or Faksim or Taksim which, I seemed to recall, whatever its actual name was, was near the centre of the city. Possibly.

I briefly caught sight of a sign, which may or may not have had Taksim on it. But by the time I'd concluded that's precisely what it had said, and that it was precisely the place I was looking for, I was past the turning, and weaving all over the three-lane motorway, sparring with the murderous trucks once more. A warning light came on my bike console in the shape of a bulb. I had entered into the horn-beeping frenzy with such gusto that my headlamp had exploded.

I had to turn around. But I was being swept along and there seemed to be no exits for miles. The road going in the opposite direction was gridlocked. Shortly after, I was spat out of Istanbul, flying high over the Bosphorus, with the sublime beauty of the Golden Horn and the mosques tumbling down Sultanahmet away to my right, leaving Europe behind and entering Asia.

I was tempted to just keep going. I wasn't really in the mood for big cities. But there was something I wanted to do in Istanbul, something I wanted to find.

Elaine had been my first serious girlfriend. Not long after we'd met in the mid-eighties in a nightclub in Birmingham, she'd gone off to Istanbul to become a stripper. I'm not sure whether the two events were connected, and these days I might have taken the hint. But back then I got right on a plane and followed her.

Actually, she wasn't a stripper; she was officially billed as an 'exotic dancer', a drama graduate trying to rack up professional credits by taking a half-equity contract in the pre-*X Factor* days when the route to fame was a little more prescriptive.

At the Parisian nightclub, Elaine would twist and twirl in boas and feathered head-dresses, the climax of the show being reached when, just as the stage lights were killed, she would twang off her bra to the sound of audible gasps and much shuffling of hands in the darkened auditorium. How innocent it all seemed now.

One night, during a particularly energetic twanging manoeuvre, Elaine had fallen off the stage and broken her foot and that was the end of that. We returned to England. There was briefly talk of marriage, but I eventually left her for no good reason other than life's then seemingly infinite supply of beautiful, smart, talented women.

In 1986, Istanbul was a city of three million people. It was the year before my mum died and the first city abroad I'd ever visited. The smells and the sounds and the things I'd seen are still imprinted on my memory, a memory that tells me that the entire population sat around sucking on bubbling hookah pipes all day, wearing funny slippers and selling carpets.

All the taxis had been fifties' American cars, with fin tails and cracked leather bench seats. Back then, the place seemed impossibly crowded and foreign. I'd felt like a Graham Greene character strolling through a Freya Stark photograph. I'd loved it, wandering around with the look of an Amish teenager visiting the Big Smoke. It's one of life's little tragedies that you can do something for the first time only once.

After about an hour, I managed to find Taksim, I suppose it must have been still where it was two decades earlier, but unrecognisable in almost every respect.

Now there were 18 million people shoehorned into the city, it felt like one of those rag stunts where as many students as possible try to cram into a phone box.

I stopped outside a hotel and walked up the steps. A man dressed in black combat gear asked me to remove my crash helmet, then my jacket, then my shoes. He invited me to pass through an airport-style metal detector. It beeped. I emptied my pockets of coins and keys and passed back through again. It beeped. He scanned me with a ping-pong bat and waved me through.

The hotel had no free rooms. It was the Turkish Grand Prix that weekend, the receptionist told me, and the city was full. I felt like bursting into tears. Seeing my pathetic expression, she kindly called round a few places and, finally, found a small place nearby, off Taksim Square, with one spare room due to a cancellation. They would hold it for me for 10 minutes, she told me, but I must hurry.

I raced back out to get my bike. I contemplated the prospect of entering the Istanbul traffic again, and concluded that it might be 10 years and a population increase of several million before I was in a position to claim the last free room in town. I doubted they'd hold it for me. So I left my bike outside the hotel and walked around the corner into Taksim Square.

Everywhere I looked, there were McDonald's and global chain hotels and Western high-street shops and huge billboards advertising the Grand Prix. And everybody seemed far too busy driving a Range Rover and yelling into their mobile phone to sit down and smoke a pipe or try and flog me a rug. Nobody was wearing funny slippers. And have you noticed how songs don't have proper lyrics any more?

I found the hotel and, yes, they still had a room, and did I know how fortunate I was, what with not booking ahead and it being the Grand Prix and all? They would have to charge me for double occupancy, the room had no window and the air conditioning was broken.

'Okay?' the receptionist asked me.

'Dandy,' I said to her.

'Do you know the Parisian?' I asked the receptionist. 'I think it is near here somewhere.'

'The Parisian? What is it?' she said.

'A nightclub. Girls dancing.'

'Lapdancing?' she said.

'Not exactly,' I replied. 'More like the Moulin Rouge.'

She thought for a while, and eventually shook her head.

'Never heard of such a thing in Istanbul,' she said.

I took my bags to the room. For a while, I had to leave them in the corridor while I worked out how they and me could all fit in the space at the same time. But with one bag in the bath, and the two panniers stacked on top of each other, and using the chair and the bedside table as stepping stones, I eventually made it to the bed.

Steve McQueen would have thrown a baseball against the wall. I just lay there perspiring for a while.

Then I texted the Germans. I had met them at a petrol station just before the Bulgaria-Turkish border earlier in the day.

Matthias had wandered over. 'Wow, you have been to

214

many places,' he said, pointing to all the country stickers on my panniers. 'Where are you going now?'

I told him I was going to Istanbul.

'So are we,' and he indicated over to a red VW Golf, where three other young men were sitting in the back seat, and to another young man who was filling the tank. 'We are from Düsseldorf, going to Istanbul to party for the weekend.'

'Maybe we could meet up for a drink tonight?' I'd said to Matthias.

'Great,' Matthias had replied. 'I will give you my handy.'

'And I will shake it,' I'd said.

'No, my handy. My cell. In England, you call it a mobile, no?'

'I did know that. It was a joke.'

'But in English, this is called a hand isn't it?' he asked, holding out his hand.

'Yes it is,' I said.

'I have found a hotel just off Taksim Square,' I punched into the phone. 'I am just going out for a walk. Let me know where and when you want to meet up.' I pressed send.

With that, I stepped back on to the bedside table, then the chair, opened the door, walked into the cool of the air-conditioned corridor, down the stairs and back into the chaos of Istanbul. I went looking for the Parisian.

As I walked, I thought about how mobile phones have utterly changed not just the way we travel, but the way we live, the way we think. If I had not had a mobile, then I would have had to make concrete plans with Matthias back at the border.

But now I was connected with him. I would have been doing something different had I not had it, just as the Turks I walked past would have been doing something other than talking into their phones.

Back home, it amazes me when I'm travelling to work in

the morning, and all these people are walking down the street with one hand clamped to their ear, chattering away into their phones. What on earth are we all talking about? How did we ever survive when all we had to do was walk in silence or gaze out of the train window? It's as if aloneness now is a terrible disease that can be defeated, eradicated. All I know is that being alone and silent and uncontactable is one thing, and often not remotely lonely; being alone and silent and contactable is a different thing altogether.

'Do you have the time?' a young man asked me.

I told him.

'Ah, you are English. My goodness, I could have sworn you were Turkish,' he said.

I look about as Turkish as Boris Becker, but I let it go.

He walked with me along the street. Waiting for a response from the Germans, holding a mute phone in my hand, I was happy to have somebody to talk to.

'Is this your first time in Istanbul?' he asked.

'No, I was here in 1986,' I told him.

'Goodness, 1986. That was the year of my birth,' he said. 'I believe it has probably changed very much in that time.'

I told him it had changed a lot, seemed more aggressive somehow, less friendly. But that this maybe wasn't something just peculiar to Istanbul.

'My father says this about the world as well,' he said. 'That it is changing very fast, and not for the better.'

'I think most of us old codgers think like that,' I said.

'How old are you,' he asked?

'I'm 42,' I told him.

'Goodness, I am surprised,' he said. 'I would have thought you were no more than 30.'

I laughed.

'My name is Mike.'

'Tariq,' he said.

We shook hands.

'Do you live in Istanbul?' I asked Tariq.

'Goodness, no,' he said. 'I do not think I would survive very long in a city such as this. I am from a small village in Cyprus, on holiday here. I only arrived yesterday.'

The wide-eyed, innocent way he surveyed everything around him made him look like an Amish kid in the Big Smoke for the first time. I envied him.

We walked on for 15, maybe 20 minutes, chatting. I was looking down every alleyway, at every building that looked like it could conceivably have once been a nightclub.

'What are you looking for?' asked Tariq.

'Oh, I used to have a girlfriend who worked as a dancer at a nightclub when I was last here,' I said. 'I'm trying to remember where the place was. Memories, you know?'

'A nightclub dancer?' Tariq said, looking shocked. 'Goodness. That does not sound a very respectable job for a girlfriend to have. I hope that you did not marry her?'

I laughed again.

'No, I did not marry her,' I said.

My phone beeped. It was a text message from Matthias. They were having trouble finding a hotel room and were running late. He would text again when they were nearby.

'Who was that?' Tariq asked. I told him about the Germans, and how they were struggling to find a room after driving all the way from Düsseldorf.

'Goodness, that is a long way,' Tariq said.

He was quiet for a moment.

'Well, I hope you will not think it too much of an imposition, but if you have some time to spare while waiting for your friends, I would very much like to buy you a beer,' he said. 'I love to practise my English and you seem like a very nice man, not unfriendly like some English people I've met at home.'

Back in London, closed up, I'd have maybe instinctively refused such an offer. But I thought back to the Roma village and every single act of kindness I'd experienced since leaving home, and the people I'd met through chance encounters. One of the loveliest, restorative things about being on the road, I'd discovered, is that you realise that most people have goodness in their hearts. Some people, like Tariq, have goodness in every sentence.

Besides, I'd more or less given up trying to find the Parisian. Even if it had still existed, deep down I knew that it could never really exist again. Maybe better to leave it where it was, perfectly preserved in the archive.

'Sure, why not?' I said to him.

We walked down the street for a while.

'There's a place,' Tariq said, pointing to a bar just up a side street. Just before we went in, I texted Matthias the name, telling him that's where they could find me once they were sorted.

I followed Tariq through a door and down some stone steps. On the way up the steps was a guy with mad, staring eyes, looking right at me, shaking his head. I was happy he was leaving.

Through another door and we entered a large, dark underground room. There were about 100 people in the bar, sitting on banquettes and armchairs, gathered around tables, drinking, talking.

As my eyes adjusted to the light, I realised that those 100 figures were all women, all blonde, like a casting for a Timotei commercial. Beep, went my radar. But Tariq had already bought the beer. We stood there surveying the room and wide-eyed little Tariq looked like he'd died and gone to heaven.

'Let's grab a seat,' he said and headed off towards a banquette and table in the corner before I could say anything. I followed him. I needed to get him out of there.

I slid on to the velvet seat.

'Tariq,' I said. 'This is a very dangerous place ...'

A girl came over and sat beside me, blocking my exit. She asked me what my name was and then what I did for a job. I told her and asked her the same. It would have been rude not to at least have acknowledged her. 'My name is Anka,' she said. And her line of work? 'I am Ukrainian,' she replied.

I said that that seemed to be as good a job as any. She laughed like a bad film extra and stroked my arm.

Tariq had also found a friend. I was now very concerned for the poor, naive, Amish kid.

'Tariq,' I whispered to him. 'Do you know what sort of bar this is? You have got to be careful.'

But Tariq seemed quite happy lapping up the attention of the giggling young woman, and brushed aside my worries.

'Mike, look around you. This is a perfect bar, no?'

The waiter sidled over.

'Would you like to buy the young lady a drink?' he asked me. 'She usually has champagne.'

'No, I wouldn't,' I replied. 'I'm afraid I've got to be off to meet some friends. I only popped in for a quick drink with Tariq here.'

I turned to Tariq and told him we should go, but he said he was happy right there, what was the problem.

I had to make a quick decision. Something was going to have to be sacrificed: my wallet and/or kneecaps, or Tariq's innocence. I'm sad to say that Tariq's innocence bought it.

I squeezed past Anka, and tripped quickly along the edge of the dance floor to the door. But the door would not open. The handle seemed to have some kind of child lock on it, so that while it could be operated from the outside, from the inside it just flopped impotently up and down.

Besides, even if I could have opened the door, it was doubtful that the five members of what looked like the Turkish Olympic heavyweight boxing team that had gathered to watch me janking on the handle would have permitted me to leave.

The manager appeared as if from nowhere, like a lank, greasy-haired version of the shopkeeper in Mr Benn.

'Sir, sir, before you go, you must pay this,' he said, letting a formidably unctuous smile form on his thin, reedy lips.

I looked down. The bill in his hand was roughly the size of my monthly mortgage bill.

'I'm n-n-n-ot paying that,' I said. 'I only had one beer, and that was paid for by my friend Tar—'

I pointed out to the manager where my friend Tariq was sitting, except, of course, now there was just an empty velvet banquette. My Ukrainian friend had also gone.

One of the heavies cracked his knuckles like a Sweeney villain. The manager's eyes narrowed into slits. I started trembling.

'You, a rich Westerner, come here and dare tell me you won't pay,' he spat, his face contorted with rage. 'It is all about the principle with you bastards, isn't it. We are poor Turkish people and you think we're savages, stupid pigs.'

I had one of those thoughts that really should have stayed internal, refused an exit pass by the filters, but somehow the words were already out there, floating towards the Shopkeeper and Knuckles and the gang.

'You should jolly well stop talking like that because you're just making an absolute idiot of yourself,' I said, enunciating suddenly like Hugh Lawrie's Lieutenant George.

The Shopkeeper paused for a second and looked at me, quizzically. Perhaps I had pricked his conscience. Perhaps I'd made him see the error of his ways, held up a mirror to the inhumanity and suffering he was inflicting on his fellow man. Not to mention the Ukrainians.

'It is you who is the idiot, you stupid fuck,' he said.

Perhaps not.

He pinned me to the wall with his hand on my chest.

'There, up on the wall, are the prices,' and he pointed to a small piece of paper poking out from behind the fire extinguisher. It was true. There was a tariff. It looked like one of those Magna Cartas written courtesy of a magnifying glass on to a postage stamp that people labour over in order to earn a place in the *Guinness Book of Records*.

'Or, if you prefer, we can go into my office to discuss it.' He pointed to an open door leading off the room, beyond which there were some stone steps leading down. I doubted any discussion held down there would have enhanced further my enjoyment of that particular evening, but may well have given me an insight into the level of emergency dental care in Istanbul. I declined his kind offer.

I picked out two 50 lira notes from my wallet and thrust them at him, which was far, far less than he wanted, but still made my sip of beer around £40 or, to give it some true perspective, more expensive than Norway.

The Shopkeeper looked at the money. I could see him making some rapid calculations: 100 lira gets this arsehole out of my club; or we drag him into the office and have some man fun. Then empty his wallet.

It was a win-win situation for him and he revelled in the power, my balls on the line and, quite probably, on his carpet. For a minute, as knuckles cracked and I coveted the sphincter of a Hurtigruten captain, it seemed it could go either way.

He snatched the notes. On some signal the hard men melted away, the child lock was deactivated and I walked up the stairs.

I passed a male tourist and his new best friend on the way down. I looked hard at him, staring straight into his eyes, subtly shaking my head. And he looked at me for a second, then looked away and carried on walking down.

And then I was back on the street, drawing deep breaths from the thick Istanbul night.

I quickly texted Matthias. I envisaged the Germans pitching up at the club and entering, looking and failing to find me, then having to go through the whole terrifying ordeal. They might even eventually come to the conclusion that the club was so organised that they'd posted English dupes at petrol stations in Sofia.

They texted back to say they were on their way. But I had lost my appetite for any more excitement that evening. I walked slowly back through Taksim Square towards my hotel.

'Do you have the time?' a young man asked me.

I told him.

'Goodness, you are English. I could have sworn you were Turkish.'

He walked with me for a while.

'I hope you don't mind me talking to you, but I like to practise my English,' he said.

'No, I don't mind at all,' I said. 'In fact, do you want to go for a beer, then we could talk some more?'

He looked surprised but, after a beat, said sure, why not. He knew a great place just around the corner, he said.

'Sounds good,' I said, and we walked off together.

Hassan was a student from northern Cyprus, on holiday in Istanbul. He'd never been to the city before. He was wide-eyed with the chaos around him.

We'd gone about 100 metres down a quiet side street when I grabbed him and threw him against the wall, my hand gripped tightly around his throat.

'How fucking dare you,' I said, spitting in his face with rage. 'How do you sleep at night? I was here before you were born. I loved this fucking city. Before. When it was ... Why me, huh? What do you see? What the fuck am I, huh? Before, it was all so ... before ... when everything was so ...'

The words were now spewing out, senseless, incoherent.

'Before ...'

I held him in that position for a full minute or so. He was frozen with fear, unable to breathe, his face turning scarlet. I stared into his eyes like a feral animal. I believe I had enough anger coursing through me at that moment to punch through his chest and rip out his heart.

I could feel him trembling. He was only young. I released his throat gently, lowered my arm and put my hands against my face. It was wet. I heard Hassan run off.

I stood there for a while. Glazed. Numb. I tried to light a cigarette. My hands were shaking so much that it took three or four attempts, leaving charred shadows halfway down the length.

I closed my eyes and breathed deeply. Then I started walking again. Slowly.

By the time I got back to my tiny room, the anger had gone. Completely. I felt a calmness descend.

I lay on the bed thinking about everything that had happened that day. About Elaine. About my mum who'd waved me off on the plane to Istanbul and been there to meet me when I'd returned, wide-eyed with my adventure.

I thought about the next morning, when I would leave Istanbul and start heading out into the wild, remote spaces of eastern Turkey. I was really looking forward to that.

And then I had a thought about Hassan. The thought was this: what if he really had been a student from northern Cyprus on holiday?

# 24 Faraway

In *Zen and the Art of Motorcycle Maintenance*, Robert Pirsig talked about his motorbike and the moods it had and its living, breathing soul. And you think, for Christ's sake, I know you've had a nervous breakdown, matey, but it is only a machine.

But here's the thing. You spend hour after hour, day after day, listening to your bike, and you do begin to hear it speak. Some days, there's a sweet mellifluous, contented purr and on others a distinct grumbling and weariness.

And the really weird thing is, you start to talk back to it, encouraging it, patting it gently on the petrol tank like you would a horse when it's done something desirable, like stop in time in an emergency, for example, and gently scolding it when it does something not so clever, like wobble or slip on a bend.

And you know logically that this is errant nonsense, that maybe you need to seek out more human company, that a BMW R1200GS is not a horse, despite its dead-sheep saddle and coterie of flies, but simply a marvellous piece of Teutonic engineering, that the only variable here was the lump sitting astride it, and that if I were reading this instead of writing it, I'd be making that twirling gesture against my temple, but …

I'd been talking to my bike a lot in Turkey. There was an us-against-them siege mentality when the average daily fare on the road included mad, snarling dogs, insane truckers who come at us two abreast on blind bends so I would just have to close my eyes and go for the gap in between them, rockfalls and tarmac rendered molten by the heat.

Then there were the cliff-top roads with no guard rails, goats, donkeys, children trying to thrust watermelons or hazelnuts into my hands at 70 mph and car drivers who were complete strangers to the indicator switch.

There was even a village I passed through where a landslide had deposited a mosque, intact and upright, in the middle of the road. Talk about divine intervention. I rode through it. I didn't remove my boots. Apologies.

And all along the Black Sea coast in northern Turkey, when I'd been asked where I was going, I'd been warned about the activities of the PKK Kurdish separatists in the far southeast; how they had landmined the roads I would be passing along, and how I should avoid travelling with military convoys as they were the favoured shooting gallery for the snipers.

Was it any wonder that I was talking to a motorcycle? And drinking a lot of raki?

But Turkey. What a country! I had always assumed, based rather solipsistically on the fact that I had only ever previously visited Istanbul and the south-coast resorts, that that was about it.

And so, looking at my globe at home before I left, I had imagined that Turkey, like Greenland, must have been stretched out of all proportion by that Mercator chap. But as it's towards the middle of the planet, I can see now that that couldn't be the case at all.

All day, day in, day out, I rode. Through the lush verdant mountains skirting the Black Sea coast, with their tea plantations, and through stunning Ottoman villages like Safranbolu and Amasya, then down into the brown, scorched 45-degree furnace that was Eastern Anatolia. I could really have used my CamelBak. I hoped Andreas was getting good use out of it.

Up again from the brown, arid flatlands on to the high, grassy plains and the heather-covered meadows – like Oz after Kansas – that lay towards the borders with Georgia and Armenia. And when, in the evenings, I sat down with my map and sophisticated measuring device, I could see that I'd only covered about half a cigarette lighter.

After a week and a thousand miles of riding in Turkey, I'd reached the eastern limits of my trip. I was at the tenth-century ruined city of Ani, its great, crumbling walls, nearly a mile long, rising out of the empty plains to greet me. Ahead, just over the deep gorge of the Arpa Cayi River, lay Armenia, all sinister fortifications and watch towers, the sun glinting off the guards' binoculars like flickering fairy lights. All points east of here would have required a visa. Though I seemed to recall Pub Guy having a theory involving vodka and Armenian border guards.

I walked around the ghost city, completely alone. This place was as far off the tourist trail as it's possible to imagine. The long grass that covers the site swirled in the hot breeze. The acrid smell of burning tezek, cakes of dried dung used for fuel, drifted across from an adjacent Kurdish village, its stone houses with earthen roofs looking, if anything, older than the buildings of Ani.

I wandered along the streets, past mosques and churches with ancient Armenian inscriptions and faded frescoes showing scenes from the Bible.

In the distance, I noticed a speck, which became a dot, which eventually became a man. It took him around 30 minutes to get to me. On arrival, he held out his hand and unfurled his palm. It contained a few ancient, battered coins.

'No, thanks,' I said.

He furled his palm and turned and started the long walk back to wherever he had come from. I sat on a lump of the cathedral wall and watched him go, eventually disappearing into the heat haze rising off the vast treeless plain.

I left Ani and headed south. After about an hour, the metal road ended and I was suddenly riding across an infinite landscape of red-clay desert and scrub.

There were boulders strewn everywhere, like I was riding on the moon, and the desert floor plunged into dried river beds and then up banks so steep I thought the bike was going to topple over backwards. To my left, somewhere close, was the border with Iran. I was miles away from the nearest help should anything happen to me, and had no idea where I was going, but I felt marvellously, miraculously, happy, weaving between the rocks and the low bushes.

Trying to construct a mental route map between where I live in London and this desert was difficult. This bike and me had been riding around the M25 not long ago, and now we were here, a dot in a vast brown landscape, the bike's wheels, boats excepted, never having left the surface of the earth. It seemed outrageous that the London Orbital could, if you took the requisite combination of turnings, have led to this place.

After an hour of seeing nobody, I came across a young raggedy boy, herding his sheep. I stopped and asked him the way to Dogubayazit, and he just pointed ahead into the nothingness. In the mountains to my right, a violent electrical storm was unleashing itself, lightning jabbing the peaks. Shortly after, fat globules of water fell, rapidly making the clay as slippery as ice. My visor, already caked with dust, became opaque, like filthy frosted glass, so I removed my helmet and strapped it to the rear rack and rode on, gingerly.

And then, shimmering in the distance, rising surreally above the desert, was the bulk of Mount Ararat, like an immense collapsed Christmas pudding topped with cream, a trail of wispy cloud snagging its peak like a flying ace's silk scarf.

I always knew that Ararat would be the very furthest point I could get from London. And now I was here. A large part of me imagined I would never, could never, get this far. From here on in I would be making my way home.

So, as the bike pointed due west for the first time in three months, I opened the throttle and hurtled, helmetless, across the desert, touching 70, maybe 80, miles per hour, egging the bike on, patting it on the petrol tank, slipping and a sliding and a hollering and a screaming in the pouring rain; the exhilaration and sense of freedom quite indescribable.

For about two minutes, anyway, until the smell of burning filled my nostrils. I pulled up and killed the ignition. There was smoke rising from my radiator grill. The engine was oil-cooled. I'd only discovered this a couple of days before when the same thing had happened after I'd pulled in for petrol.

Seeing me looking puzzled at the smoke pouring out of the bike, the garage owner had come over.

'Your bike is oil-cooled,' he'd said.

'I know that,' I'd said. 'Tsk.'

'In this heat, it will use much oil.'

'I know that.'

'You need to fill it up more often here.'

'I know that.'

'Or else it will overheat.'

'Obviously,' I'd said. 'Tsk.'

'Would you like to buy some oil?'

'Of course,' I'd said. 'That's why I stopped here.'

He'd gone off, returned with a bottle of oil and handed it to me.

'Thank you,' I'd said.

We'd stood there for a minute or two. I was subtly scanning the bike.

'Nice garage you've got here,' I'd said.

'Would you like me to show you where the oil goes?' he'd asked.

'Yes, please,' I'd said.

Now, in the desert, it had happened again. I put the bike

on its stand, ferreted around in the pannier for the bottle of oil, unscrewed the filler cap and drizzled in the gloop.

While I waited for the engine to cool down, I looked around.

About half a mile away was a tented Kurdish village. I could see some people milling around, and some sheep grazing on the scrub. Behind the village, Ararat. It was so peaceful, so still, so raining.

I decided I would camp, right there.

I took my bag of camping gear off the bike. I hadn't camped since Sweden. As I emptied the contents on the floor, the frying pan fell out. I looked at it and laughed. That all seemed so long ago.

The tent was up in 10 minutes and I crawled inside, sitting there with the flap open, looking out into the rain.

Suddenly, there was a boy standing in front of my tent, about 10 yards away. He looked like the little shepherd I'd asked for directions earlier. He was wearing jeans pulled up high, almost to his chest, and a yellow shirt that must once have been smart but was now threadbare and stained with dust. He must have been around 12 or 13, but something about his face looked worn out, tired, making him seem old before his time. It must be a hard life, out here, I thought.

He went over and walked around my bike, and stroked my sodden sheep. Then he turned around to me, pointed to the animals away in his village, and smiled.

I nodded and smiled back.

I climbed out of my tent into the rain. He came over and stood in front of me.

I said hello and asked him his name.

He didn't speak any English.

I reached out my hand and, after a pause, he reached out his. His face may have been old, but his hand was smooth, tiny held in mine.

We stood there for a minute, awkward. I was frustrated that I couldn't ask him anything about his life. I had so much I needed to tell him. So much I wanted to ask.

He looked over at my bike again.

I pointed to him, then I pointed to myself, then I pointed to the bike. His face broke into a huge grin.

I lifted him up on to the pillion seat, climbed on myself and fired the engine. Then I took off across the scrub, slowly at first, then getting faster, faster, in the rain. His hands dug through my T-shirt and into my skin. I could hear him screaming. I slowed down. The screaming stopped. I turned the throttle, the screaming started again.

Finally, I pulled up outside the tent, put the bike on its stand and lifted him off. He stood there grinning. He didn't look old any more. He looked like a boy.

He put his arms around me and squeezed tightly, then he ran off towards the tented village.

'Hey,' I shouted after him. 'Could your family use this?' I'd picked up the frying pan and was holding it in my hand. I'd decided I was going to dump it anyway. I pointed to it and then pointed away, to the tents.

He walked back. He looked at the pan for a second, then he reached out his hand and took it. Then he ran off towards his home once more.

I climbed back inside the tent and zipped up the flap. I lay there, listening to the rain, now gentle, tapping against the roof.

I closed my eyes and talked to her. It was not my usual conversation. Something was different.

I forgive you, I whispered. It's time …

There was a rustle outside the tent. I unzipped the flap. The boy was standing there.

He reached out his tiny hand and in it was a parcel, wrapped in paper. I took it and opened it. It was some bread and cheese.

'Thank you,' I said to him. 'Thank you.'

He smiled and ran off once more.

I put my palms up and held them against my face. For the second time in Turkey, it was wet.

# 25 The road back

The road heading south from Lake Van crossed a plateau, then before me was a landscape of red rock that looked like a giant brain. The unmetalled road plunged into a series of gorges that twisted and turned, following riverbeds long divested of water. The temperature was well over 100 degrees. I always preferred to ride with my visor open, but here it was impossible. Imagine, if you can, sitting in a sauna holding a hairdryer switched to turbo an inch from your face. Then imagine that the 12-volt motor had been removed from your hairdryer and replaced with the engine of a Boeing 737. That is what it was like riding with the visor up.

I passed groaning, weaving trucks so overloaded with timber that they looked as precarious as an drunken game of Jenga. The drivers would always beep their horn as I passed. Oncoming truck drivers would wave, maniacally, often with both hands off the wheel. I wished they wouldn't.

I stopped at a garage for petrol. As ever in Kurdish Turkey, and most other places in Turkey for that matter, I was immediately mobbed by men looking at the bike and asking me questions: always 'how fast?' followed by 'how much?', then gazing at the bike with awed reverence.

It was always men. Women, I had disappointingly discovered, were supremely indifferent to motorcycles; if women responded to them the way that men do, I'd still be on the road. Perhaps next time I'll ride a giant shoe.

Tea was always brought out as a matter of course and, as at every garage in Turkey, I was presented with a man-size box of tissues. Finding space on a motorcycle for dozens of breezeblock-sized boxes of tissues was problematic. But refusal was impossible without causing major offence. Believe me, I'd tried.

And so I took them graciously and cleaned my visor with them, my sunglasses, my windscreen, my exhaust pipe, rocks by the side of the road, mopped up oil spills, plugged holes in dams and, just when I'd managed to get through a whole box, the petrol gauge would start flashing and soon I'd be saying '125mph', '£9,000' and 'thanks for the tissues, just what I needed'.

As we drank tea, the garage owner showed me the newspaper. The day before, he explained, there had been a big bomb blast in Diyarbakir, the Kurdish capital, just down the road. Many had been killed. The PKK separatists were being blamed, but the garage owner smelled the work of the Turkish secret service. The army was on high alert, he told me, and there had been kidnappings and many shootings on these roads.

'You have to be careful,' he said. 'Do not be on the road after dark. It is very dangerous.'

The army was everywhere. Every mile or so there was a roadblock, with a queue of trucks and cars waiting to pass through. Helicopters thundered overhead. I waited patiently for my turn to present my papers to the soldiers. Tanks and armoured cars trained their cannons and machine guns on us. The atmosphere was tense.

Finally, it was my turn. '125mph', '£9,000' I told the young soldier in response to his questions. Then he told me about his ambitions to travel to England, about his family in Ankara, and his love for Galatasaray Football Club.

'Do not be on the road after dark,' he said after about an hour of chat, and waved me through.

This was a routine repeated at the next dozen roadblocks. All the questions about the bike, and the soldiers' post-army plans, and their family and how Galatasaray couldn't kick their way out of a paper bag compared to Trabzonspor or Fenerbahçe.

Then it was dark and the next roadblock and all the ones after that had been abandoned for the night and the soldiers snugly tucked up in their barracks, where doubtless the arguments about football were continuing.

Now I was riding alone along the road in a rocky landscape softly lit by a gibbous moon, eyeing the shadowy ridges, wondering where a sniper would sit and contemplating how many tissues it would take to stem a bullet wound.

I started whistling, but my initial somewhat glib assessment of the situation lasted only as long as it took for me to think I'd spotted something moving high up on a ridge. Mr Glib was quickly replaced by, at first, Mr Jumpy and then, shortly after, by the double-barrelled charms of Mr Sphincter-Failure.

Something had changed for me on the road very recently. It was only a subtle change, but suddenly I was a little more afraid of being in dangerous situations. Whereas previously, I'd been fairly cavalier, now, increasingly, I wanted to survive; wanted to see what might happen tomorrow.

As my mind focused on the ever-increasing inevitability of me getting mown down in a hail of gunfire, or having my head blown off by a rocket-propelled grenade, I pulled over and quickly retrieved my iPod from the tank bag.

I'd never ridden along listening to music before, because clearly that would be hazardous on a motorcycle. But whereas listening to music on a normal road might prevent you from hearing a car horn, and thus failing to take evasive action, I doubted that, on a deserted road in these parts, hearing an incoming RPG would leave you much time to do anything apart from mutter: 'Fu—'

I put on my headphones, replaced my helmet, clicked play, put on my gloves and pulled away again quickly. From my *Best of MGM Musicals* came the soothing tones of Debbie Reynolds 'Good mornin', good morrrrrrrrnin ...'

It's something the world has seemingly known for some time, but only latterly discovered by me, about just how totally music can affect your moods. In no time, I was riding with a happy heart, joining in with Debbie and Gene and Donald, all thoughts of snipers and landmines and RPGs gone.

The iPod shuffled into its next song. If there's another disadvantage to listening to music on a motorcycle, it's that, what with the thick gloves and the iPod being tucked away in your pocket, and the desirability of keeping two hands on the bars, you're kind of stuck with what you get shuffled.

On this occasion it was 'The Flight of the Valkyries'.

On the shadowy ridges, there were small figures moving everywhere I looked.

I finally arrived in the town of Siirt, about 100 miles from the Iraqi border. I rode along the main street, weaving around the cows and the sheep that grazed on the mounds of rubbish in the dark. I pulled up outside a hotel.

A man from inside came running out with a worried expression, holding his head then fussing over me like I was a long-lost relative, given up for dead. He pointed along the very long, very dark road I had just ridden down and then held his left arm out straight, pulling an imaginary trigger with his right index finger.

'Oh that,' said Mr Glib, who was always very brave after the event. 'No big deal.'

'Bullshit,' said Mr Sphincter-Failure, who Mr Glib would maybe do well to pay more attention to in future.

Mr Fussy didn't speak any English, but gestured towards my bike parked in the street and wagged his finger. Then he did his rifle impression again, after which he pointed into the hotel lobby. Although not yet quite fluent in Kurdish sign language, I surmised that this meant he wanted me to put my motorbike into the hotel lobby.

As far as I could see, there were two major problems with this plan. Firstly, hotel lobbies, especially ones with carpets as fine as that one, were not specifically designed with the parking of filthy, oily motorcycles in them in mind.

Secondly, there was the small matter of the ten steep steps leading down to the hotel entrance. From his subsequent hand gestures and shrugs, I further surmised that he considered such a manoeuvre a mere trifle for a man who had just run the gauntlet of the PKK.

Of course, had I been at some stage Kickstart champion, he might have had a point. But sadly, I was not. I tried my best to communicate this to him by impersonating a man falling off his motorcycle and clutching his leg in considerable pain.

Mr Fussy scratched his head again.

He disappeared into the hotel and re-emerged with half a dozen men who had hitherto been engrossed in a football match on a flickering black and white television in the corner of the lobby. They didn't look best pleased at being dragged away from the game.

They positioned themselves around the bike and lifted it, luggage and all, about 250kg in total, and carried it down the steps. At the bottom they put it down and returned, grumbling, to the match.

Mr Fussy went and took up his position behind reception. I jumped on my bike, started it up, rode it into the lobby and up to the front desk. There, I checked in without dismounting. I didn't have to do this, of course, but Mr Smartarse thought it might be funny. The world's most northerly McDonald's, and now this.

With a big motorcycle now in the middle of the small

room, the men had to move their seats so they could still see the game.

After the ride with the Valkyries, followed by the exhaustion of watching other people carry my motorbike down some steep stairs, I needed a drink.

I walked back along the main street, past the grazing cows. This was a deeply conservative part of Turkey and, being after dark, women were completely absent from the pavements and teashops. Men sitting outside drinking tea stared intensely at me as I walked along. The atmosphere seemed tense, hardly surprising given the events in Diyabakir and out on the roads.

I ducked into a supermarket. I asked the man on the till where they kept the beer.

'No beer,' he said.

A youngish guy, listening to the conversation, waited until the man on the till was serving somebody else. Then he sidled up to me.

'Pssst. You want beer?' he said, sotto voce. His hair was gelled into a quiff and he'd folded back the cuffs of his jacket, giving him the look of a teddy boy, or spiv.

'You know where I can get some?'

'Sure. Come with me.'

We walked back into the street. He linked arms with me as we strode along. Up an alleyway, then down another street, then through a courtyard filled with grazing sheep and goats. The spiv seemed nervy, edgy, his eyes darting around. Out of the courtyard and into another alleyway. It was a labyrinth.

I was trying to remember the route we'd taken in case I needed to get away quickly.

Into another courtyard. The spiv headed down some stone steps and beckoned me to follow him.

'I don't suppose you're on holiday here from northern Cyprus are you?' I asked him.

'No, I am from Siirt,' he replied, looking puzzled.

At the bottom of the steps there was a nondescript-looking door. The spiv rapped on it three times. A small panel opened and my man had a whispered conversation. The panel closed again.

We stood there for a while. Mr Glib had stayed behind in the supermarket. Mr Sphincter-Failure was along for this mission.

I imagined the headlines at home:

### DYING FOR A DRINK

Britons' obsession with alcohol plumbed new depths yesterday when a Wandsworth man was found decapitated in a street in south-east Turkey, near the Iraqi border.

In a desperate quest for booze, Mike Carton, 38, had apparently allowed himself to be taken to an address in Siirt, a known terrorist hotbed, where he'd been forced into an orange jumpsuit and bundled into a cage.

'You okay?' the spiv asked.

'F-f-fine,' I said.

There was a commotion behind the door. Was that a cage being hastily readied? A knife being sharpened? I wanted my iPod.

The panel opened. Nothing happened. Then a hand emerged. It was clutching a bottle of Efes beer. My man took it. Then the hand disappeared and re-emerged holding a brown paper bag. My man took this, too.

The hand then turned upwards.

'It'll be two Turkish liras,' the spiv said.

I placed the money in the palm and it withdrew like one of those novelty moneybox coffins, the panel sliding shut afterwards.

'You must put the bottle in the bag,' my man said.

We returned to the main street. My friend whistled and a car pulled up with a smashed front windscreen.

'Get in,' he said.

The driver didn't speak English. I sat there as we sped through town, destination unknown.

Eventually we pulled up outside my hotel. I thanked the driver and walked down the steps into the lobby, where I stared in disbelief at my motorcycle for a second, before remembering.

Then, hiding my brown paper bag behind my back, I sneaked past the guys now watching another football match and up to my room where, having double-locked the door and slid on the security chain, I opened the bottle and glugged down half in one go.

It was the finest beer I'd tasted in my life.

I got up at dawn, anxious to hit the road early and avoid the mistakes of the previous day. Unfortunately, the men had finished watching football and the lobby was empty, save for me, the motorbike and the manager.

Further calamity. It was not Mr Fussy on duty. It was his colleague, Mr Furious.

The only resemblance to his colleague that I could ascertain was that he didn't speak English. In his attitude to my motorbike, he couldn't have differed more. He stood there, pointing at it, and then raising his hands while looking at the ceiling, as if in supplication.

Then he started shouting. Roughly translated, it probably went something like, 'This is a hotel. Why did you think it appropriate to ride your motorcycle down the steps and park it in my lobby, huh? If I came to your house, would I drive my car through your door and park it in the kitchen? Do you think we are all savages? I bet, if I went to your room, I would find evidence of alcohol too, huh.'

To which I replied, 'Of course I don't think you are all savages. I only put my bike in the lobby because your colleague said I should. I was as surprised as anyone. I'm sorry to have upset you. It looks like there's been an honest mistake made.'

Roughly translated, this probably sounded like, 'Up yours, arsehole, I'll park my bike where I bloody well want.'

I checked out. I didn't ride my bike up to the desk this time.

The man took my money, tutted again, shook his head and disappeared.

I walked out of the lobby and went to have another look at the steps. There were still ten of them. And the intervening hours had done nothing to diminish their steepness.

It seemed like I had two choices. I could go back to the desk and try and ask Mr Furious if he had a copy of the bus timetable between Siirt and London, changing at Zagreb. Or I could go back to the desk and try and ask him for help in extricating my bike.

I pinged the bell. I hoped that he hadn't been up to my room yet and looked in the bin.

He emerged. I put my hands together in prayer, then pointed to the bike, then to the steps, then I shrugged my shoulders.

He shrugged his shoulders back. To be fair, I supposed that he couldn't see the problem. If, a few hours previously, I had ridden my bike down the steep steps in arrogant imperialistic fashion, then how hard could it be to just ride it back up again?

I beckoned him to follow me to the steps. I demonstrated as best I could via a series of tortuous mimes that it would be impossible to ride the bike up the steps. For one thing, even if I had the skill – and the sphincter – the bottom of the engine block would smash into the concrete.

Had we been able to talk, he would at that stage have asked me why the block hadn't caught the steps on the way down. And I would have told him, and we would have laughed at our silly misunderstanding, and drank some tea, and mended some cultural bridges. But we couldn't. All I could do was point at the steps and then go to my bike and point to the engine block and punch my palm with my fist.

Eventually, he seemed to understand the problem. After some requisite head-scratching, the manager disappeared, returning presently with some planks of wood. Then he popped off again, and re-emerged carrying an armful of bricks and misshapen concrete with steel prongs sticking out. This journey he repeated several times until the foot of the steps looked like a small collapsed building.

Some small boys carrying pastries on trays balanced on their heads stopped at the top of the steps to see what was going on.

The manager laid the planks up the steps, as I feared he might, wedging bricks and bits of rubble underneath. He seemed to be a lot happier now, not unlike a man digging a bear pit in the jungle, filling it with sharpened bamboo poles and then covering it with palm leaves.

Some more passing small boys carrying trays stopped to see what was going on. There would be no pastries delivered on time in this town that morning.

The manager laid the last plank and wedged in the last bit of rubble. Then he stood back and presented his work to me like a magician's assistant.

It was, by any standards, a truly appalling piece of engineering. The planks were not tied together and there were nails sticking out all over the place. The rubble was already beginning to slip and tumble down the steps.

I reassessed. It seemed that I now had three choices. Wait until the small boys had grown into men so they could help me carry the bike. Ask for the bus timetable. Or go for it.

I walked back to the bike in the lobby, then paced out the run-up to the foot of the ramp. I don't know why I did this, but vaguely recalled Eddie Kidd going through similar motions before a stunt, perhaps even the stunt that put him in a wheelchair. The boys were so excited now that some had even removed the trays from their heads.

I gave the ramp a last once-over and saluted the crowd with the thumbs-up. I received a small spattering of applause. I then returned to the bike, mounted it and started the engine. After offering up a silent prayer to Allah, because he had the best local knowledge, I revved, slipped the bike into gear, dropped the clutch and sped towards the ramp.

Somewhere between the potted date palm and the gilded portrait of Kurdish leader Abdullah Ocalan, I passed V1.

As the bike angled skywards, I could feel the planks being spat out behind me and the rubble giving way, but there could be no hesitation. My feet dangled out uselessly from either side. There was no longer any ground to rest them on. On and on. Upwards and upwards. My buttocks were so clenched they could have skinned a walnut.

And then I was on the pavement, still upright, still alive. I looked back at the steps. Once again, there was a small, collapsed building at the bottom of them.

I felt like Steve McQueen in *The Great Escape*. The small boys clapped and cheered wildly, jostling round and patting me on the back, offering me pastries and asking me questions. I couldn't understand them, of course, so I took a calculated guess and answered '125mph' and '£9,000'.

The manager looked slightly disappointed, and shrugged his shoulders again as if to say, 'What was all the fuss about?'

But I thanked him all the same. Liberating my bike had felt like a victory. A real victory.

# 26 Dancer

The Roman amphitheatre was, according to my guide-book, 'the best-preserved in the world' and 'top of the must-see list in Turkey'. I was reading this sitting drinking tea in a street-side café, the aforementioned architectural wonder not 50 metres away.

But instead of making my way across the dusty street, I drained the bitter dregs of tea from my tulip glass, climbed on my bike and rode away, taking with me a tremendous sense of guilt.

This guilt had been building for quite a while. A long trip like this seemed akin to visiting a fantastic zoo. You start off minutely examining and contemplating, wide-eyed and earnest, every stick insect and meerkat, but after a while you're looking at a snow leopard or a unicorn and thinking: 'Whatever.'

It was like the deadlands, where very little can stir the soul; when your everydays are filled with the extraordinary – snow-capped mountains, whirling dervishes, minty toothpaste-coloured lagoons, sunsets like a Florentine painting – you start to crave the counterpoint of the mundane, the normal. Otherwise it can all start to get a bit meaningless.

Maybe I just needed to go home. But then the thought kicked in; the thought that, two months hence, I'd be back in the cold and the rain, trudging along grey streets, complaining about how dull life was, how the drip, drip routine was corrosive and I'd be planning a bike trip again.

It reminded me of something I once read about Dave Stewart of the Eurythmics, who'd self-diagnosed himself as having 'Paradise Syndrome', the affliction of pop stars and billionaires who, unburdened by structure, grind to a halt, paralysed by the fact that they can have whatever they want.

I recalled, stuck in my then shitty job, how I felt reading about him complaining about the fact that he had everything he ever wanted from life. 'Tosser,' I think was my mature and considered opinion.

I thought better of ever trying to explain to anybody why I couldn't be bothered to cross the street to explore one of the architectural wonders of the world.

Later that day I came across a bunch of people who had just found God. Or it certainly looked that way, as they wafted, glassy-eyed and beatific across a car park. I asked them what had happened, and they pointed skywards.

I was introduced to Lars, who told me the price of salvation was 120 euros and would take approximately two hours.

Predawn the next morning there were 30 of us gathered in a field. There was a full moon hunkering low on the horizon, as immense as if looking through a powerful telescope, its craters and lakes like bleached birthmarks.

We clambered into two baskets and levitated slowly upwards, the exalted, cathedral-like silence punctuated only by the occasional, violent staccato bursts of fiery breath. And we drifted, up and up, like stately elevators, a red halo now framing the saw-tooth volcanic peak of Mount Erciyes to the east, the recently black escarpment nearby now burning ochre, a giant screen on which two heart-shaped shadows kissed.

As we reached and cleared the top of the ridge, there was a collective gasp as the fairy chimneys and the conical witches hats and the phallic columns of Cappadocia filled the plain to the horizon.

Lars was now Willy Wonka, the showman, taking our balloon down, gliding through the trees and among this alien Terracotta Army, the huge air-filled beast dancing nimbly between the stacks, before shooting us back up and over the rock-cut chapels and monasteries of Göreme. If there was any sense of the jaded in me, it was certainly gone now.

I glanced around at my fellow passengers. They looked like the people I had met in the car park the day before; as if they too had found God. I know I looked the same.

We landed. I thanked Lars, made my way back to the bike and switched on my mobile. I had two text messages.

The first said: 'When you arrive Zagreb? We get plenty messed up, but it's gonna cost you some blood. B.'

The second read: 'Where are you? We are in Bodrum. We miss you. The Aussie honeymooners. xx'

Spooky. Bodrum was a place I had some business.

I texted back.

The first read: 'Soon. What do you mean, blood?'

The second read: 'I'm on my way.'

I rode south from Cappadocia, across the Anatolian plateau and up into the Taurus Mountains. I was flying quickly around the bends, recklessly even, the false sense of invincibility that can infect you on a motorcycle – like riding with angels – burning strong. I was in a hurry to get to Bodrum.

But there was an atmosphere on the roads that day, a dissonance, like there sometimes is, where the synchronicity was missing.

Everybody seemed nervous or distracted, things that you are far more attuned to with the vulnerability that comes with riding a motorbike. You can instinctively tell if somebody is on their mobile, or having a row with their passenger. Bad driving just becomes so obvious.

Maybe it was the full moon, but the near misses came thick

and fast. Something was going to happen; I knew it, everybody else on the road seemed to know it.

I came round a bend. Ahead of me was a crowd gathered in the middle of the road. As I drew nearer I could make out the body of a man, lying on his back, hideously twisted and contorted into an impossible shape, thrown clear from the mangled wreckage of the car some 50 metres away.

I noticed a big, dark stain on his trousers around his crotch, and then the woman, a wife or girlfriend maybe, bent over him, bloodied, sobbing. I pulled over and sat on my bike at the side of the road, some distance away, smoking a cigarette. I don't know why I didn't just ride on. It seemed somehow more respectful to wait, quietly.

An ambulance arrived, and they gently, tenderly, straightened out the man, put him on a stretcher and loaded him into the back. Then the woman climbed in, too, slowly, reluctantly. I followed them down the mountain, hurtling along, sirens blazing, although there was little traffic on the road now.

The sirens suddenly stopped and the ambulance slowed and, after a little while, pulled over in front of a mosque.

They were probably having breakfast as I floated over Cappadocia was all I could think, as I rode past, very slowly, the angels gone.

The pick-up truck crawled slowly along the Bodrum esplanade and stopped right outside the restaurant. On the side, in lurid pink lettering, were the words: 'Halikarnus – The Club.' On the back, on three small podiums, were three young women, dancing like they were being attacked by wasps, or 'throwing shapes' as I believe it is now called. They were wearing tiny bikini tops and strips of black cloth for underpants, with which they appeared to be flossing their nether regions.

We had just been discussing underpants. By 'we', I mean

me and Sue. And by underpants, I mean mine, whose regular turnover thereof still seemed to be a particular obsession of Sue's (I told her I was putting clean ones on every other day, as per instructions, but it was still a terrible lie).

It was glorious to be back with Joe and Sue. Now we were the gang again, tripping across the MGM lot, Sue organising our days: where we were going to stay, what we would do, where we would head afterwards. I told them my tales of the road since we'd parted, and I heard theirs. It felt like I had come home. So happy was I, in fact, that I had even decided to give up smoking.

'You look different somehow,' Joe said to me. 'Have you lost a bit of weight?'

'It's possible,' I said to him.

'You gotta get your photo taken with them,' Sue was telling me, moving mercifully away from the subject of my pants and pointing to the dancers. Sue might have been the same age as me, but managed to make me feel like I was 14.

'I don't want to,' I said.

'Just get over there,' she barked.

So I meekly moved towards the pick-up truck, hands in my pockets, dragging my heels like a petulant teenager.

'Don't worry, I am not a pervert,' I said to the girls.

'They are Russian. They don't understand you,' the driver told me, as the girls moved to the far side of the truck and looked at me like I was a pervert.

I guess we've all got photographs of ourselves that we'd rather didn't exist. I've got two. The one Sue had just taken of me. And one from 1986, the last time I'd been in Bodrum, showing me wearing a leather glove on one hand and sporting a denim jacket with cut-off sleeves, the gloved hand pointing to the stars, the head titled downwards to the floor. For, during a brief spell that summer, I too had been a dancer at the Halikarnus, Turkey's world-famous open-air nightclub.

I asked the driver to explain this to the girls. I grinned at them and said 'yes, yes' and stuck up my thumbs. But I don't think the driver's English can have been too good, because they were still looking at me like I was a pervert.

But yes, it was true. And yes, it was a long story, involving Elaine, the broken-footed exotic dancer from Istanbul, and an offer from the owner of the Parisian nightclub, who also happened to own the Halikarnus, to go down to the south coast so she could rest her poorly foot and I could, I thought, sit by the pool, drink free beer and generally freeload. It had seemed the perfect plan.

But then there was another broken foot, this time belonging to a male dancer at the Halikarnus, and a performance coming up that evening and, wouldn't you know it, no understudy, and the troupe, nice Home Counties drama-school youngsters, all scratching their heads and then looking at me trying to sidle past inconspicuously with my free beer on the way to the pool and, collectively, a string of light bulbs had appeared over their heads.

No, no, I'd protested. I told them that I danced like a puppet whose operator had Parkinson's, could have been, even at that tender age, the world dad-dancing champion, was unable to move without pulling the sex face.

But they wouldn't have it; as trained dancers, perhaps they thought that because God have given them the ability to listen to music and move accordingly, it was a shoo-in that, with a bit of rehearsal time, I should be able to pick it up.

Besides, part of me actually believed, being 22 and full of brio and unquenchable self-belief and in a foreign country, that maybe I could pull it off.

And so began my career as a dancer. Every night, I'd go out there on stage, murdering Danny in *Grease* or Tony in *Saturday Night Fever*, strutting my stuff in front of paying punters. One night, standing there centre-stage in just a pair of shorts festooned with love hearts (I think it might have been a Beach Boys surfing homage), I totally forgot what I was supposed to be doing and froze. For maybe a full minute I just stood there, hands covering my crotch like a footballer lining up to defend a free kick, gormlessly looking to the wings for help.

The help never came. The next day, there was a photograph of me, in full colour, on the cover of the local newspaper, looking like a man in a Whitehall farce whose lover's husband had just discovered him in the wardrobe. Even 20 years later, thinking about how utterly terrible I was makes me want to stuff my head inside my T-shirt.

I had told all of this to Joe and Sue in the deluded belief that they would offer mature counsel, perhaps Sue turning to me and saying, 'Though age from folly could not give me freedom, It does from childishness,' where after we would sip our red wine and sit quietly ruminating on life's discursive narrative.

But they didn't. That's why I was now standing next to some half-naked women with my thumbs up, trying to convince them that I was not a pervert.

'You've got to go back to the club,' said Sue next.

'There's no way I am going back there,' I said. 'Why would I want to revisit the scene of past humiliations?'

We walked along the esplanade, Sue insisting on taking me there herself, holding my hand along the way, telling me everything would be okay, like it was my first day at school. But the walk there was a slow accumulation of dread. I really didn't want to go back and I wasn't sure exactly why.

'I'm nervous,' I said to Sue, as we approached the entrance.

'What of?' she said.

'I don't know,' I replied. 'Something.'

'He used to be a dancer here,' Sue was telling one of the doormen. He told his mate and they both had a good chuckle.

The story was relayed to some of the young people in the queue, who looked like they'd just been told to imagine their parents having sex, then to the girl on the cash desk, then the cloakroom girl and, my, how I sprinkled their evening with a little joy and pixie dust.

'Off you go,' said Sue, leaving me at the door to enter the club alone. 'Everything will be okay.'

I walked through the metal detector – they're everywhere in Turkey these days – then through the whitewashed tunnel and out into the vast, spectacular space, open to the stars; the dance floor with the floodlit backdrop of St Peter's castle, the colonnaded terraces, the DJ's booth.

It was more or less the same. Sure, the near-naked Russian podium dancers, the foam-filled dance floor and the techno music might have been different. As was my aversion to the noise. But as I grabbed a beer and took a seat, the memories started to come flooding back.

I looked at the stage and thought back to 1986 and the photograph of that fresh-faced dancer – with the leather glove and the cut-off waistcoat – frozen in time. And I could recall, as if it were yesterday, his innocence, his energy and limitless horizons.

In the photograph, he didn't know, of course, that shortly after his mother would be dead. He couldn't know that his last summer as a child was drawing to a close, that the photo-taking would soon stop again.

As I sat there, watching the Class of 2006 take to the stage and begin their routine, I thought about the punctuation marks of the 'then' and the 'now' and everything that had happened in between.

I started to understand the feeling of dread on the walk over. I had never wanted to come back to this place. In my mind, I think, it had always represented something too raw and painful, a huge and terrible watershed in my life.

But now I was sitting there, the dread had gone and all I felt was a calmness descend. It was as if, after a period of not being able to see my life behind or in front, I could see it again as a line running from left to right. I closed my eyes and remembered and couldn't help but smile.

We left Bodrum the next morning. I took up my usual position behind the Yamaha, Sue's devil horns sticking up from her helmet.

As we rode along, she constantly pointed things out to our left and our right, so I effectively spent the morning as if watching a tennis match.

'Didya see all that stuff I pointed out?' she said, when we stopped for a break.

I had to confess that I hadn't seen much beyond the normal view of Turkey seen from a motorcycle on a Turkish road.

'That's because I was winding you up, you gallah,' she said, and tickled me in the ribs.

We rode on, through charred, apocalyptic landscapes devastated by forest fires, and along narrow, serpentine dirt roads clinging to the coastal bluffs. A wave of noise, ear-splitting even in a helmet on a motorcycle, followed us through tunnels of trees as cicadas drummed us along. Below us, the iridescent turquoise waters washed gently against the rocks.

About mid-afternoon, we stopped again for some shade and a glug of water in a remote orange grove. It was almost too hot to ride, but Sue had some kind of plan about where we would stay the night and it might have been just around the next corner, or not. Just as it might have been around the last dozen or so corners, but hadn't been.

'I'm starving,' I moaned to Sue.

'Whingeing again, huh?' she said.

In truth, Joe and I were not unduly concerned with the trivial logistics of food or accommodation We were men, after all. Joe was the kind of guy who could fashion us a bivouac shelter from the dead wood on the ground, or knock up a cicada casserole, or repair a puncture using the skin off his own foot. I could, if pushed, put a condom on my head and juggle oranges. We were a good team.

Along the track in the distance, through the heat haze, a figure emerged. The only human beings we'd seen for the past few hours was the odd toothless old shepherdess crone, but this woman was statuesque, wearing a sarong and a bikini top and with a swagger like Jessica Rabbit.

It was like a scene from an eighties rock video. I had to rub my eyes to make sure I wasn't suffering from sunstroke. With her Gypsy black hair blowing in the breeze, she was as miraculous a sight in middle-of-nowhere Turkey as Ursula Andress emerging from the surf. I think the Idiot might have even chimed in with a ding, dong.

My mind raced ahead, pathetic (and deluded) old romantic that I am. What a story to tell our children.

'So, Dad, tell us about when you first saw Mum again,' they'd say, as we all snuggled on the sofa in front of our roaring fire drinking our red wine having just returned from a long walk in the country. Internet dating? Pah!

She got closer and closer. But just at the point when the eye minus distance plus perspective should have equalled her being right besides us, she was in fact still about 20 metres away. By the time she was introducing herself as Jasmine, Joe, Sue and I were all craning our necks skywards. I offered my hand in greeting. It disappeared.

'Hi,' Jasmine said, in a voice not dissimilar to Barry White. 'Where are you guys from?'

It was only at that point that I noticed the webbing sticking out from under her hairline and the dark shadow around her chin.

'Well, we're from Cairns, Australia,' Sue said, before adding, somewhat superfluously, I felt. 'We're married.'

And she put her arm around Joe's waist and pulled him close to her.

'And this is Mike. He's from London,' she continued, then

added, somewhat even more superfluously, I felt. 'He's all on his own.'

'Really?' Jasmine purred. 'I'm on my own, too.'

'Fancy that,' said Sue.

'I live close by. Would you like to come back to my place for some lunch and a cool drink? You must get hot riding your bike.'

'We're pretty well set, here, thanks anyway, Jasmine,' Sue said, although Jasmine had seemed to be addressing the question to me alone.

'But, Mike, weren't you just saying how hungry you were? We could meet up with you later.'

This was not the kind of plot twist I wanted to tell my kids about at all. But suddenly all eyes were on me. I fumbled around for some words, but beyond erm and ah they proved elusive. I eventually managed to construct a sentence using the words hungry, erm, not, erm, go, erm, haven't we got to … in that order, and Jasmine looked a tad crestfallen, but pursed her lips and gave me a wink as she shrugged her docker's shoulders and turned and sashayed away up the track.

Sue pursed her lips and winked at me, too, as she pulled on her crash helmet, the devil horns glowing scarlet in the white light.

We rode together for a few more days, then it was time to say goodbye again. That was hard. But Joe and Sue were planning to travel a bit more along the Turkish coast from where I'd just come, and I still had a long way to get home. We hugged and took some final, valedictory photographs.

'Come visit us in Queensland,' said Joe. 'Or join us for our next road trip.'

'I will,' I replied.

'Next year?'

'Maybe not next year. I think I'm going to stay still for a while.'

'No good ever came from staying still,' said Joe. 'We are designed to move.'

'I want to stop soon. Wake up in the same bed every morning.'

'Think that would stop the desire to be moving?'

'Maybe.'

'Never worked for me. Man finds other ways of travelling when he's cooped up. Look at the Aboriginals back home. Stuck in settlements, unable to move, they drink themselves to death.'

'Sounds like Britain ...'

'Put a bear in a cage at a zoo and he'll rip his fur out.'

'I'll think about it.'

'Ages away.'

'Back in Hungary, when I told you about my dad, you had a go at him for leaving.'

'I know. I've been thinking about that.'

'Wasn't he just trying to escape, wanting to be moving?'

'Probably.'

'Everything touches everything.'

'That's the problem.'

'I'm not sure it is.'

'Is the Pom off again?' said Sue.

'I'm going to miss you two,' I said.

'See you next year, on the road,' she said.

'Maybe.'

'Remember your pants,' Sue said. 'Every other day.'

And with that they were gone in a trail of dust, Sue pointing wildly left and right from the pillion.

# 27 Bazoukie

I couldn't be totally sure, but I think I was engaged to be married. For the past seven days in Athens I'd had a constant companion by the name of Cousin Althea. In certain traditional Greek families, this constitutes a very serious courtship indeed. And the Boltsis clan, of which I had somehow managed to become a member, was most assuredly such a family.

A week earlier, after waving goodbye to the Aussies, I had ridden up to Izmir, then across on the small ferry to the Greek island of Chios, just eight miles from the Turkish mainland.

On the short ride across, I'd looked up Chios in my guidebook. As recently as 1822, Turkish troops had stormed the place to exact a terrible revenge on the islanders for taking part in an independence uprising. Some 30,000 Chiots were slaughtered, 45,000 more enslaved and nearly all the island's buildings razed to the ground. I thought this might be a prudent time to lower the Turkish flag that had been flying from my luggage and bury it in my pannier.

As I watched the Turkish shoreline recede, I felt a sadness wash over me. I had spent five weeks riding around the country, covering over 5,000 miles. There had been some anxious moments in the volatile areas around the border with Iraq and Syria, for sure, but if there's a warmer, friendlier, more gentle people in the world, I'd yet to meet them.

The ferry docked. I had to ride my bike through a sheep dip. Then my boots were hosed down with disinfectant. I'm not sure how effective this was in terms of killing germs. But it seemed like there might be 75,000 reasons to make some kind of gesture.

'Your rear tyre is bald,' said the man on the hose.

'Thank you,' I said.

'Those Turkish roads are terribly, huh?' he said.

'Terrible,' I replied.

Sterilised, I was ushered me into the customs office to have my papers checked.

'Did you have a good time in Turkey?' asked the official, flicking through my passport.

'Not really,' I said.

He snapped the book shut. 'Good. Welcome to Greece.'

The seafront parade of Chios Town reminded me of any number of sleepy Greek island settlements I'd visited over the years in reality and in my imagination; a couple of bars and restaurants overlooking the water and a cluster of shops behind.

The place looked deserted, though, and I figured that being the furthest island outpost from Piraeus, and with the summer season drawing to a close, they must have to work very hard to attract the visitors on whom, doubtless, based on my vast knowledge of the Greek tourist industry, Chios's economy must depend.

The fact that I'd never previously heard of the island only confirmed, in my solipsistic mind, that here was a place on its financial uppers. Poor little Chios.

At the end of the bay I found a hotel, parked the bike and walked into the reception. Instead of the run-down lobby I was expecting, I entered a palatial room of marble and glass, with uniformed bellboys and guests swanning around dressed as if they had just stepped out of *The Great Gatsby* and walking miniature poodles.

Standing there in my tattered jeans and biker jacket, I felt very self-conscious. The woman behind the desk eyed me suspiciously and made me wait for a minute or two while she tidied some paperclips. She took a last drag of her cigarette then lit the next one with the stub.

Disgusting, I thought. How could anybody do that to their body? It had been a week since I'd quit smoking, and I was positively pious with contempt for those pathetic addicts. I don't know why the brain should work this way, and it's especially rich coming from a man whose numerous visits to Allan Carr's stop smoking clinic over the years means that I have a favourite chair. Maybe we reserve our greatest contempt for those that remind us of ourselves. Germans, anyone?

The paperclips arranged to her satisfaction, she asked what I wanted.

'A room would be nice.'

They didn't have any free, she said, sucking hard and revoltingly on her fag. But, hang on, what was this, a late cancellation and, yes, there was a room, a very small one, but it will be fine for just one person and the cost was 200 euros.

'I'm only here for one night.' I told her, that I'd be catching the ferry to Athens in the morning.

'That is the cost per night,' she said.

Two hundred euros! That had been my weekly accommodation budget in Turkey.

By now there were other guests waiting at the desk, all glam and manicured and poodled-up. And smoking. So I did what any self-respecting person desperate not to look like a cheapskate would do, and instead of saying, 'But this is a poor, sleepy Greek island. Would 200 euros suddenly injected into the economy not herald street parties and precipitate a run on Chios real estate?' said, 'That would be great, thank you'.

As she turned around to get my key, I stuffed my pockets with mint imperials from the bowl on the counter.

I went to my room and had a nap. I woke up two hours

later and shot into the shower. It was 9 p.m. I hadn't eaten since breakfast and, you know what these small, sleepy, out-of-season Greek islands are like; restaurants would be closing down around now and not reopening again until, say, May.

I walked past the same woman on the desk. She was still smoking a fag. I wondered whether, like the Olympic torch, the flame had been passed from fag to fag since the last time I saw her. I pocketed a few more mints on the way, and walked out into the night.

Through some bizarre quantum leap I'd been transported to Oxford Street on Christmas Eve, which in turn had been relocated to Puerto Banus.

A million people, maybe two, were jammed along the seafront. Men on souped-up motorcycles were flying along the parade on their rear wheels, ducking in between the Ferraris and Lamborghinis that were stuck nose to tail.

Everybody was in couture. This I knew, because their clothes and bags and shoes carried their designer's mark in large lettering. Loud techno pumped out of the bars I'd failed to notice on my earlier ride from the ferry. It was dark, but everybody was wearing sunglasses.

I walked right along the strip, then walked right the way back again. My sleepy, out-of-season-Greek-island-fantasy-mind was looking for a small taverna with cheap plastic tablecloths tethered with those plastic pegs that keep popping off. There, I would order a plate of calamari and some hummus, and perhaps a glass or two of ouzo, which would be brought to my table by a portly man sporting a white, stained vest and a large moustache who, later on, might be persuaded to produce his bouzouki and bang out 'Zorba the Greek'.

In the end, I had to settle for a platter of nachos smothered with guacamole and a bottle or two of Mexican beer with a lime in the top, served by a glamorous young waitress with a short skirt, an American accent and no discernible moustache.

She was from Chicago, visiting her family's ancestral home-land for the summer.

'What's happened to Chios?' I asked her.

'What do you mean?'

'How come it's changed so much?'

'You been here before, then?'

'No. It's just that I thought it might be a bit, well … You know the movie *Shirley Valentine*?'

'Uh huh.'

'Well, a bit more like that: sleepy tavernas, toothless old fisherman, bouzouki, bit of picturesque poverty, that kind of thing.'

'That is such a Hollywood cliché,' she said. 'Chios is one of the wealthiest places in Greece. Always has been. First there was the gum from the mastic bushes that they sold all over the world, and now most of the shipping dynasties live here. It's a crazy place.'

A couple of lads dressed in Versace came to the bar and ordered a trayful of B52s. The sound system pumped out more techno. Outside, the Ferraris and the Lamborghinis were still going nowhere.

I finished my food and started walking back towards the hotel.

My mobile beeped. I looked at the screen. It was a message from my ex-wife. I hadn't heard from her for over a year.

Had she finally realised that she couldn't live without me? Was she begging for forgiveness? Had she made some dreadful mistake?

I wished I could say that I'd been indifferent when I saw her name flash up, but frustratingly there was still something, albeit very dim, but still some residual, lingering thought that maybe, just maybe, everything might work out.

I opened the text.

'Louis has been missing for a week. I'm out looking for him every day, but I think he might be gone. x'

Louis was our cat. I hadn't been the world's biggest fan of them, but when my ex had moved in with me, she'd brought along Louis. It was part of the package. I was in love. What can I say?

In Darwinian terms, Louis had no right to be alive: he slept on hot manhole covers in the middle of the road so he got hit by cars; he got beaten up by every other cat in the neighbourhood, and squirrels, and magpies; he lacked any feline grace, falling off fences in slapstick fashion or walking into walls; if he was asleep on top of you and a noise spooked him – like somebody getting a text in the next street, for example – he would leave Freddy Krueger lacerations in your chest. He was a shit cat of the highest order. I missed him terribly.

I put my phone in my pocket and stood there, looking out across the sea to the twinkling lights of Turkey.

The next day, I'd taken the overnight ferry bound for Athens. There had been no cabins available, so I'd dug out my sleeping bag and found the last remaining floor space, in a corner by the fruit machines, where, courtesy of the insomniac truckers nudging away and a rather perky Aegean, I had spent a sleepless night rolling from one side of the ship to the other in the manner of a man on fire trying to put himself out.

We arrived in Athens before dawn. I stood bleary-eyed on deck with the smokers in the grey light as we waited our turn to enter the port of Piraeus, to the north of us sitting under a Piraeus-sized smog.

I looked at the smokers, inhaling that disgusting filth into their lungs, waving my hand around ostentatiously in front of my face lest any of them would think I was as degraded and weak as them. The man standing at my shoulder lit his next cigarette from the stub of his previous one. I tutted.

We bobbed around for 30 minutes, our flotilla of patient

ferries like a Spithead review. The sun finally poked its head over the hills and the colour switch was flicked and there came that collective, palpable relief that people feel when another night is done. Even at this hour, the sun was very strong. It was going to be a hot day.

I drove off the boat and into the insanity that was Athens's rush hour. The nearest supplier of tyres, according to my list of BMW service dealers, was in the Athenian suburb of Chalandri, exactly on the opposite side of the city from Piraeus.

My attempts to locate Chalandri were not aided by the fact that all the road signs were in algebra, nor by the seeming abundance of Parthenons which I passed with regularity, nor indeed by the constant accusations by my fellow road users of being a 'malakas' (think those early Nescafé ads featuring the coffee-bean shake).

It was nearly two hours later that I pulled up outside the BMW dealer in Chalandri. Well, when I say BMW dealer, I mean former BMW dealer, the site of the operation, according to the lone security guard sitting in his hut in the huge empty car park, having being moved across town to somewhere close to Piraeus a couple of weeks previously.

I went to the cabin on the corner of the street and bought some cigarettes. I opened the packet and smoked three in a row, lighting the next with the stub of the previous one.

Then I sat down in the gutter and, head in hands, rocked gently back and forth, muttering to myself.

'You okay?' a voice said from somewhere beyond my palms.

I looked up to see a man, not unlike a thirtysomething Leo McKern.

'Nice bike,' he said. 'That's mine over there.'

I looked over to see a motorbike, a Honda Africa Twin, parked next to mine.

'Your rear tyre's bald.'

'I know.'

'You should get it replaced.'

'Thank you.' I lit another cigarette.

'You smoke like a Greek,' said the man.

'Thank you.'

'My name's Ilias. Ilias Boltsis,' and he put his hand out in greeting. 'You don't look so happy. Where are you heading?'

So I told him about my night in Chios and the sleepless night on the ferry and my Athenian morning and my tyre odyssey and the nasty men in their cars, as if Ilias was going to say, 'There, there. Did Mikey have a scary nightmare?', which he didn't. But he did say: 'Chios! That's where my family is from originally. Did you like it?'

'Of course.'

'That's it,' Ilias said. 'You're coming home with me.'

'Dennis Neilson,' screamed my London brain.

'Okay, then,' whispered my meek, cowed voice. I'd quickly mulled over the options. Getting cut up into little pieces and melted down into glue would be an infinitely preferable fate to being alone again on a motorcycle in the Athens traffic.

We walked over to the bikes.

'Why have you got this thing on your saddle?' asked Ilias.

'It's to keep you cool when the weather is very hot,' I said.

'In Athens it is very hot,' said Ilias. 'But my saddle is never a problem.'

We both stood there for a while, staring at my dead Polish sheep, now caked and grime-encrusted and looking like a sheep's arse.

'It was useful in Turkey,' I said.

'You have been in Turkey?'

'That's how I came to be in Chios.'

'Did they disinfect you?'?

We rode away. But instead of going back to a bedsit with pentagrams carved into black-gloss walls, we pulled up outside a four-storey apartment block.

'This is my family home,' Ilias said. 'On the top floor lives my sister Olga and her husband. I live on the second floor and my parents on the first.'

There was an English-language school at street level.

'That is run by Olga,' Ilias said. 'Her students would like to meet you, I'm sure.'

After insisting that I ride my motorcycle up three steps, through the front door and park it in their hallway – a mere trifle for me now – Ilias marched me into his parents' apartment, where I was introduced to his mother, the matriarch known to all as Mrs Chrysanthi.

I was instructed to take a seat at the table and within minutes Mrs Chrysanthi was plonking an enormous plate of moussaka in front of me, flanked by mountains of feta cheese, spinach pies, aubergine, homemade bread and sardines in garlic.

I was instructed to eat, but whispered to Ilias whether it would be more polite to wait for everybody else.

'This is just for you,' he said.

I ate it all, bar perhaps a bit of garlic, and Mrs Chrysanthi looked at the garlic and whispered something to Ilias.

'What did she say?' I asked.

'She's wondering why you don't like her food,' said Ilias.

Lunch over, and Mrs Chrysanthi turned her attentions to my laundry and was calling me '*pethi mou*' or 'my child' and telling Ilias that he should introduce me to Cousin Althea.

Olga was making up my room, Cousin Poppy had popped round and was fussing over me.

'What did you think of Turkey,' she said.

'Oh, erm … it was …'

'Not as nice as Greece?'

'No way.'

There followed a succession of the neighbourhood's single women, who just happened to be filing through the kitchen to say hello. I felt like I'd been scooped out of a raging sea.

I was sitting on the Greek kitchen set of a movie that could only have been created by the clichéd minds of Hollywood scriptwriters. I was happy that my unoriginal brain was being plied with bromides once more.

Ilias, meanwhile, was phoning around all his friends and relaying to me the social programme for the next week and possibly the rest of my life.

'Tomorrow we will find you a tyre. The day after, I will show you around.'

'But I was going to be leaving tomorrow,' I told him.

'Mike, Mike, Mike,' he replied. 'You may already smoke like a Greek. Now you have to learn to relax like a Greek. You can only live for today. Never for tomorrow. It will always take care of itself.' And the subject of my departure was closed.

And so began my two weeks of staying put.

Ilias and his girlfriend, Litsa, took the day off work and we rode our motorbikes out through the pine forests and along the Sea of Corinth. We stopped for lunch at their favourite hilltop restaurant and at some waterside cafés. After, we rode around Athens, with its single Parthenon, and met up with their friends for iced coffees in Piraeus. I was taking a lot of photographs.

The next morning, Mrs Chrysanthi delivered, as she would do every morning, a breakfast of toasted sandwiches to Ilias's flat. It was a magnificent apartment in the best bachelor tradition, with sinks not plumbed in, the kitchen cabinets mostly still flat-packed in their boxes and a windsurfer complete with sail leaning against the living-room wall. The television was huge, though.

'Your mom looks after you like a king,' I said.

'Like all Greek mothers,' Ilias said, laughing. 'I am 36 years old, but I am still her little boy. It will always be like that, even if I get married. I don't know what I would do without her.'

I glanced over at Ilias. It was easy to imagine what he had looked like as a little boy. He still looked like a little boy.

'I think mothers are the same all over the world,' he said. 'I bet your mum still treats you like a child when you go home.'

I told him.

He looked mortified.

'I'm really sorry,' he said.

'It was a long time ago,' I said. We sat munching in silence for a while.

'Mike, tonight I have a special treat for you,' Ilias said. 'We are going to go to bazoukie. It is the finest Greek entertainment.'

'Sounds good.'

'But first, my sister Olga has asked me if you'd mind visiting her school downstairs to meet her students. They'd be really excited to practise their English on you.'

'Sounds good,' I said.

I was paraded in front of the young pupils who, ranged from around four years old to 12 or 13, seemed very shy and reticent. Eventually, one young boy raised his hand and asked me: 'Where London Queen live?'

I answered. They was a palpable buzz in the room. They seemed to regard my command of the English language as putting me in the same intellectual bracket as Einstein. It was my turn to be smart. I liked the feeling.

Another question. 'What name you?'

I answered with all the élan and witty elegance of Stephen Fry, or maybe even Oscar Wilde. I was a giant.

A young girl raised her hand.

'Yes?' I said, pointing to her.

'I was wondering,' she said, in perfect English. 'Whether it was always appropriate to use the present continuous with normal verbs when talking about the near future?'

All eyes were upon me. I felt like I was back on the stage

at the Halikarnus wearing a pair of shorts festooned with hearts.

'Erm, that is indeed an excellent question,' I stuttered. 'And, erm, in the world of normal, erm, verbs, one would usually, erm, not sometimes refer to the near future with, erm, the present continuous, but, erm, if the question is whether it's always appropriate, then I would have to say, erm, that you would probably need to, erm, define what, in any particular context, constitutes appropriate, apropos of erm, and that's really a whole different matter ...'

The children sitting with big animal alphabets in front of them looked mightily impressed. The inquisitor slightly less so.

'We should go,' said Ilias.

That night, a dozen of us hit the town and spent until sunrise at that most bonkers of Greek institutions: the bazoukie bar.

It took a while to get going, the early acts receiving just muted applause. The waitress came over and plonked a bottle of Jameson's on the table.

'These are only the warm-up acts,' said Ilias. 'Just wait until the big stars come on later.'

At some stage well after midnight, the big names started to appear and the flower-throwing started. At first there was just the odd bloom arcing its way stagewards, but soon after the room was a hailstorm of carnations.

'It is how we show our appreciation for the singers,' Ilias said. 'We used to throw plates, but the authorities said that too many people were getting hurt so it was banned. Banned! The world is going mad.'

I asked him what would happen in Greece when they banned smoking, like in many other EU countries.

'Ban smoking? In Greece?' he said, taking a long, thoughtful drag on his cigarette. 'Mike, Mike. Have you gone crazy? Plates they can take from us. Smoking, never.'

A waitress came past. I wanted to take part in the flower-throwing. Not to would have been like being in Rovaniemi and not going to a thrash-metal gig. I ordered two sets of the standard five trays.

'How much?' I asked.

'Fifteen euros,' she said.

'Wow, 15 euros for a load of old carnations! Can't give 'em away at home. Only people who buy them are drunk men at petrol stations, late home for dinner …'

'Fifteen euros,' she said again, and held out her hand.

I gave her the money and took the flowers. Ilias and Cousin Althea and the rest of our table plunged their hands into the trays and started flinging the blooms about.

The waitress was still standing there, chewing gum, hand outstretched. She was beginning to annoy me a bit.

'Yes?' I said to her.

'I am waiting for the rest of the money.'

'I just paid you,' I said. 'Fifteen euros.'

She rolled her eyes. 'Per tray,' she said.

By now our wooden trays were sitting empty, their erstwhile contents either on the stage getting ground underfoot or else still, just, finishing their parabolic journeys towards neighbouring tables.

'Can I scoop some of them up and give them back to you?' I asked.

'From the dirty floor?'

'I can see how that probably wouldn't work.'

'One hundred and fifty euros,' she said.

I counted out the money. Fifteen ten-euro notes. I handed them over.

She counted them again in front of me. Then sashayed off.

I took a long slug of Jameson's.

'You okay?' asked Ilias. 'You've gone quiet.'

'Great,' I replied, and took another slug.

'Now, Mike, I meant to tell you this at the start of the

evening,' Ilias said, suddenly looking grave. 'Because you are
with Cousin Althea this evening, it is your duty to protect her
honour.'

'Her honour?'

'Should a single carnation land on her, it would mean
another man was vying for her attention. For the sake of the
family and your own honour, you would have to fight him.'

I laughed politely. I thought back to the tow rope and the
dead sheep. Was this another one?

'It is no joke, Mike,' he said, nodding solemnly. 'Honour in
Greece is everything.'

For a while, I sat there scanning the air for incoming, slapping away any blooms flying in the vicinity of Cousin Althea
like a one-man Patriot missile defence system.

Concentrating on incomings was made more tricky by the
fact that every ten seconds or so there would be a toast, when
one of our party would raise their glasses and we'd all stand
up and take a sip of whisky, a frenzy of clunking.

Well, my Greek friends would take a sip of whisky. I have
never quite mastered the art of sipping, and soon my coordi-
nation was such that I would have been unable to stop a beach
ball hitting Cousin Althea.

At some unseen signal, the entire club en masse climbed
on to the stage or up on their tables and started dancing like
drunken tightrope walkers. At this same unseen signal, I
slumped into my arms on the table. It was around 5 a.m.
Within seconds I was asleep, Althea, for all I knew, sitting
next to me under a growing pyramid of carnations with just
her head poking out of the top.

During that fortnight, there would be many more evenings in
bazoukie bars. And by the end I was no mean slouch at
drunken tightrope walking.

Cousin Althea seemed to forgive me for leaving her
honour unprotected and we even went out on a couple of

uncharperoned dates, afternoons of sightseeing with all the innocence of a Doris Day movie.

I got to know cousins Costas and Georgiou, and many more cousins whose names I forget, heard about the family's triumphs and tragedies and even managed to learn some more Greek. Well, 'malakas' isn't going to get you far.

We watched family wedding videos and laughed as Ilias's father set fire to the crotch of his trousers with a welding torch. Ilias and I talked away whole afternoons, slowly peeling back the guarded layers to the substance beneath.

I felt part of something, no longer just a spectator flashing by; by simply not moving, I travelled much further. For I was slowly learning, first from Joe and Sue, and now with the Boltsis family, that no matter how much I try to kid myself that I can exist quite happily in isolation, meaningful human contact is, for me anyway, the only thing that brings a full life. In that fortnight, I found a level of love and care I had long-forgotten existed.

Ilias had predicted that it would be raining the morning I planned to leave, just as he had told me it would be raining every time I suggested that I might leave tomorrow. 'Tomorrow, tomorrow,' he would say. 'Have you learned nothing from the Greeks?'

But the weather was fine, as it had been all those other mornings.

As I went around the apartment, slowly gathering all my stuff together and packing it in my panniers, Mrs Chrysanthi appeared with the last toasted sandwiches. She grabbed both my cheeks, kissed me and said something to Ilias.

'What did she say?' I asked.

'Just that she considers you her son,' Ilias replied.

'Thank you, Mrs Chrysanthi,' I said.

I took a photograph of her and Ilias together, arm in arm.

Packing finished, Ilias and I sat down and started on the sandwiches.

'Thank you for coming over to me at the roadside,' I said to him. 'I have enjoyed it staying with you. More than you could know.'

'My pleasure,' he said. 'You will always be welcome here. Any time.'

'Thank you,' I said again.

A pause.

'You are a truly lucky man to have a family like this,' I said.

'I know. But you have your freedom,' he said, 'to travel the world and have adventures.'

'Maybe,' I said. 'But if I had what you had, I'm not sure I would have left in the first place.'

Ilias helped me carry my luggage down the stairs and within ten minutes it was all secured on the bike.

The entire Boltsis family had come around to see me off. One by one, they approached with gifts. There were books on Greek cookery and a Greek dictionary from Olga and Cousin Poppy. Mrs Chrysanthi gave me a pair of smart leather shoes and a stuffed stripy fish that said 'I love you' in English when you squeezed its belly. Cousin Althea gave me a set of worry beads. She looked sad as she handed them over.

Ilias approached and gave me a posh, silver pen. He looked even sadder than Althea.

'Watch out for those Albanians,' he said.

Then he disappeared and came back with a piece of old tarpaulin.

'You'll need this to cover your luggage,' he said. 'I'm telling you, the weather's going to be bad.'

I looked up in the sky again. Not a cloud. But I took the tarpaulin and stashed it under the cargo net.

'You could always stay for another few days,' Ilias said.

'I really should be heading home,' I said, hugging him. 'I've got a long way to go.'

I climbed on my bike and rode off into the Athens traffic.

On the outskirts of the city, as the highway passed the exit for Chalandri, the sky turned black and, before I had time to pull over and dig out my wet-weather gear, the heavens opened. It would rain remorselessly for the next two days.

# 28 The Comb-over Kid

'I hope you have good insurance for your bike. And plenty of money,' said the guard, standing at the Greece/Albania border.

'I do,' I said. 'At least I think I do.'

'That,' he said, pointing beyond no-man's-land, 'is the country with the most worst roads, the craziest drivers and the most corrupt police in the world. They'll stop you every few kilometres, find something wrong with your bike that'll cost you money every time.'

'Great,' I said. 'Anything else?'

'There are many guns,' he said. 'Everywhere. Some say two guns for every citizen. Armed bandits have been robbing travellers recently.'

He finished scanning my passport, handed it back and opened the barrier.

'Have a good trip,' he said, waving cheerily.

One thing the border guard didn't mention, however, was the wildlife. Because, had he done so, I would probably not, just a few kilometres down the road, have ridden towards the pair of metre-long strips of intertwined rubber on the road with quite so much casual indifference. Would probably not have been quite so surprised to witness said rubber strips stand to attention. And would perhaps have been better prepared to one-handedly fend off two rather annoyed snakes – and boy those things can shift – snapping viciously at my ankles, an entirely understandable reaction when somebody has tried to run you over while you're engaged in a spot of reptilian rumpy pumpy.

The fact that the attack came from the right, so my throttle hand was alternately employed in fight and flight, made my stuttering progress along the road reminiscent of a man with appalling clutch control.

As welcomes go, Albania's was certainly memorable. I'd only been in the country five minutes and already it felt like I was starring in *Raiders of the Lost Ark*. I didn't know it then, but by the time I'd finally make it out of Albania, I would feel like I'd been through the entire Indiana Jones trilogy.

I pulled over in the next town to compose myself. The main street was piled with mounds of rotting rubbish being scavenged through by packs of dogs.

A Porsche Cayenne drew up. An old man climbed out, dropped the tailgate and retrieved a goat from the back. A brand-new Bentley with blacked-out windows cruised past, dodging around the donkey-hauled carts and elderly women stooped double carrying huge bundles of straw. Parked alongside the street were rows of gleaming top-of-the-range BMWs, Mercedes and Range Rovers.

These were testimony, not to the economic powerhouse that isn't Albania – one of the poorest countries in Europe, where the average annual salary is under £3,000 – but to the affluence of the people busy filling in their claims forms in Stuttgart and Sloane Square. For it is they who are the unwitting donors of the estimated two-thirds of all the cars on the road in Albania that have been stolen in western Europe. 'Do business in Albania,' runs a German joke. 'Your car's already there.'

And I know it isn't helpful to propagate stereotypes – notice how I haven't said 'German? Joke? Isn't that an oxymoron' – especially as stereotypes are the very things travel is meant to challenge. But it was easy, sitting there, surrounded by more fancy motors than the Chelsea players' car park, to see how Albania had become a byword in some circles for organised crime.

I rode to Gjirokastra, a town perched high on a rocky perch overlooking the Drinos valley. Gjirokastra was the birthplace of dictator Enver Hoxha, and the soppy old sod's sentimentality meant that the town was spared the levelling and Stalinist building programme that swept across the rest of the country.

I rode up the steep cobbled streets, winding between nineteenth-century Ottoman houses roofed in slate. I passed the Greek embassy. There were queues snaking down the road into the distance.

At the top of the town was the magnificently sinister and brooding castle. Flying high above it was the large Albanian flag, with its fearsome-looking double-headed eagle on a blood-red background, its message, in heraldic terms: come and have a go if you think you're hard enough.

I walked through the immense gates and up a dark, cobbled passageway dripping water down the walls that gathered in calcified pools at the bottom. At the end of this passageway, now deep in the bowels of the castle, was a large snarling dog of indeterminate pedigree attached to a large ring on the wall by a chain of indeterminate length. It was Dungeons and Dragons. I wished I had a bullwhip.

The dog charged towards me, frothing and growling, and the chain snapped it back about three feet in front of me so that the dog's back legs overtook its front ones and it ended up in a heap on the floor. The dog looked surprised, incredulous even, and let out a yelp, which helps explain I guess why he was chained to a wall and I was riding a motorbike around Europe.

I walked passed a selection of field guns and tanks parked in the vaulted recesses of the gloomy corridor, the barrels appearing as ghostly silhouettes in the half-light, and up a stone staircase into a series of interconnected whitewashed rooms.

Everywhere there were guns. Thousand upon thousand of them in piles and stacked against the walls, like a huge weapons amnesty: rifles, machine guns, howitzers, shotguns and pistols.

The curator came over.

'This is the gun museum,' she said.

'Really?' I said.

She shook her head. I was confused. (Bear with me on this one.)

'But they are not our guns. No, they are mostly German and Italian.

'We had many more,' she went on, before adding: 'But a lot disappeared during the "transition" after Hoxha's death. Nearly a million guns were stolen from the army as well.'

'Is that right?'

She shook her head. (Pay attention.)

I walked out on to the ramparts. There, on a narrow ledge, right at the edge of the castle, was an eviscerated jet fighter, a US plane according to the decals on the wings and fuselage. It must have been one hell of a landing, maybe something beyond even the top guns of the Hurtigruten fleet.

The curator had followed me out.

'How did that get there?' I asked, pointing to the wreck.

'The communist party used to tell us that it was a US spy plane forced down and captured by our heroic defenders,' she said. 'It was carried up here by helicopter. But later we found out that it was just a NATO training plane from Italy that had run out of fuel. The stickers were put on afterwards.'

I rode on over the southern mountains to Saranda. Then along the coast road to Vlora, through olive groves and pine forests, past terraces of agave and along miles and miles of the stunning deserted beaches and turquoise waters of the

Ionians, dodging the ancient trucks, buses, donkey carts and Lamborghini Diablos as I went. I passed a disused submarine base, the barracks all flyblown, a submarine-sized tunnel disappearing into the mountainside like a Disney ride.

Ghoulish stuffed dummies hung from trees, the Albanian custom to ward off evil spirits. And everywhere there were the mushroom-shaped concrete bunkers, like Daleks popping their heads through the earth. Hoxha had 700,000 of them built – one for every four citizens – between 1950 and his death in 1985 to defend Albania as it grew ever more internationally isolated and he grew ever more bonkers, eventually, in the best dictator tradition, dragging an entire country down with him.

Nothing can prepare you for the sight of those bunkers, so ubiquitous are they. They were made to be indestructible – there's a story that Hoxha asked the designer to make them rocket-proof, and then, also in the best dictator tradition, made said designer cower in one while he shelled it – and so they stand, in every field, on every street corner, in every olive grove, along every beach, like the entire landscape has been riveted.

Albanians have been busy painting many of them in blobs and candy stripes, and have found myriad practical applications, as storage for tools, or for illicit love trysts. I imagined Hoxha, sitting on a cloud, or possibly somewhere warmer, watching the Coca-Cola salesmen walk right past while the citizens were too busy snogging to notice or care.

I stayed the night in Vlora, one of Albania's major ports.

The hotel manager came outside to greet me. He had undoubtedly the worst comb-over I'd even seen, a great big gelled tongue of hair that reared up in the wind like a cornered cobra. I was mesmerised by it, but was trying so hard not to stare at it that I just gazed intently into his eyes. I'm surprised he didn't call the police.

Until my own hairline started receding, I didn't really

notice other men's hair. Now it's one of the first thing I clock. I notice other men clocking my barnet, too.

Hair is extraordinarily important to a man. If we had the equivalent to those women's mags that feature photos of female celebs' flaws, like their cellulite or their chubby ankles or their bingo wings, it would just be called *Slaphead!* and have cover-to-cover pictures of male celebs going bald.

Even better if they're caught trying to cover it up. Forget spiralling personal debt, failing schools and a nation addicted to Prozac. Catch Jude Law coming out of a hair clinic and hold the front page.

And don't get me started on all that guff about women liking sexy bald men like Vin Diesel or Bruce Willis. Let's be honest here. There are balding movie stars and there are balding sub-editors. Telling me not to worry about it would be about as consoling as me going up to a woman on the treadmill and saying: 'I don't know why you're bothering, love. Men love fat chicks.'

I felt guilty about thinking bad things about the Comb-over Kid a bit later on, though, when, in response to my query about whether the hotel had an iron, he came to my room, put a towel on the floor, knelt down and pressed my shirt for me. At least, out of the wind, the flap stayed pasted to his head.

I was out on the town by 11 p.m., walking up and down Vlora's main drag in my nicely ironed shirt. Tourism is in its infancy in Albania and I attracted a lot of attention whenever I stopped and asked for advice about good places to eat or somewhere to get a drink.

That attention stopped at 11.01 p.m. In fact, everything stopped at 11.01 p.m. One minute there'd been thousands of people promenading, the next just me watching a bunch of tumbleweed pitchpoling down the street. The search for a restaurant, any restaurant, became frantic. Shutters were coming down like the entire street had narcolepsy.

The difference between Albanian and Greek nightlife had been startling. For one thing, at 11 p.m., in Greece the evening was only just beginning. For another, at 11 p.m. in Greece, it was midnight in Albania, a fact I now realised by looking at the clock on the town hall. Maybe Sancho Panza at the border might consider including that snippet of information in his pep talk.

I walked back to my hotel. I wondered if the nice manager might knock me up a sandwich, so I mimed to him that I hadn't managed to eat by rubbing my tummy and shaking my head. He shook his head back at me and smiled. We stood there for a while. Albania was a study in confusion.

I tried again. This time just miming putting something in my mouth and pointing to the kitchen. The Comb-over Kid held up his finger then disappeared round the back, re-emerging a few minutes later with a sandwich. This, combined with the business with the iron earlier, only made me feel more of a cad for thinking bad things about his hair.

I ate the sandwich in the lobby. Once finished, the manager rubbed his tummy and smiled.

I smiled back and nodded.

The manager looked disappointed, annoyed even.

I set off the next day in fairly low spirits. I'd been four months on the road and covered around 12,000 miles. It would be fair to say I was exhausted with the constant movement, the fatigue of riding every day, the packing and unpacking, the solo breakfasts and dinners, the near misses on the road, the hellos and goodbyes. I was also thinking a lot about Louis, imagining him lost and confused.

If somebody had given me a pair of ruby slippers at that point, I might have been clicking away. But there was still one place I felt I had to go.

My phone beeped.

'When you coming to Zagreb?'

Two places.

At the foot of the Llogaraja Pass, I spotted another motor-cycle traveller heading towards me. You learn to spot the luggage profile a mile off. We stopped for a chat. I asked him where he was from.

'Austria,' he replied.

'Really?'

'Yes. Not Australia. Austria.'

He sounded like Herr Flick. I couldn't imagine it was a mistake many people made.

'You have to be very careful on these roads,' he went on. 'The driving is crazy. I have nearly been killed many times. And there are no helicopters for airlifts or hospitals close by. If you crash, you could just bleed to death by the side of the road. Bleed to death. All alone. Have you thought about that?'

I said that I hadn't, but that I probably would do from now on.

'This country is very dangerous,' he said. 'Very dangerous. What is the road like up ahead?'

'Oh, terrible. There are sheer drops, and places where the road has washed away and plunges down the cliff, and mad, snarling dogs in the villages that try and attack you, and people shooting at you and there are huge snakes, every-where.'

'Really?' he said.

'Really,' I replied. I'd made it all up, of course, apart from the snakes. And the mad, snarling dogs. But Herr Flick struck me as the kind of person who thrived on the prospect of calamity, of impending doom. The type who would definitely have a dismembered motorcycling friend of a friend or two.

'This sounds very bad,' he said.

'Try not to think about it,' I said.

The road started to climb on the Llogaraja, twisting in sharp switchbacks. The road gained 1,000 metres in height in rapid time, the sides guarded by a low castellated wall that would doubtless prevent skateboards from coming to much harm, but not any forms of transport more than, say, two inches off the ground. What is it with dictators and poorly guarded roads? There's a thesis right there. Research grants have been given for less. A gallery of curled photos gazed out from most bends.

Over the pass and inland, along horrendously disfigured roads, rutted and potholed. Herr Flick had been right about that. Romanians and Poles, I take it all back. I passed by fields of abandoned cars, shanty towns and fetid green rivers choked with rubbish. I rode alongside ancient trains, their carriages missing doors.

In the pothole-riddled city of Shkodra, strap-hanging commuters stared back at me through the smashed windows of their bus. Overhead, the clouds were yellow from the high-sulphur petrol sold in Albania that's long been banned in the rest of Europe.

All of this might be less shocking if I'd been in some other part of the world, or in another time. But I was in Europe, in 2006, just north of Greece and only 100 miles across the Otranto Straits from Italy.

That Albania is a poor country is unquestionable. But there was something else that struck me about the place. Looking around, there didn't seem to be much of a culture of maintenance. Rubbish was discarded in the street. Broken windows went unrepaired. The roads were falling apart for want of a little attention. Supermarkets had rows of empty shelves.

In terms of GDP, I'd been to much poorer countries, but I'd rarely seen a place with such widespread decay or dereliction, neglecting itself.

I stopped in a café. I repeated my earlier mime of pretending to put something in my mouth. The café owner just shook his head and turned to walk off.

I looked around to double-check I was in a café and not,

say, in a hardware shop. Yup, the signs were all there: people sitting at tables, eating and drinking. No racks of nails or hammers.

I called the owner back and repeated my mime. Again, he just shook his head, more vigourously this time, and walked off.

For the first time in my life, I harumphed. I didn't even know what a harumph was until it came out of my mouth. Then I turned and flounced towards the door.

'Where are you going?' said a man sitting at the table nearest the door.

'Well,' and I think I harumphed again. 'The owner clearly has no intention of serving me so I thought I'd take my custom elsewhere.'

Who uses a phrase like 'take my custom elsewhere'? A harumpher, that's who.

'He is going to make you a sandwich,' the man said.

'But he refused, twice,' I said. 'He kept shaking his head.'

'In Albania, that means yes,' said the man.

I thought back to the gun museum and the Comb-over Kid.

'That explains a lot,' I said.

'Would you like to sit down here with me?' the man asked.

I nodded my head and sat down. The man introduced himself as Shume.

He looked like a young Peter Lorre, and spoke in low, guttural tones. He had the kind of sad, hangdog face and life-less voice that even if he was telling you you'd won the lottery, you be reaching for the lithium.

I asked him how his English was so good.

'I worked in London as a builder for a few years,' he said. 'I was illegal. Got caught and deported last year.'

'What will you do now?'

'Go back,' he said.

'Is there no work for you here?' I asked.

'A little, but the wages are so poor that you can't afford to live. I have been in London. I have seen how it is possible to live. I cannot forget.'

The owner brought over a sandwich.

'Coffee?' he asked.

I nodded.

I told Shume what I had seen on my ride through Albania, that it seemed to be a country in the grips of a depression.

'There is money in Albania, but the politicians and the gangsters steal it all for themselves,' he said. 'Maybe one day, far off, when we join the EU, things might change. People here always relied on the state to take care of their basic needs.

'Now, the state is smaller but many people don't want to take care of themselves. They give up. What can you do?' He shrugged his shoulders.

I asked him whether people were getting sentimental about the communist days.

'Some, especially older people, are beginning to think that the old days were easier. But we wouldn't have been able to have this conversation back then. There would have been police agents following you, or sitting on the next table monitoring us.'

We sat there for a minute or two in silence.

'But now we are free,' Shume said, finally.

My coffee never did arrive. Eventually I said goodbye to Shume, wished him luck and went back outside to the bike. I took out my mobile and sent a text message to Gasho in Montenegro, a respondent from the Horizons website. Montenegro was only 50 miles or so up the road. I told him I was on my way.

I'd sent him an email a few weeks back saying that I'd be heading to Montenegro at some stage and he'd invited me to stay with him in Bar.

Although I'd initially planned to explore Albania for a few more days, I now had the urge to get out. This was tinged with guilt, a pointless, futile guilt, after my conversation with Shume, as it was so easy for me to do. Or so I'd thought.

I got a text back from Gasho. It read: 'Meet you at the border in an hour.'

I rode through northern Albania, past thousands more of Hoxha's bunkers and hulking derelict factories whose skeletal remains were rusted and calcified. I stopped to have a look at one in the middle of nowhere.

Two youths came past on a scooter heading in the direction from where I'd just come. I noticed them pulling over about 100 yards up the road. They dismounted and one of them tied a scarf around his face. Then he started walking towards me. The other one stayed by the scooter.

He had what looked like a Kalashnikov slung around his back. As he got a little nearer, he took it from his shoulder and held it in his right hand. It was unmistakably a Kalashnikov.

I had no idea of what was going to happen. For a split second, I stood there, all the benign and quixotic explanations rushing around my brain. They're out hunting with AK47s? They're lost? He wants to look at my bike? He's from northern Cyprus and wants to practise his English? It all went into slow motion. I stared at the scarf tied around his face. Then I stared at the gun. I remembered the border guard's warnings. I thought about Herr Flick. He was about 60 yards away now.

My legs were growing rapidly heavier and my hands had started to tremble. Any longer and I would become frozen and whatever was going to happen would happen. Weirdly, there was a grain of comfort in this thought, the passive prostrating before the aggressor, curling up in a ball, at the mercy of others. Fifty yards. It was now or never.

I swung my leg over the bike, kicked it off the stand and

pressed the ignition. As I smashed the bike into gear and released the clutch too quickly, causing it stutter before catching, I hunched my shoulders, waiting for the sound of the gun. The bike picked up speed, I stayed in a crouched position on the saddle, braced for the impact. It never came.

For the next 20 miles or so I rode like a maniac, touching maybe 100 mph on some of the decrepit roads. Finally, when I felt I'd put enough distance between me and the gunman, I slowed down. I breathed deeply. I could still feel my heart pounding. I breathed deeply again. Montenegro, where Gasho was waiting for me, was now only about 10 miles away. I was looking forward to seeing a friendly face. I breathed deeply once more. My heart was slowing down again.

A Mercedes came around the corner on the wrong side of the road at a ludicrously high speed. The driver touched his brakes, but the wheels locked on the rucked surface and the car veered first to the left, then to the right, where it went into a spin. Now it was side on and careening straight towards me. There was a wall on my side of the road and nowhere for me to go.

Like the incident with the two youths just a few minutes before, everything went into slow motion again, just like when you drop a wine glass from the table and have time to imagine the broken pieces and cleaning it up even before the glass hits the ground.

I felt a wave of calm as the driver and I locked eyes momentarily and even had time to think 'I am about to die'. It wasn't a remotely scary sensation. It was, bizarrely, almost comforting.

I closed my eyes, passively, and waited, not for the physical impact but, like the wine glass, for the noise.

There was a ungodly sound of squealing tyres and an acrid smell of rubber. I felt the wave of air. And then the only noise I heard was a scraping of metal on stone as I opened my eyes and looked over my shoulder to see the Mercedes disappearing over the wall and into space.

I pulled up. My whole body now in spasm, my hands clamped rigid around the handlebars. After a minute or so of deep breathing, I turned around and went back to the half-demolished wall, expecting to find a wrecked car at the bottom of the mountain.

But instead, when I popped my head over what was left of the wall, I saw the Mercedes about 20 feet below me, in a field, next to a bunker, with its wheels splayed out like a collapsed giraffe. The driver was standing next to the car, clutching a hubcap in his left hand. I shouted down to him and stuck up my thumb. He looked up, his face wearing a dazed, blank expression. I would find out later that the thumbs-up gesture in Albania is a grievous sexual insult.

I should have waited for the police. I only needed them to turn up and arrest me and I'd have had the full Albanian collection as prophesied by the Greek border guard.

But I ran back to my bike and rode off, at first recklessly, then more cautiously, towards Montenegro.

# 29 Land of the giants

Through the border post and the potholes immediately gave way to immaculate tarmac surfaces. I pulled over and looked around for Gasho. There was nobody around. I wasn't unduly concerned. At least I wasn't in Albania.

Thirty minutes passed and of Gasho there was still no sign. I received a text.

'Where are you?' it said.

'I am waiting at the Montenegro/Albania border for you,' I replied.

Five minutes passed. Another text.

'Which Montenegro/Albania border?' it said.

What an odd question. How many border posts could there be?

I fished out my map. From Shkodra in Albania to Bar, I could see now, you had two choices of route.

Route one took you on 30-mile road due north through the badlands of Albania that contained AK47-wielding bandits and psychotic Mercedes drivers. After that, you proceeded to Montenegro's capital Podgorica. Having negotiated that, you hung a left, took the road right around the expanse of Lake Skardar, then rode over the mountains for 40 miles or so, did a left at Budvar and then rode down the coast for another 20 miles until you got to Bar. Alternatively, at Shkodra, you could bear left, ride through 10 miles of flat countryside, cross the border at Sukobin and be in Bar minutes later. For some reason, it was at that border crossing that Gasho was awaiting my arrival.

I finally rolled into Bar two hours later, well after dark. Gasho was there to greet me, standing at the bar in Bar, and did so with great warmth. But I suspected that after the border debacle, the neutral standing one normally has with someone one has never met and about whom one knows nothing was already showing a deficit.

'How was Albania?' he asked.

'Interesting,' I said.

Gasho laughed.

Gasho was enormous. About 6 foot 8 inches and probably the same distance around the chest. A group of people sitting at a table by the door got up and went to leave. They were also enormous, if anything taller than Gasho. Two women walked past on the way to the loo. They must have be 6 foot 4 inches. After the experience in the Turkish orange grove, I checked out their feet and hands and Adam's apples. All seemed in order. I felt like I'd left Albania and arrived in Brobdingnagian.

'You are all so tall,' I said to Gasho.

'The second tallest nation in the world,' he said. 'Only the Watusi of Burundi are taller.'

'How come?' I asked him.

'Nobody knows for sure,' he said. 'Some claim it's because we've never been invaded, so our nation is racially pure.'

If I'd sailed to Montenegro and seen Gasho waiting on the beach, I'd probably have had a little rethink about my invasion plans, too. Unless, of course, I'd been with my Watusi mates from Burundi.

We ordered some more beers and sat and talked for a while.

'I read that Montenegro won its independence from Serbia this year?' I said.

'That's right,' Gasho replied. 'You are sitting in the world's newest country.'

We raised a toast. I looked around. The bar was heaving. A group of midgets came in. Six foot if they were an inch.

'Tourists?' I asked.

'Yes,' Gasho replied.

'Good summer for visitors?' I asked.

'The best yet,' Gasho said. 'Tourist numbers are up, rich Europeans are flocking to buy cheap properties here, or stay in some of the glitzy hotels springing up along the coast.'

Gasho was sitting pretty. He owned a bar and a pizza restaurant in Bar. Both were packed every night. His wife was pregnant with their first child. The future for him was exciting.

The Balkan war had devastated tourism and investment in Montenegro, but in the ten years since it had ended, change had happened so fast it was dizzying, he told me.

'Foreign companies are buying up plenty of land. Israeli diamond dealers, Kazakhstani bankers, South African gold mine owners, they're all investing in property here,' Gasho said. 'It's a problem for some. Montenegrins are being priced out.'

'You might end up losing your ranking on the world height chart,' I said.

Gasho laughed. He took a sip of beer and looked out of the window.

The next day we went for a ride up the coast, under the brooding shadow of the Black Mountains from which the country gets its name. We passed the beach where, I believe, for the price of a couple of satsumas and a cucumber, Daniel Craig turned himself into the world's sexiest man.

We passed the Sveti Stefan, a gorgeous cluster of former fishermen's cottages and chapels clinging to a rock and linked to the mainland by a slender causeway. We stopped to take in the view.

'From 2008, all this will be a luxury hotel,' Gasho said.

After, Gasho sped off, riding lightning quick around the tight bends of the coast road. I was struggling to keep up, riding on my very limits and beyond.

We pulled over at a café and I complimented Gasho on his high-speed riding, the sublime shapes he was making with the bike, riding on the edge.

'I love the English ironic humour,' he laughed. 'How do you say it? "Taking the piss." The reason I am riding so slowly is so you can see the sights. We can ride properly if you'd prefer.'

'No, no, this is great,' I said. 'I normally ride like a crazy man. It's good to take it easy for a change.'

We rode along the narrow roads that encircled Kotor Bay, southern Europe's deepest fjord, with the water an almost impossible shade of indigo. Vertical bluffs towered above us, from which eagles launched and danced like kites on the thermals. Beside the road, pomegranate trees and orange groves.

Despite it being October, it was still gloriously hot. Montenegro was going to walk the trip's Tallest People award, short of me taking a disastrously wrong turning on the way back to London. And it was definitely in the frame to win the Most Stunning Landscape category, as well.

Gasho started to push on, and soon I was trailing several bends behind. It was hard to believe that anybody could ride a motorcycle that fast. To be honest, though, every biker I'd ridden with on this trip was much quicker than me, despite the fact that I was trying really hard. Maybe riding a motorcycle was a bit like learning to ski jump: you had to master the art when you were young and fearless (and stupid).

Gasho stopped to wait for me, during which time he managed to clean out his carburettor and learn some Mandarin. When eventually I pootled round the corner, he asked me if there was something wrong with my bike.

'It does seem very sluggish today,' I told him. 'That's why I'm taking it slow. Don't want to risk it.'

Gasho had to get back to Bar in time to open up his restaurant. 'It's a shame your bike's playing up,' he said. 'We could have had a good race back along the coast.'

'Yup, that's a real pity,' I said, with the sincerity of someone who'd just been told that the shot from his own gun that had somehow found his own foot had ruled him out of the big push. Gasho left me there to make my own way back.

I stood there for a while, smoking a cigarette, gazing across the water of Kotor Bay.

My mobile beeped. I looked at the screen. It was a message from my ex-wife. I had been dreading this.

'Louis has been found. He's lost an eye, is emaciated and semi-conscious. I took him to the vet. They've done their best, but say he's in pain and it would be kinder to put him to sleep. I'm on my way there now. Just thought you should know. Sorry. x'

Standing by the side of the road, I felt devastated. I knew that I wasn't just grieving for Louis. The last living connection between me and my ex-wife was gone.

I rode back to Gasho's house.

'How was the ride?' he asked.

'Great,' I said.

'Tomorrow we can go further up the coast,' he said. 'There are some beautiful beaches.'

'I've got to leave tomorrow,' I said.

'Why?' he asked. 'I thought you were going to hang around for a while. Don't you like Montenegro?'

'It's beautiful,' I said.

'Then why?'

'Because … something's happened.'

'What?'

'It's not important. I just need to be moving on.'

You'd have thought after my experiences back in Turkey, I'd have been more careful. But for the second time on this trip,

I had misjudged time and distance and was now in a spot of trouble.

I had left Gasho at first light in order to get to Sarajevo by sunset.

The journey, first up and over the mountains, then along the Tara Canyon, at a mile deep and 50 miles long, the world's second-largest, then across the treeless, moonscape plateau of Durmitor National Park, had taken me much longer than I had anticipated.

This was down to a combination of factors. Firstly, my map-reading; secondly, the fact that I was stopping every few miles with my jaw on the floor to take in the landscape and the trees with their golden autumnal plumage; and thirdly, and I concede that this may overlap with the first factor, the road showing on the map that crossed the high plateau of the Durmitor National Park was not really a road in the traditional sense of the word. Well, it wasn't a road in any sense of the word, really, just a boulder-strewn groove worn into the rock. Progress was Kickstart slow.

By the time I eventually got to the Bosnian border, darkness was closing in fast, as if on a rapid dimmer switch, and the colours of the moorlands were fading one by one, until there just remained an unremitting, bleak monochrome.

Gasho had specifically warned me about the hazards of travelling after dark between the Bosnian border and Sarajevo, citing a whole catalogue of recent incidents on that road involving armed robbers and not a little violence.

Now that I was passing through the Republika Srpska, the Serb part of Bosnia, all the road signs had reverted once again to some form of algebra. I stopped to look at a sign, and on it roads fanned off in all directions like the smoke trails of a Red Arrows manoeuvre. One of the flight paths might have ended with the word Sarajevo. Or I might have been staring at a vast periodic table and therefore considering turning left to the electron configuration of ununbium. I was still 50 miles short of Sarajevo and things were not looking good.

The rain, light at first, was now torrential, being propelled horizontally by the cold, howling easterly; big, fat globules of water exploding against my helmet like paintball bullets. I looked around the empty, bleak landscape for signs of life, of a sanctuary, of a light maybe, or a wisp of smoke, but there was nothing apart from the ghoulish shells of bombed-out houses, their windows like empty eye sockets, countless Halloween masks lining the road. It felt like the Apocalypse.

A temporary sign with a big arrow pointing left, beyond which the main road had disappeared down a mountainside, sent me off on a diversion. The tarmac soon ended and I was shortly slipping and sliding on mud tracks that twisted and turned through a dense forest. I put my headlamp on to full beam, but it hardly penetrated the opaque shroud that hung from the trees.

There was nobody else on the road. I rode with my feet dangling down on both sides, ready to leap off should the bike lose its grip and topple off into a ravine.

After half an hour, I stopped to consult my map, using the headlight to see where I might be and which nearby town I might be able to head for. The map was, of course, useless. I had been on the equivalent of a farm track, meandering around all points of the compass. I had absolutely no idea where I was.

I had my tent. I could stop in this forest, in the middle of bandit country, put it up and hope for the best. But then I remembered what the *Lonely Planet* had said about camping in these former killing fields, that there were unexploded mines everywhere, and on no account should you wander away from the roads without the company of a man dressed as a giant caterpillar clutching wirecutters and wearing a welding mask. One-man, tent-peg roulette sounded like a sure-fire way into the Darwin Awards Hall of Fame.

I lit a cigarette. Everything always felt better after a cigarette. Except my lungs, of course, and my mouth, and my throat. As I smoked, I followed the bike's headlight beam. In the distance, something was shining. I walked towards it. It was a small marble obelisk, cradled by tall pines. It displayed about a hundred male names, grouped in family clusters, their date of death all the same 1992 day, their ages ranging from 14 to 82.

I pressed on in the darkness and the rain. After another 20 minutes I was spat out of the forest and on to a main road. I rode through a ghost town. Up ahead, a car, a white Audi, was crawling along. I pulled out and overtook it, watching his headlights recede in my mirrors until they were pinpricks.

The pinpricks started to grow again, the smudges of light expanding to fill my mirror again in a matter of seconds until the full-beam glare was blinding and I had to squint to see the road ahead.

I slowed down to let him pass, but he slowed down too, driving two feet behind me. I sped up. He sped up. My heart was pounding. He began flashing his lights at me and blaring his horn, and when I glanced over my shoulder, I could make out some shadowy figures leaning out of the back windows gesticulating wildly and yelling.

This was the very road that Gasho had warned me about, where the car-jackings and the violent robberies had occurred. And here I was, riding along it in the dark, being chased by a bunch of Balkan Asbos. If there was a fine line between adventure travel and stupidity, I felt I had crossed it then.

The road started to climb and twist. I opened the throttle. On dry, mountain roads, a car would be no match for a motorbike, but on that sodden surface I could feel my wheels slipping, my line getting ever more erratic. I knew I wasn't going to be able to outrun him.

I pulled over, jumped off the bike and frantically dug out my D-lock from the pannier. It was the only thing I had that might be effective as a weapon.

Meanwhile, the Audi had stopped, around 50 yards behind me. I could hear its engine revving, the rain sheeting across the headlamps' twin beams. The engine was cut and the lights died. There was now no noise at all, save for my breathing, rapid, shallow. But I didn't feel afraid at all, had a half-cocked grin on my face. The human mind is miraculous. Anticipation can paralyse us. In the thick of it, the mind quietens, then steps back, abdicates, and we float free. Alive.

The car's engine fired up. It revved for a moment, then lurched forward, accelerating straight at me. I just stood there. Staring at the lights. At peace.

At the last moment, the Audi swerved and roared past, the occupants screaming at the top of their lungs. They had had their fun. The bravado I had been running on for the past four months seeped out into the night like air escaping from a balloon. My mind came back. I replayed the scene. My knees started to tremble.

Eventually, the tungsten glow of Sarajevo appeared on the horizon and soon afterwards I was weaving in between the rattling trams and the EUFOR armoured patrols and through the lakes of standing water.

Soaked to the skin, I forewent the pleasures of trawling round town looking for a cheap bed and instead headed for the Holiday Inn, that iconic symbol of the siege of Sarajevo, still hideously pockmarked, still luminous yellow – it reminded me of that Far Side cartoon showing a deer with a target on its backside and his friend saying: 'Bummer of a birthmark, Hal.'

I parked my bike under the bullet-scarred canopy at the front and walked into the reception area. It was full of important-looking army personnel in camouflage fatigues, talking to men and women in smart suits whom I assumed to be representatives from the various NGOs.

'Ma'am, I explicitly said in my email that I needed a suite,' an American army officer was telling the woman behind reception.

'I'm sorry, but they're all taken,' the woman replied. 'There's nothing I can do.'

'You ain't heard this last of this, ma'am,' the officer said, and turned on his heels before marching off smartly in a huff. Marching in a huff is spectacularly funny. It was the campest thing I'd seen in an army uniform since Bombadier 'Gloria' Beaumont.

'You need to move your bike. It is blocking the way,' the concierge said. 'We have a Spanish delegation arriving.'

I went outside and put the bike on the pavement. Just then the Spanish convoy arrived. Four large, black 4x4s with Spanish flags flying from the grilles. Hotel staff raced to open the car doors. Around a dozen people in suits emerged and entered the hotel.

I walked back in after them. It was heaving in the lobby now, as the great and the good talked in clusters.

I went back to the desk and completed registering.

'You are on a motorbike?' a voice to my left asked.

I turned round. There was a man in his mid-forties wearing Gucci loafers, brown corduroy trousers and a baby blue shirt with white cuffs and collar. Around his shoulders was draped a pink cashmere sweater. I was guessing he was Italian.

'I also ride a motorbike,' he said.

'You are from Sarajevo?' I asked.

'No, Italy,' he said.

We chatted about bikes for a while.

'My name is Franco,' he said.

'Mike.'

'So, what brings you here?' he asked me.

I told him I was writing a column for a newspaper about men having a midlife crisis.

'Ah, in Italy we have this phenomenon as well,' Franco said. 'I think maybe we are the best in the world at this.'

'How come?'

'Ah, you know,' he said. 'Italian men worry when they're getting older.'

'It's the same everywhere, it seems.'

'But we Italians, we have this reputation as lovers, macho men. It's not so easy when they start to feel not-so-young.'

'Still, Italians have got all the right toys to deal with it.'

'You mean Ferraris and Ducattis and the rest?'

'Exactly.'

'We're all so predictable, eh? It's true. This is why I say Italians are the best at the midlife crisis.'

'Silvio's a great poster boy.'

Franco laughed.

'And Blair,' he said.

'And Blair. But Berlusconi's worse. That weave's a riot.'

'We are having an argument about whose politicians are having the worst midlife crisis,' said Franco.

'Better than talking about their politics,' I said.

'Probably adds up to the same thing,' said Franco.

Franco's phone beeped. He looked at the message.

'Why are you in Sarajevo?' I asked him.

'Well, four years ago or so I was working for the Genovese judiciary,' he said. 'Then, one day I decided on a change. I'd been thinking about doing something different for a while. The International War Crimes Court were looking for judges, so I applied.'

'Wow. Was that some kind of ultimate midlife crisis?'

'Maybe,' he laughed.

'Sounds a bit more useful than poncing around Europe on a motorbike.' Thanks for that, Wayne.

'Oh, my wife and I did a lot of travelling around by

motorbike beforehand,' Franco said. 'Europe, South America, Asia. But we recently had a baby, so that's all had to stop.'

The receptionist handed me my room key.

'Where did you come from today?' Franco asked.

'From Bar in Montenegro, over the mountains.' I told him about my experience on the road outside Sarajevo.

'You have to be careful on those roads,' he said. 'There have been armed robberies and hijackings recently.'

I was going to say, yes, I'd been told, but that when I'd left Montenegro I hadn't really been concentrating too much on my own safety.

Then Franco would have asked me why, and I would have told him that I'd been upset because my cat had died.

Then Franco would have said something like 'that's terrible'.

And I would have stood there thinking about all the things he'd seen and heard at the War Crimes Court over the past four years.

'Yes, I was lucky,' I said.

His phone beeped again. He looked at the message.

'I've got to go now,' he said. 'What are you up to tomorrow?'

'Hadn't made any plans.'

'I've got the day off. I'd be happy to show you around town.'

'I'd like that,' I said.

Franco left for his appointment. I went into the Internet room off the hotel's lobby and checked my inbox. There was an email from Boris in Zagreb.

'Come to the party this Saturday night at the Pit,' it read. 'There's going to be hundreds of bikers from all over the Balkans, strippers, lots of meat and drink. We will get very messy.

'But,' it ended, rather ominously, just as the previous 23 text messages had done, 'it's gonna cost you some blood.'

I figured this might be a small price to pay for a night of debauchery Zagreb-biker style, and imagined myself slashing my arm with a broken bottle before rubbing my A-negative against the open wound of a giant, bearded Croat called Ox, and thus sealing our union in perpetuity, or at least until one of us forgot the other's birthday and the whole thing would descend into an ugly tiff.

I thought about it for a minute or so, then sent Boris a reply: 'I'm on my way. See you at the weekend.'

Next day I met Franco on the steps of the Catholic cathedral. He was wearing a different, but still immaculate, ensemble of corduroy, pastel shirt with white cuffs and collar, Gucci loafers and cashmere sweater, topped off with a quilted jacket. I was wearing my only non-bike outfit of jeans and a jean-jacket. He looked like Noel Coward. I looked like Shakin Stevens.

We walked through the Ottoman houses of Bascarsija, the old Turkish quarter, past the mosque where the muezzin was standing on the minaret, calling the faithful to prayer without the aid of a microphone.

We walked along the polished-cobbled alleyways. On the ground were the Sarajevo Roses, where the holes of the shells that killed citizens in the siege have been filled in with red cement, the 'petals' cascading away from the blast point like dandelions blown in a wish. We crossed the Latin Bridge, where a single bullet in 1914 precipitated another mass slaughter.

I asked Franco about his work at the court.

He couldn't go into too much detail, but talked about the harrowing people-trafficking and genocide cases he'd had to preside over.

He talked about what the future might hold and seemed a little worn out. 'Nothing much happens quickly in Bosnia,' he said. 'Each of the three ethnic groups who rotate the presidency has the right of veto and they tend to use it. Four years after I arrived here, the same issues are being debated. Things are changing, but it is complicated and slow.'

We drove out to visit the tunnel museum, sited in the house at one end of the tunnel that Sarajevans dug under the airport to bring relief to, at 43 months, the longest city siege in history.

There, we watched a film of the siege and I recognised from my walk around town earlier many of the buildings that were being pummelled as people cowered from gun and artillery fire.

Seeing people gunned down in cold blood when it's in black and white and they're wearing military fatigues or fashions long gone is one thing. Watching it in colour, when they're wearing jeans and T-shirts, and they're falling down, with their skulls open, in the car park of your hotel, is quite another.

'Look at this,' Franco said.

He pointed out the laminated maps on the wall from the time Sarajevo had hosted the 1984 Winter Olympics. On them, next to bobsleigh runs and the figure-skating arena, the museum had superimposed tanks and a red ring denoting where, just eight years later, the circle of Bosnian Serb artillery murdered over 10,500 Sarajevans and wounded another 50,000. It was a chilling juxtaposition.

We drove back into town and, parking the car, walked along Zmaja od Bosne, known during the siege as Sniper Alley, where many of the buildings were still pixelated from bullet and shell holes. The extent of the damage was staggering. Apartment blocks still contained burnt-out stairwells and corners of common ground and children's playgrounds were roped off because of unexploded ordinance, ghoulish skull-and-crossbone pennants hanging limply from the tape.

'It's staggering,' I said. 'The war ended 10 years ago.'

I thought about the differences between countries I had passed through recently. From first-world Greece into crumbling Albania, then into Montenegro, where five-star hotels were springing up and into where foreign multinationals were pouring money. Then across the border into Bosnia, where the roads were abysmal once more and the landscape pocked with minefields and the ravages of war.

I knew that Bosnia was the main theatre of the Balkan conflict, but still, after the Second World War, entire countries had been rebuilt in rapid time. It was puzzling. I mentioned it to Franco.

'This is going to sound stupid and naive,' I said to him. 'But it seems to me that it's the majority Muslim countries that are still suffering the most in this region. Western investment is pouring in to the others.'

'There's plenty of money coming to Bosnia, too,' he said. 'But like I said, things move very slowly here.'

In the surrounding hills, that banked up behind the city like grandstands, where the Bosnian Serb gunners had drunk beer and had their human target practice, the rumbling of thunder and low-scudding clouds, pierced occasionally by a shaft of sunlight, created a chilling son et lumière.

'Can a city wear its grief?' I asked Franco.

'Maybe.'

We walked on.

I asked Franco about his wife and his new child and he reached into his wallet and showed me a photograph of a smiling woman clutching a tiny baby.

'They live in Genoa,' he said. 'They come here for weekends, or I go home.'

'You must miss them desperately,' I said.

'I live for weekends,' he said. 'They are arriving tomorrow.' His face lit up.

'You are welcome to stay with us for the weekend,' Franco said.

'That's kind, but I don't want to get in the way,' I said. 'Anyway, tomorrow night I am supposed to be partying with the Zagreb bikers.'

'Oh, God,' Franco said, laughing. 'Be careful with those guys.'

# 30 Boris

'For the last time, I do not want your blood.'

This, not from an ungrateful, giant, bearded Croat called Ox, but a rather petit nurse at a Zagreb hospital, working through the queue of bikers at their annual donation fest. She was smiling with clenched teeth, clearly getting somewhat weary of my insistence that 'my blood is as good as anyone's'.

'No ... It ... Is ... Not ...' she said, saying the words very slowly now, with an emphatic, dramatic pause between them.

'Why not?' I asked.

'You are British?' she said.

'Yes,' I replied.

'Then you probably have mad cow disease,' she said.

There wasn't really any answer to that, apart from to make a pathetic mad mooing noise, which I did. But the nurse didn't seem to notice, because by then she was too busy processing the biker behind me, with his strong, pure, Croatian blood.

I was left to turn around like the weedy boy not picked for the team and, for the second time on this trip, go back past the queue of shame, and past the trays of red wine and sausages that I was now not going to sample because I was horribly diseased, probably.

If there's a polar opposite emotion to the puffed-up sanctimonious glow of anticipation when you're about to do something genuinely altruistic, it was the empty feeling I had then. Which was ironic, really, seeing as I was a pint fuller that everybody else.

'It is all shit. Do not worry about it. They are dipsticks,' said Boris, later, as we sat drinking beer at a pavement café.

Boris drained his can, crushed it on his forehead and let fly with a sonorous belch. 'Now we go to the Pit. Follow me.'

By now, Boris had perhaps drunk enough to not be considering anything more complicated than falling over. But for some reason he thought it a good idea to jump on a powerful motorcycle and speed off through the Zagreb traffic. Just in case balancing on two wheels wasn't difficult enough, Boris rode the first 50 metres pulling a wheelie.

'The cops here are idiots, plonkers. They never pull over bikers in Zagreb,' Boris told me at the next set of traffic lights.

We waited for the lights to go green.

'But if they try to stop us,' Boris added. 'We will make a run for it. We can cut across the parks. They'll give up. Just follow me and everything will be cushtie.'

It seemed to me somewhat unfair that my blood had been refused when, if anybody was showing the signs of a fondness for tainted Aberdeen sirloin, it was Boris Trotter here.

'Let's go,' he yelled. 'Yeehaa.' And he was off again on one wheel.

I had met Boris for the first time the evening before in my hotel's bar. He had been waiting for me at my hotel. In fact, he had booked my hotel for me and texted me the address.

He was on his mobile when I walked in. He was shouting into it in the manner of a man who hadn't quite grasped the remarkable characteristics of phones in that they negate the need to yell at somebody who just happens not to be in the same room.

He waved at me and gestured for me to sit down. I looked

at him. Late twenties, I'd have guessed, with cropped hair and intense blue eyes. I liked him immediately.

Boris finished his call.

'Mike, Mike, great to meet you at last,' he said. 'Luverly, jubberly.'

'Luverly, jubberly?'

'Yes, luverly, jubberly. You know, who dares wins.'

A pause.

'Thanks for booking me a room,' I said.

'Is it okay?' Boris replied. 'I can find you something else if you don't like it. Not a problem. Cushtie.'

'Cushtie?'

'Yes, cushtie.'

A pause.

'No, it's fine,' I said.

Boris ordered us some Karlovacko beer and some Ozujsko beer, and some brandies of the plum, then herbal, variety, as chasers.

'You try some different Croatian drinks,' he said.

In the corner of the bar, a television was showing an episode of *'Allo, 'Allo*. It was in English with Serbo-Croat subtitles. Boris was watching it out of the corner of his eye.

'You like this?' I asked him.

'Oh, yes, very much,' Boris said. 'English comedy's very popular in Croatia. You perlonker.'

On screen, the fake gendarme was having a whispered conversation with René.

'God moaning,' he said. 'The resist-once are going to ex-plod the whaleway brodge with a bum.'

'Does that work in Serbo-Croat?' I asked Boris.

Boris was almost falling off his chair in a manner I'd not seen since Amsterdam. I guessed that it must do.

Boris's phone went again. Again he barked into it in a stac-cato fashion, before ending the call.

'Dipsticks,' he said. 'I've got to go. I'm organising the party at the Pit tomorrow night and the sorts are asking for more wedge.'

'The sorts?'

'Yes, the sorts, the strippers,' he said. 'I'll pick you up here tomorrow afternoon and we'll go and give some blood.'

And with that he was gone, and I was left alone with my two beers and two brandies and the opening bars from the theme tune of *Terry and June*.

Via half the bars of Zagreb, we'd eventually got to the Pit, the city's biker headquarters. It was rammed with leather and beards and there were countless toasts with cherry brandy, and glasses, once drained, were smashed on the floor, where the shards were crunched in to form a paste with the pools of beer and other unidentifiable liquids.

In the car park, packed with customised cruisers and trikes, there was a pig roast, barrels of beer, and guys pulling wheelies.

The strippers appeared and started gyrating around poles, thrusting their thong-clad bums in punters' faces. Soon after, the bikers were ripping off their shirts and joining the girls on the poles. The room was an ocean of smiling faces, a piss-up of Bacchanalian proportions. My head was swimming. I went to the toilet to splash some water on my face. I looked in the mirror. There he was staring back at me. I returned to the mayhem.

Above the noise of breaking glass and Motörhead, Boris was shouting something at me.

'What?' I yelled, leaning in closer.

'Your face has changed shape, man,' he was shouting.

I knew exactly what he meant. For since hitting my forties, there'd been this bizarre Cinderella thing going on, where on the stroke of midnight, or thereabouts, my face had developed the habit of turning into a pumpkin: a crumpled, collapsed, fleshy mess.

I'd rather hoped that it was all in my mind, that the saggy and drooping reflection that I'd latterly been getting to know in bar and nightclub toilets was down to dodgy mirrors or bad lighting.

But no, here was Boris, calling over his friends to check out the freaky, morphing Englishman and pointing at me saying: 'That's really weird, man.'

And always accompanying John Merrick at the witching hour was Victor Meldrew, because suddenly I was looking at the strippers and thinking, 'Just what is the bloody point of that?' and then across at the bikers and the dancing and the drinking and just seeing it all as so utterly ridiculous, like somebody had pulled back a curtain to reveal the old bloke at the controls.

Even the Idiot had long since stopped getting involved. He'd been catching sight of my imploded face in the mirror behind the bar and listening to my bellyaching.

God knows he's an optimist, but he'd lost a lot of heart on this trip, taken a lot of hits.

I went out with Boris into the car park.

'I'm sorry,' I said. 'I don't know what's wrong with me. This is a fantastic party and your friends are great, but …'

'That's okay,' said Boris. 'I'll take you back to your hotel.'

Before, I'd always wanted to make some excuses, as if shutting down at midnight were an aberration, say, 'That won't be necessary, my friend. I'm just going to pop off to the loo for some crystal meth and I'll see you up on the pole in a minute.'

But now, in Zagreb, at the Pit, I just knew, with blinding clarity, that I didn't want to do this any more. Would not be doing this any more. It felt fine.

'You're probably just tired,' said Boris.

'I am,' I said.

'We still on for tomorrow, though?' Boris said. 'For a tour of the city?'

'Cushtie,' I replied.

We pulled on our helmets, jumped on our bikes and pulled away.

Maybe Boris had revised his opinions of the Zagreb police, or perhaps me, because there were no wheelies or screeching tyres as the noise of the party was swallowed by the dark, moonless night, and we rode cautiously across building sites, through industrial estates and along the deserted back streets.

The next day, Boris and I walked through the huge fruit and vegetable market in central Zagreb, where it seemed you could buy anything you wanted, as long as it was a tomato.

Boris inspected one, turned it in his hand, polished it, then put it back on the stall.

'How's the trip been?' asked Boris.

'Pretty good overall,' I said.

'Not sure I could do a long trip like that on my own,' Boris said. 'I would go nuts.'

'It's just like normal life; good days, bad days. It's just that everything's intensified.'

'I would miss my friends.'

'They're always there.'

'Still ...'

'Toughest bit is all the people you meet. You're only ever in each other's lives for a short time. It's hard to get anywhere. It's frustrating. At home, you know each other's back stories, histories, where you've been. You don't have to start from scratch every time.'

'I would like that.'

'It's not easy.'

'To just be, I don't know, like an actor.'

'An actor?'

'Yeah, if you're feeling shit, you can play the miserable guy. If you're feeling good, you can be the happy guy. Nobody's going to know if that's you or not.'

'Funny.'

'What?'

'That's what I thought. But it's not really working out that way.'

'If there's a girl in a bar, I can tell her anything, change my name, my job. She doesn't need to know the truth.'

'I'm bored having to explain myself the whole time,' I said. 'Like last night. I felt bad for wanting to leave the party.'

'It wasn't a problem. We got you home.'

'But I didn't want to be at the hotel.'

'You should have come back.'

'I didn't want to be at the party.'

'You going Radio Rentals, Mike?'

'Very possibly,' I said.

We jumped on our bikes and headed into the hills beyond the city. We pulled up outside some large iron gates, flanked either side by vast walls entirely covered in ivy and topped with a string of cupolas stretching as far as the eye could see.

'This is the Mirogoj,' Boris told me. 'The most beautiful cemetery in Europe.'

We parked up and walked through the gates, through an archway and into a majestic arcade, again ivy-clad, supported by marble columns and lined with tombs sporting wonderful sculptures.

'All of Croatia's famous sons and daughters are buried here,' Boris said.

We walked in silence for a while, reading the stones. We stopped. In front of us was the grave of a four-year-old child.

'That must be the worst thing in the world,' Boris said. 'Losing a child.'

'I couldn't begin to imagine.'

'You have children?' Boris asked.

'No,' I replied.

We walked on.

'You have brothers, sisters?' he asked.

'One of each. I'm the youngest.'

'They have families?'

'Yes, two kids each. They're grown up now.'

'And your parents. Are they still alive?' Boris asked.

I told him about my mum.

'I'm sorry,' he said.

'How about yours?' I asked him.

'My mother is alive. My father is dead.'

We walked further along the arcade in silence, save for the odd scrunch of the fallen leaves underfoot, stopping occasionally to inspect a tomb.

'Did you get on with him?' I asked. 'Your dad?'

'He left my mum when I was young. Never saw much of him after.'

'How come?'

'When I did, he was drunk. Could get nasty. He was in a car crash a few years back. My mum got a phone call from the police.'

'I'm sorry.'

'I wasn't at the time. Just got on with my life. Didn't know him really. Blocked him out. There was a part of me that wasn't sorry that he'd died.'

'And now?'

'I miss him.'

'Is he here?'

'No.'

We walked some more.

'Your dad is still alive,' Boris said. 'You are lucky.'

'Could say the same thing to you about your mum.'

'Sure.'

'I don't really know him,' I said.

'You can do something about that.'

'I don't know how.'

'There's time.'

'Sometimes it feels like he's all I've got left ...'

'You've got a brother, a sister ...'

'... and that when he's gone, there will just be a big hole. No cushion, no buffers, nothing between me and ... This is going to sound crazy ... almost like he's the last witness to my existence, my history.'

'... if you had kids ...'

'Does that make a difference? I can't say. My friends, they've got kids ... I've envied them all these years, having two parents alive. I felt guilty for feeling it, but the resentment was there. All those "what are you doing for Christmas?" conversations. But now, they're seeing parents die, or growing fragile, and there's a kind of clamour, a rising panic, that they're moving to the front line, about to get cut adrift ... It feels like we're all in the same boat again.'

'It's normal ...'

'When my mum died, despite the resentment and the anger, it always felt like it was a mistake, some freak of nature.'

An elderly man walked towards us, carrying a small nosegay of red roses and a teddy bear. He looked up, smiled, dipped his head, walked on.

'A couple of years ago, I got a call from my sister telling me to get to the hospital quickly. My dad had put something in the oven, cracked opened the Teacher's, fallen asleep. When I got there, he was lying in a gown, face mask on, drips coming out of his arms. He was struggling to breathe. The nurse told me that he'd been lucky. If he hadn't managed to crawl to the phone, the smoke would have killed him.

'I looked at him. He's been a bricklayer his whole life, strong, unbreakable. He was tiny in that bed, ancient, shrunken. It had side panels on it, like a cot. There was a vile rasping sound coming from his throat, a gurgling. He opened his eyes. He smiled, weakly. For a few seconds, we just stared at each other. I knew then … I knew then that if those eyes hadn't opened, that when those eyes don't open, a door closes, and everything on the other side of it is gone.'

We walked in silence for a while, under the arcade, reading the gravestones.

'That's the face I see in the mirror,' I said.

# 31 Limoncello

How much is too much limoncello? I only ask because a litre of the stuff seemed to be having a rather violent effect on Gisella, who was standing in the doorway of her Umbrian kitchen in her nightie at 2 a.m., yelling obscenities at her partner Robert. But Gisella hadn't touched a drop.

No, the main gist of her angry invective seemed to be that Robert and I had demolished an amount of the sickly after-dinner liqueur that would ordinarily last an Italian family a couple of generations. Such behaviour to her, she was saying, warming to her theme, was about as mature as injecting mercury into your eyes.

I suddenly felt ashamed of myself. I chose to express this, however, by allowing a stupid, sheepish grin to spread across my face which, looking back, I don't think conveyed much remorse. Robert's face just looked smudged.

Only a sozzled prat would try to justify himself by claiming that here was your classic genetically informed culture clash, that, being Italian, Gisella could never hope to understand the pleasure in getting completely mullered, or the imperative that drives the Scots (represented here by Robert) or the English (hello, there) to excess in alcohol. It's an atavistic response to the depressing weather, the poor light, the, erm, war-time rationing ...

But as soon as I tried to assemble this plea-bargaining into some kind of coherent form, Gisella was theatrically waving her arms about in exasperation and stropping off back to her room. Talk about stereotypes.

Earlier that day, I had arrived on Italian shores at Ancona, via the night ferry from Split. Can there be a more exciting way to depart a country than by boat, at night, watching the lights of the coast dip and bob and then one by one melt into the blackness?

This boat trip, in particular, felt symbolic, significant. I had made it through Eastern Europe, Turkey and now the Balkan states. With only Western Europe ahead, it seemed like the really difficult stuff was behind me.

At Ancona, I'd had a choice to make. If I turned right and headed north, I could go to Florence, Milan, pop over the Alps, whizz through France and be home in a few days. Actually, looking at the map of Europe, if I rode like a maniac, I could be home by this time tomorrow. Tomorrow. After nearly five months on the road, it felt weird to put the words home and tomorrow together in the same thought.

I closed my eyes and conjured up images of London, the faces of friends and family, my dad.

I thought about walking into my apartment and being able to close the door on the world. Then I thought about the tenants that would be there until December.

I thought about being able talk to anybody and everybody again without having to wave my arms around and shout loudly.

I wondered whether things would look differently, smell differently, feel differently.

I wanted to laugh at satirical jokes and argue about politics; feel the autumn leaves crunching underfoot on the footpath in the park, the crisp chill in the air and hoary frosts and swirling fogs and ruddy-cheeked children who'd soon be asking for a penny for the guy, mister, and Pearly Kings and comely milkmaids and West Brom leading the league and ...

Richard Curtis's England sang me its siren song. Then the grumpy old man reminded me that that particular vision of home had been exposed for the hopeless piece fiction that it is.

I thought about the rain and the grey skies and the cold. I thought about the *Daily Mail* and *Celebrity Love Island* and the traffic jams and the alarm clock.

That would all come soon enough. I decided to follow the sun for a while longer, have a look around Umbria, then head through the Italian south and across to Sicily, island-hop across the Med and finish off with a big loop of the Iberian Peninsula. That way, I would be home in time for the snow and the roasted chestnuts and the *Morecombe and Wise Christmas Special*.

Besides, there was still one place I'd promised myself I'd go. The need to visit it had diminished considerably during the trip, but it still felt like a piece of unfinished business, a place that had been haunting me, where a line needed to be drawn.

From Ancona, I'd ridden across Marche and Umbria, and all was as you'd expect – if Ricardo Curtis had been the architect and landscape gardener – with the fortified towns clinging precariously to their hills and the cypress trees and the burnt-orange rolling fields.

I went to Assisi and lit a candle for Louis in the cathedral, and then stopped in a nearby sleepy, walled town for lunch. Afterwards I leaned against my bike in the middle of the square, lit a cigarette and, in lieu of having no further plans for the day, waited for providence to strike. And waited.

Providence was having a late, lingering lunch, because two hours and half a packet of cigarettes later I was still sitting on my bike in the square of the sleepy walled village.

A middle-aged couple walked through the square, smiling at me as they passed. I smiled back.

'Buongiorno,' I said.

'Buongiorno,' the woman replied.

'All right mate,' the man said.

They walked off down the street.

I lit another cigarette.

'Watchya doin' here then?' a cockney voice said.

I turned around. It was the man from the couple. The woman was standing about 10 paces away.

'Oh, just trying to work out where to go next,' I said.

'I clocked the plates when we walked passed,' the man said.

'My feet?' I said.

'No, the GB number plates,' he said.

'You having a good holiday?' I asked him.

'We live here. This is my wife, Gisella. I'm Robert,' he said. 'We moved here from London about a year ago.'

I reached out my hand to shake Robert's. Then waved at Gisella. She moved closer.

Robert looked at all the country stickers on my panniers.

'A long trip,' he said.

'About 15,000 miles so far, 24 countries.'

'Wow,' Robert said. 'Must have seen some amazing things.'

'Sure,' I replied.

'Where next?' he asked.

'I'm not sure. I've got some old friends in Rome. I might head down there.'

'You're welcome to stay with us,' Robert said. 'We live just outside town.'

'Are you sure?'

'Of course,' Robert said. 'Stay as long as you like.'

I looked over at Gisella. She nodded.

I followed the couple in the car along the main road, then off on a gravel track for a mile or so. Finally, the car turned off through a set of gates and pulled up in front of an old Umbrian farmhouse.

I parked my bike beside the car and followed Robert and Gisella into the kitchen.

There were all the things one might expect to find in an Umbrian farmhouse kitchen: a wood stove, russet stone floor tiles, an ancient olive press in the corner, an elderly man pedalling furiously on an exercise bike and a young oriental man sitting quietly in an armchair.

Gisella disappeared through the other door and Robert bade me sit down. He then also disappeared through the other door. I could hear a muffled conversation.

'Hello,' I said to the oriental man.

He nodded back, then returned his gaze to the wall behind me where it had hitherto been fixed.

'Hello,' I said to the elderly man on the exercise bike.

He didn't nod back, but just continued staring vacantly at the same wall that the oriental man was finding so compelling.

I turned and looked at the wall. It was a fine wall, no doubt, but I could find nothing about it that could explain such devoted study.

'Do you speak English?' I asked the oriental man.

He nodded his head. Eyes back to the wall.

The pedalling continued.

Minutes passed. Then more minutes. I counted the rivets on the olive press. Twice.

Gisella and Robert reappeared. Gisella didn't look too happy.

'Right, Gisella's going to cook dinner,' Robert said. 'Why don't I show you around?'

We walked out into the garden. Robert gestured to the olive and lemon groves below and then to the acres of rolling hills beyond.

'All belongs to the farm,' he said.

'Quite a place,' I said. 'Must have cost a bomb.'

'It's not ours,' Robert replied. 'Did you see the man on the bike in the kitchen?'

I said that I had vaguely.

'That's Gisella's uncle. He owns the place, has lived and farmed here his whole life,' Robert told me. 'But his dementia has got worse and so we came out here last year to look after him.'

'And the other guy?'

'That's his nurse, Ramon. From the Philippines.'

We sat down to dinner. Oxtail stew, the tender meat tumbling off the bone. Ramon spoon-fed the uncle. Gisella didn't say too much. She still didn't look that happy. Robert seemed a little less sure of himself now, a bit more reserved, and looked occasionally over to Gisella after he'd spoken, as if for approval.

Soon after dinner the uncle and Ramon went off to bed. About 30 minutes later, Gisella followed.

We polished off the wine, then the home-made grappa came out. We put a fair dent in that too.

At about eleven, Robert and me retired to the armchairs and got into that comfortable attitude and banter that you know will span several bottles and half the night.

'I can think of worse places to live,' I said.

'It's great,' Robert said. 'But … well, Gisella's Italian, so she can talk to people. But I don't speak the language, so, well, sometimes I feel a bit isolated.

'That's why I came back to talk to you in the square, really,' he said. 'Don't get much chance these days, and when I saw that your bike had British plates, well, I thought I'd say hello.'

We talked about British football, and British politics, and British life with the misty-eyed sentimentalism of a pair of blokes who hadn't been there for a while.

'How did you guys meet?' I asked.

Robert told me that he'd met Gisella seven years previously when he was running a market stall in London and she'd been a regular customer.

'She was working at the Italian embassy. So sophisticated.

I was just this cockney barrow boy, I thought she was way out of my league. But she succumbed to my charms and agreed to go out on a date.'

'And now you're here!' I said to him.

'And now I'm here,' he laughed. 'Funny old world, ain't it?'

Robert told me about growing up in Scotland.

'You sound like an East Ender,' I said.

'The accent's gone completely,' he said. 'My mates back home take the piss. But I'm a proud Scot. Play the pipes.'

And around midnight, I think, Gisella made her first appearance at the door and gently asked Robert what time he was coming to bed.

'Soon, dear,' he said to her. She withdrew. He winked at me, then got up and retrieved a bottle of limoncello from a cupboard.

'Home-made,' he said.

He poured us each a tumbler full.

'You're obviously not married,' Robert said. 'If you can take off for six months.'

'Recently got divorced.'

'Is that okay?' he said.

'More or less,' I said.

'If I was ten years younger, I'd do the same.'

'Divorce?'

'No, go off on a road trip, on my own.'

'You've got Gisella. This,' I said, giving the kitchen a sweep with my arm.

'I know.'

'We always want we don't have,' I said. 'It's what makes us such sunny creatures.'

Robert laughed.

'So what happened?'

'To what?'

'To your marriage?'

'Oh, you know, people change. Same old story.'

318

'You married long then?'

'About 18 months.'

'People don't put in the work any more. Haven't got the stomach.'

'She got a new job.'

'Typical.'

'Sent her off travelling. Meeting new people. Every time she came home, something else had shifted, like she was plugged into a charge and I was running down my batteries. Small things. She grew, I shrunk. That's it.'

'Is it? Is that all it is? What about promises, vows?'

'I'm not sure she was paying much attention during that part of the ceremony. Especially the bit about forsaking all others.' I laughed.

'How can you think that's funny?'

'Isn't everything funny, ultimately?'

'I'd have killed her. Then I'd have killed him.'

'I don't think they'd have let me out on parole to go off on a motorbike trip.'

'What's happened to women?'

'I'm not sure they've changed all that much.'

'It's all aggro these days. It's gone too far the other way.'

Robert topped up the tumblers.

'When I was a young man, you knew what was what.'

'I'm starting to think that that's the rub,' I said.

'People don't change that much. Men are men, women are women. It's politicians that cause the trouble, making laws, giving people ideas. All that political correctness bollocks.'

'When I met my future wife,' I said. 'I was in my early thirties, captain of the rugby club, confident. World at my feet. I enjoyed my job, travelled a lot, there was an eternity of time ahead of me to achieve anything I wanted.

'Then that all started to change. I stopped playing sport, stopped going out with my friends so much, stopped enjoying my job. I had a beautiful wife, a nice house, great holidays. I had nothing to complain about, but at the same time I couldn't find any enthusiasm for anything much. Apart from moaning. I was great at that. It was like I was depressed, sleepwalking. All I wanted to do was stay at home in the evenings. Close the curtains on the world. It was like one night I went to bed a happy-go-lucky bloke, and the next morning I woke up a grumpy old git.'

'People go through phases. Everybody gets down. There's still no excuse …'

'Oh, sure. It just so happened that just when it felt like my world was collapsing, hers was taking off. The whole balance shifted.'

'That's what women do, they grind you down,' he said. 'Remember every little detail. Store it away. Throw it in your face years later.'

'It helps to at least acknowledge your own contribution.'

'It's the modern world, that's all, emasculating us. It feeds on the neuroses of women, telling them they can have it all. They believe all that shit. '

'And what do we believe? That it should all be ours, because that's the way it's always been?'

It was 2 a.m. The bottle was empty. Gisella was at the door again, remonstrating with Robert, rather more forcibly this time, that he should really call it a night. She saw the empties on the table, hit the roof and flounced out.

Robert got up, said goodnight and slowly made his way towards the door. A few minutes later I was in bed.

It was difficult to get to sleep. For one thing, there was a spider the size of a dinner plate hovering over the bed. For another, there was the sound of shouting and furniture being thrown around downstairs. I dug out my earplugs and closed my eyes.

The next morning, things were quiet at the breakfast table. The uncle pedalled his bike and Ramon stared at the wall.

Robert looked sheepish. I tried to smile at Gisella, but, what with banging the plates on the table and flinging bits of toast around, she didn't seem to notice.

After coffee, I said to Robert and Gisella that I should probably be going. I waited for the 'No, stay as long as you like', but all I got was Robert saying, 'Right, then.' Even Ramon nodded.

I went outside and loaded up. Robert stood next to me, looking at the motorbike. When the packing was complete, Robert disappeared into the garage and re-emerged with a set of bagpipes.

'I've got to pipe you away,' he said, in his broad cockney accent. 'It's traditional.'

Robert huffed and puffed and the opening notes of 'Will Ye Not Come Back Again' wafted out into the still Umbrian air, as incongruous among the cypress trees and lemon groves as it was ambiguous in its title.

Looking at the different expressions on Robert and Gisella's faces, it fitted the occasion perfectly.

# 32 Life coaches

'Have you got any rooms available for tonight?'

It seemed a reasonable enough question, but the woman behind the reception desk was looking back at me as if I had just asked her if she had a spare kidney.

'Of course we have a room, the season is over,' and her tone suggested that my impertinent arrival had completely ruined the computer game of solitaire she had been planning to spin out until April.

'We have 300 rooms. They are all empty.'

That was a relief. I'd spent the morning negotiating my way through a mass vehicular rally of charming anarchists called Naples, followed by a ride through the Rat Pack song-sheet: past the Isle of Capri and along the Amalfi coast road through the outrageously picturesque towns of Sorrento, Positano and Amalfi itself.

The 'Road of a Thousand Bends' might be enough to induce paroxysms of whooping at every vertical crag plunging into the shimmering sea, at every ancient tile-domed church and fingernail of beach. But for the locals, frustratingly robbed for the summer of their serpentine racetrack by the choking tourist traffic, now was the time to reassert their Italianness by driving like murderous lunatics.

The fact that there was a slow-moving idiot with a GB sticker on a luggage-laden motorcycle, cooing at the scenery like a migratory bird blown off-course by an unseasonable wind, seemed only to fuel their appetite for revenge.

And so it was that, in need of a stiff drink, I flopped into the first hotel I found and gratefully accepted one of the 300 rooms.

The woman at the desk used the hand not guiding the mouse to place hearts on clubs to call the porter. She didn't take her eyes off the screen, though, and it took her three attempts slapping the desk before she finally located the bell and produced a ding.

While waiting for the porter to emerge, I wandered around the cavernous lobby with its shut-up shops containing the season-just-gone's must-have-had bikinis and peered through the window to the open-air swimming pool beyond, glowing neglected like a lime jelly.

The porter appeared a few minutes later, rubbing his eyes and stretching like a recently awoken cat. He looked as surprised to see me as his colleague had been.

He grabbed my panniers and walked ahead. With 300 empty rooms, it would have been reasonable to assume that mine would be fairly close to the lobby, but entirely predictable that the woman on the desk would have assigned me the one up three flights of stairs, along a corridor, up another flight of steps and then along another corridor.

As we walked, the porter, a careworn man about my age with a mop of black curly hair and wearing a green woolly tanktop, asked about my trip. He sighed dreamily when I mentioned some of the places I'd been to.

'I'd love to travel, have some adventures,' he said, exhaling dolefully. 'But sometimes I feel like I'll be stuck here for ever.' He sighed again, more heavily this time.

Up some more stairs, along another corridor. Much further and I'd have to adjust my watch, or seek sponsors.

'You married?' the porter asked me.

'No.'

'I would love to get married one day,' he sighed. 'Find my dream woman. But how will that ever happen when I am always stuck here?'

'Up these stairs here?'

'Yes, nearly there.'

'But surely you must meet lots of women during the summer?'

'Yes. But the manager doesn't like me talking to the guests too much. When I do, he makes fun of me in front of them,' he said, and sighed again. 'I'll never get to meet anybody.'

'Along this corridor?'

'Yes, nearly there.'

'You must keep pretty fit, carrying luggage up all these stairs and along all these corridors,' I said.

A big sigh. 'I keep asking the manager for a trolley, but he says it does me good to carry the bags.'

'Can't I just have one of these rooms?'

'No, you have been put in 321. It is a special room,' he said. 'You'll see.'

Another corridor. More sighing.

'Can I ask you a question?' he said.

'Go ahead.'

'Well, it's happened a couple of times, and only with British guests, but after a few days some of them started to call me Granville,' he said. 'Who is this Granville? They wouldn't tell me.'

'Erm ...'

'Well?' He looked at me with big, hopeful eyes.

'Well, he's a character in a British television series,' I said. 'And, erm ...'

'What's he like?' He looked at me again, like I had in my possession some magical key. 'Always, with British people, I ask this question and they hesitate, then say they've never heard of him.'

What would the harm in sexing up Granville a bit? The

porter would be happy. Nobody would ever know. Maybe if I'd been a Catholic, I might have been restrained by the idea of God's omnipresence. But I'm not, and it was just the two of us in this isolated spot, some 27 miles from the nearest reception desk.

Someone once told me I reminded them of Mel Gibson. I was chuffed. Had I not later discovered that they'd got in a muddle and meant Mel Brooks, I might still be chuffed.

'Well, erm, he's an heroic loner, travels the world, drives fast cars,' I said. I should have stopped there, but I was in the flow, and the porter was hanging on my every word. 'Always gets the girl. Very handsome.'

Stop now.

'Looks a bit like Pierce Brosnan. The actor who played him was tipped to be the next Bond before Daniel Craig got it.'

Stop.

'Oh, yes. Every man would love to be Granville.'

I stopped.

'I thought so,' he said. 'I thought so.' A slight swagger appeared in his step.

'Here we are,' Granville said, throwing open the door of 321 with a manly flourish and ushering me in. 'What do you think?'

'Jesus Christ!' I said.

'Yes,' Granville said.

There, in the dusk, right outside, filling the frame of the window and glowing through the diaphanous net curtains, was a 70-foot floodlit statue of the son of God, holding a pose that said not so much that I am the way, the truth and the life, but that I have just nailed a darned fine landing off the pommel horse.

'Many of our guests request this room,' Granville said.

'I can imagine,' I said. 'I bet not too many towels disappear from 321.'

Granville fussed around, rearranging my luggage on the floor several times and showing me complicated things such as how the lights went on and off when you pressed the switch, and how the door to the bathroom opened when you turned the knob.

But I wasn't paying too much attention, transfixed as I was by a 70-foot statue delivering a sermon to me about how bearing false witness was considered so bad that it made the Top 10.

'Thank you,' I said.

A pause.

'Erm, you know what I told you about Granville?'

'Yes,' he said. Concern spread across his face, like a man who'd just been told by his surgeon that the all-clear he'd been given was, in fact, somebody else's.

'Well …'

Granville was waiting for me to open the right envelope, give him the diagnosis he'd been expecting all along.

'Well … erm …'

Granville stood, braced.

'Well, erm … doesn't matter.'

Granville smiled, turned, then left the room, closing the door behind him.

I closed the curtains.

I switched on the TV. It was set to the hotel channel. There was a picture of the crowded restaurant, a suntanned holiday crowd frozen in laughter and conversation.

The walk to dinner built up a fine appetite and in the empty, silent, cavernous restaurant, I spent an age deciding where to sit – how choice creates anxiety. Two white-haired, white-tailed waiters patiently followed me around clutching a table service for one between them.

Ordinarily, I would be the guy heading for the table in the corner, out of sight, on the fringes. As a solo diner, you often don't have a choice about that.

But on this night I did, and after eyeing up the seats tucked away behind the potted palms, I eventually plumped for the table at the dead centre of the dead restaurant. I know that's not exactly shame-busting on a walking-naked-down-Oxford-Street scale, what with there being no witnesses. But I still did it, and it still felt slightly uncomfortable, and I was still waiting for one of the waiters to waggle his index finger at me and direct me to the table by the toilet. But he didn't. He just let the cutlery drop on to the table with a clang from a height of several inches.

I ordered the lamb, no the sea bass, no, hang on, how's the pork cooked? And while, after much deliberating, the elder of the waiters took my order for risotto to the kitchen and the chef no doubt emptied the sleep dust from his eyes and, also no doubt, the contents of his nose into the pan along with the Arborio rice, I sat in the restaurant alone, save for the other waiter, listening to the clock on the wall. I felt like Howard Hughes.

The next day, I rode south through the lonely toe of Calabria to the end of the road, where the map of Italy looks like it's playing keepy-uppy with Sicily. The Strait of Messina was blanketed in mist. Beyond, there was the occasional glimpse of the island, the spires in the city of Messina poking through its gossamer shroud.

I pulled over to take a photo. I remembered an article I'd read about Sicily before I'd left home. There was an interview with somebody from the tourist board in the UK, saying how the notion of modern Sicily still being in thrall to the Mafia was so utterly outdated, about as relevant today as bowler-hatted City gents and Jack the Ripper are to London.

She had gone on to say how she particularly disliked people making lame, clichéd jokes about horse's heads and the like.

At the ferry terminal in Reggio de Calabria, the Italians all lined up patiently in their cars in rows to board the boat, looking as studiedly insouciant as if they were playing a game of statues and the music had stopped. As soon as the bow doors flopped on to the dockside, chaos reigned, with every car trying to get up the ramp at the same time. Only in Italy have I ever seen such glorious, artful anarchy. The entire country should be entered for the Turner Prize.

I strapped down the bike on the car deck, walked up to the café and ordered an espresso.

The guy behind the counter clocked my motorcycle helmet.

'Be careful in Sicily,' he said.

'Why?' I asked.

'You know,' he replied, and touched his nose.

Unlike the hotels of Italy's south-west coast, the landlords of Taormina didn't seem to be having too much trouble attracting out-of-season guests. In fact, I seemed to have discovered where English aristocrats of a certain age go to escape the riffraff now the pesky natives have reclaimed Happy Valley.

For at breakfast the next day, in a dining room full of ancient dowagers shuffling around the buffet table on sticks and talking like the Queen, a rakish gentleman, who might have been the Duke of Kent, leaped to his feet, looked out of the mullioned window and brayed loudly, to nobody in particular: 'Bugger those darned clouds. Still can't see Etna.' He sat down again and, shortly after, dozed off.

An hour later I could see Etna very clearly. Having ridden my bike up its gentle foothills, at first among the citrus groves and then through the twisted and tortured black petrified lava flows, the summit now loomed above me, maybe less than a mile away, the four live craters belching clouds of fearsome black smoke.

It had not erupted since 2002, but recent activity had had volcanologists carefully monitoring Etna.

I parked up and took a cable car for the final part of the climb. It was a small module, big enough just for me and the couple sat opposite.

Are you from Sicily?' I asked the woman.

'No, we are here from Milan. We are attending a work conference,' she said.

'What do you do?' I asked.

'We're life coaches,' she said.

A few months earlier, that cable-car ride would have been the longest ten minutes of their lives.

'What are you doing here?' they said.

'Oh, just riding around,' I said.

We joined a group in a giant four-wheel-drive truck traversing the monochromed upper slopes, littered with fissures and extinct cones. Above, the summit sent puffballs of smoke up like a Roman candle. It had all the feel of a bungee jump, or a rollercoaster ride, where you know it's safe, kind of, but still …

We were turfed out of the truck. I had assumed that our guide would give us a little talk about safety and the necessity of staying close to him. But he just lit up a fag and started talking to the driver.

'Where do we go?' I asked him.

'Over there,' he pointed, without looking, in the general direction of clouds of billowing smoke.

'Is it safe?' I said.

'If you don't jump in,' he said.

I caught up with the group, wading through the sand-like ash. The cool, thin air started to warm and thicken and there was a slight hissing noise that grew and grew as we walked until it sounded like the gods were knocking up cappuccinos.

Suddenly we were staring at a vast river of fire, just a few metres away, spewing smoothly, inexorably, out of a crack in the earth and then gurgling off down the slopes, fizzing and spitting.

It was, simultaneously, the most terrifying and beautiful thing I had ever seen. The wind swung around and brought an acrid sulphurous smell that set off a crescendo of sneezing in the group and a wall of heat that did for my nasal hair.

There were no fences, no signs warning what would happen to you if you leaped in. We picked up rocks and lobbed them into the molten stream. They bounced off.

'In Britain,' I said to the life coaches, 'we would all be wearing safety harnesses and goggles and stood behind a big fence about half a mile away.'

'Why?' she asked.

'Because it's dangerous,' I replied.

'It is more dangerous to treat adults like children,' she said.

Away from Etna, I headed into Sicily's interior, through Enna, and then up along twisting roads into the mountains. Near Prizzi, at a junction on a quiet country road, a man stepped out from behind a bush and raised his hand. I stopped.

He looked at me gravely and then bowed his head. We stayed like that for a few minutes.

He looked up again. I smiled. He shook his head. More minutes passed. No other vehicles joined the one-motorbike traffic jam.

About half a mile away up the road, over the crest of a hill, appeared a cross on a pole, then the priest carrying it above his head came into view. Then came the hearse, and then a large group of people walking behind it. I arranged my face into its most solemn expression and nodded at the man. He nodded back.

It took the procession about ten minutes to cover that half a mile. It took the procession about ten more minutes to pass the point where I was standing. I felt that my face might be stuck in solemnity for ever.

I was taking my mourning responsibilities very seriously. Forget the tourist board. I'd seen too many movies about Sicily to imagine that a death here could not involve meat hooks, machine guns and chunky gold jewellery. I was also just up the road from a town called Corleone.

As the mourners filed passed, and a few of them caught my eye, I began to sweat. Fake solemnity is a tough act to keep up for long. If done badly, it is a very close relation to smirking. Any prolonged attempts at it in the headmaster's office always ended with the line: 'Finding something amusing, Carter?'

What I didn't want was for one of the mourners to interpret my solemnity for mockery.

'Hey, Enzo, did you see that guy grinning back there?'

'Sure did, Dino.

'You know what to do.'

I could always have taken the horse's head down to the breakfast buffet, though. It would have given the Duke of Kent something to take his mind off the buggering clouds.

The procession passed. The man joined the back of the group and I was free to go.

Back in Taormina, I walked up the main street looking for a restaurant. From a doorway, the theme from *The Godfather* was playing. Further down the street, the same music was drifting out into the night. I decided upon a likely establishment, based not on the menu, or the setting, but on the fact that there were two very attractive women in the window. If I owned a restaurant, I would always have two very attractive women sitting in the window.

I took a table in the middle of the room. The waitress came over and waggled her finger, then directed me to a spot just by the toilets. She fetched over a menu and, not being able to speak English, went through the specials in Italian. She was, in effect, making me an offer I couldn't understand.

She sashayed off to get help and whispered something to a spectacularly fat man. He sauntered towards me across the room, stopping to caress the heads of children, or kiss a woman's hand, or wave like a returning war hero to the table in the corner.

'I am the owner,' the Fat Man said to me.

I asked him what he could recommend.

He leaned over.

'The lobster is very good,' he said.

'Is it local?' I asked.

'Local?' he said. 'No, from Cuba, flown in live.'

'Cuba? That's a long way to go to get your lobster.'

The Fat Man leaned a bit closer.

'I do a lot of business with Cuba,' he whispered and, like the man on the boat, tapped his nose. Then he slapped me hard on the back and went off to the kitchen to drown a crustacean in boiling water.

From the restaurant next door, I could hear the opening bars of the theme from *The Godfather*.

# 33 End of the road

My helmet had shrunk. Quite how this could have happened to a lump of toughened plastic designed to withstand soaring heat, torrential rain and freezing cold, not to mention the odd impact with a lamppost, I could not say. But now, in the mornings, once I'd managed to prise it apart sufficiently enough to force the thing over my ears, it felt like my head was having its blood pressure taken.

Thinking about it, my motorcycle jacket and trousers seemed to have shrunk too – and bizarrely only since arriving in Italy. I made a vow to write to the manufacturers on my return home demanding an explanation.

I was pondering the incredible shrinking equipment when my waitress interrupted to ask if I was ready for my next course. I had opted for the 'Food of Sardinia' menu, without realising that this actually meant all of the food in Sardinia.

Having ploughed my way through three different plates of mushrooms, proscuitto, salami, devilled lambs' kidneys and olives, accompanied by a log basket of Sardinian flatbreads, followed by ravioli stuffed with cheese, macaroni and a couple of frattau – crepes smothered with fried egg and drizzled with tomatoes and herbs – then half a suckling pig stuffed with myrtle and bay leaves attended by a brace of sausages the thickness of hawsers, I was indeed ready for my trolley-load of cakes.

So it wasn't like I was overeating or anything, and I was

managing to get plenty of exercise, what with sitting on a motorcycle all day and then there was that time back in Hungary, a few months ago, when a broken lift meant that I had to walk up two flights of stairs. As I said, I will be writing to the manufacturers.

The next day, I hooked up with a bunch of bikers from Emilia-Romagna riding up Sardinia's spectacular west coast, the alabaster beaches washed by surely the bluest sea in the world.

In their dozen-strong group, 11 were separated or divorced, and this was a phenomenon I'd seen time and again on the trip: groups of newly single, middle-aged guys reacting to reverses or releases by jumping on their motor-cycles and hitting the road.

'Why do men love to go off with other men?' I asked Gianfranco, when we'd stopped for a cigarette break. But my Italian was not so great and I think, judging by the look on his face, that I had just accused him and his friends of being homosexuals.

I changed the subject by trying to ask him if he'd ever had trouble with his helmet shrinking, and I couldn't help but notice that when we all set off once more, the group seemed to be riding more quickly along the twisting cornice and it wasn't too long before I had been left behind.

Alone once again, I stopped off at some ruins and met a fabulous woman with perfect English. 'Sardinia was colonised by the Phoenicians and Romans,' she purred and, often going weeks without nuanced conversation, I was spellbound. 'Followed by the Pisans, the Genoese and the Spaniards.' And she was so knowledgeable and her voice so sexy, so mellifluous, that I thought I might just be falling in love. 'The tour is now over. Please return this audiophone to the ticket office,' the voice said. I had the thought that if it had come to this, then it was probably a good thing that I would shortly be heading home.

I took the short ferry ride across to Corsica. As the boat approached, the houses of Bonifacio, perilously clinging to white chalk cliffs 200 feet above the sea, came into view. Bonifacio must be one of the most stunning towns in the world, especially approached from the sea. But the sight of it sent a shiver down my spine. I had been there before, not that long ago, and it had been one of the lowest points of my life.

I rode up Corsica's east coast and ducked inland, climbing and twisting among the rocky crags and through the thick forests. I passed through Corte, the centre of the island's independence movement, cradled by barren mountains, whose imposing citadel sat high up on a rocky outcrop like the prow of an enormous ship. On the walls of old stone houses, spray-painted blackamoor's heads sit beneath slogans advertising the FLNC liberation movement and calling for bloody armed conflict with the great evil that is France.

My phoned beeped. It was a text message from my old friend Dave in Birmingham. The message was short, but unambiguous.

'I am in big trouble. Call me.'

In stunning Calvi on the far north-west coast, I found a birthday cake of a hotel, run by a delightful and dotty old woman who insisted on formally introducing me to her three poodles. They all then showed me my room, according to the woman the best in the joint, which, judging by the pervading smell of burning meat, I surmised was above the kitchen.

I returned to my bike to start unloading. I had made the mistake of leaving it alongside a communal washhouse which, when I arrived, looked like the last smalls that had been processed there might have been Napoleon's.

But according to the very angry old French hag that was now yelling and spitting at me like a Romanian goose, my parking there had apparently inconvenienced her so much that she had been forced to abandon her laundry and instead find a broom with which to shoo me away.

The commotion soon attracted another old hag, who worked with the first rather as a pair of border collies would with a recalcitrant sheep. When another appeared, I grabbed one pannier, but aborted the rest of my luggage retrieval. It had become a demonstration and, this being sort-of France, it would surely only be a matter of time before riot police with water cannon turned up.

The old women had put me in a bad mood. Back in my room, the smell of burning meat had grown worse. Things were unravelling. I grabbed my laptop from the pannier and headed out of the door and slipped down the last of the hotel steps on my arse, glistening wet as they were from the rain that had now started to fall heavily.

I tucked my laptop inside my jacket and ran down the street, looking for an Internet café. They were mostly closed. Soaked, I eventually found a place open opposite the citadel.

'We close in ten minutes,' the woman said behind the counter.

Normally, the Internet cafés I'd been into on the trip had been full of young people smoking, screaming and blowing large holes in people of a swarthy appearance on screen, usually via the proxy of a muscled, square-jawed man in a khaki uniform.

This Internet café was rather different. Every terminal bar one was occupied by a member of the French Foreign Legion, wearing immaculately pressed khaki trousers and shirts, with red epaulettes on the shoulders, their dazzling white kepis sitting on the desks beside the computers, on which they seemed to be doing nothing more exciting than emailing. Shoot 'em up games must seem pretty dull when you do it for real as your day job.

I took the last available space, squeezed in between a legionnaire the size of Bluto – who, for the purposes of my fantasies, I projected on to a recent past involving diamond smuggling, fairground prizefighting, a spell as a mercenary in

Equatorial Guinea and, of course, a lost love – and a small, puny-looking bespectacled legionnaire, for whom even my most febrile fantasies couldn't muster much beyond parking ticket evasion or perhaps some creative accounting.

I plugged in my laptop, attached my call-centre-style headphones and rang Dave. I hadn't spoken to him since I'd hit the road. He sounded rough, though it was hard to tell exactly as the line wasn't the best.

'What's up, mate?' I said.

'Oh, you know. Where are you?'

'Corsica.'

'Having a good time?'

'I've just been attacked by three old women with brooms, fallen down some stairs and I'm piss-wet through. I think I've screwed up my laptop as well, can hardly hear you.'

'Thanks for ringing.'

'You said you were in trouble.'

'I met somebody,' he said.

'What?'

'I met somebody.'

Shit. Knowing Dave, this could be bad. When it came to relationships, he was a million-mile-an-hour man. But it took him years to stop. His dad had died recently.

The connection went down. I redialled.

'Dave. Sorry about that ...'

'She left me, Mike ...'

'She left you?'

Bluto and the accountant stopped tapping away. They seemed to be leaning in.

'Dave, I haven't got long ...'

'I don't know what to do ...'

'It'll get easier ... time ...'

'Bullshit. This was it. This was my last chance ...'

The woman at the counter was pointing to her watch.

'Last chance? You're 42 ...'

'I loved her, did everything I could. Jumped through fucking hoops … bitch.'

I realised that Dave was quite drunk.

'Don't do anything stupid.'

Bluto and the accountant moved closer.

'I quit my job.'

The woman from the counter was now clearing the plastic cups from the desks.

'Don't do anything else stupid.'

'Every fucking day the same. Same train. Same office. Same broken flickering fucking light over my desk. Same stupid people, same stupid shit coming out their mouths. Going home to their same stupid relationships … every day … what's the point …'

'What will you do?'

'Don't give a shit …'

The woman tapped me on the arm and pointed to her watch again. The legionnaires were packing up to go.

'Dave?'

Silence. The line had gone again.

The woman was walking back to the counter with the empty cups. I redialled quickly.

'Dave?'

'Yeah.'

I could hear him crying.

'It'll work out …'

'I give up …'

The woman came back. She drew her flat hand across her throat.

'Dave?'

'Yeah.'

'Remember when we were 12? At Yardleys? Somebody stole your swimming trunks. You had to go in the pool naked in front of the whole class.'

'Yeah.'

'That was me.'

'What?'

'I took your trunks. Stuffed them down the back of the radiator.'

'Bastard. I thought it was Miff ... you were supposed to be my best friend.'

'Sorry.'

'Bastard.'

'Waited a long time to get that off my chest.'

'Bastard,' Dave said, half laughing, half crying.

Next morning Calvi sat still under a glorious, crisp, clear autumnal sky. I loaded the bike and left town, heading for the port of Bastia to catch the ferry to the French mainland.

After a few miles, I pulled off the main road and followed a track down through ancient olive groves to the sea. The track seemed familiar, but narrower, somehow, smaller.

I wasn't sure I would recognise the place, but as soon as the adobe-tiled roof and white walls appeared around the corner the memories came flooding back. It felt like I'd been here yesterday.

A few years back, I'd stupidly agreed to honour my commitment with my soon-to-be ex-wife to a long-booked holiday with another couple. A happy couple.

We'd stayed for a week here. My wife's eyes had sparkled with the future – oh, that all made sense afterwards, when I had the full picture – but the misery of that week, the foursomes for dinner, the separate bedrooms, my desperate, pointless attempts to prove myself still worthy of her, had left me hollowed out, broken, humiliated. I had been like some gruesome fallen-out-of-favour court jester, hanging on for grim death. It was probably the worst week of my life.

For ages after, I'd hated myself for what I had been prepared to put myself through; how low I'd sunk. Those years had been like a word ladder, starting with euphoria and ending with desolate, just a letter at a time.

Throughout the trip, I'd been revisiting places we'd holidayed together – Romania, the Turkish coast, Greek islands, Croatia – places I had thought now so indelibly tainted with sadness that I would have to avoid them for ever.

But one by one, I had been reclaiming them for myself, creating fresh memories. It felt like splashing on a new coat of paint: what lay beneath would always be there, but that wasn't the first thing I would see any more.

I looked at my motorcycle, dirty, scratched, bruised, the panniers covered in stickers of places I'd been, some peeling and faded, almost unidentifiable now. Nobody would ever know I'd been there, except me. I thought about the journey that had brought me here, back to this place. I worked backwards, fast rewind, and ended up in South Wales, with Kevin. He was teaching me about the lifesaver, about target fixation.

'If you're going round a bend and there's a tree, if you stare at it, then that's where you'll end up,' he'd said. 'It's a natural law. Look where you want to go and the bike will always follow.'

I stared over the fence of the villa, its windows shuttered for the winter, the grass overgrown and littered with decaying leaves, blown in swirling eddies by the cold north wind.

Now I could see that week for what it really was; could understand those agonies, that fear of loss and aloneness; could, finally, forgive myself.

I closed my eyes and tried to recapture the wretchedness I'd felt the last time I'd been stood in this spot. But all I could see were shadows and all I could hear was the sound of distant echoes. For, finally, miraculously, it seemed that those people had gone.

I opened my eyes. Overhead, thousands of starlings were flying as one, the black mass dancing across the sky in pulsing waves and corkscrews before exploding like a vast firework.

# 34 The final bend

Morning, somewhere. My eyes were closed and I was in bed. I lay there for a while. It was a game I had grown used to. In that world of half sleep, I always figured I had about 20 seconds to try and guess where I was before the brain woke up fully and it all came to me. It's when psychologists tell you to write down your dreams, before they get fanned to the four corners. Sometimes I was whole countries out.

I couldn't guess this morning. Nothing. I opened my eyes. Scanned the darkened room. Trying to remember. Still nothing. Where would I be going this morning? What language did they speak downstairs? Would it be snow outside, or an inferno? Was I alone or were there friends next door? Where the fuck was I?

My eyes grew used to the gloom. Where were my panniers? My camping bag? My crash helmet? All my clothes spilled across the floor?

There was a dressing gown hanging from the back of the door. I didn't pack a dressing gown. I remembered.

I reached over and switched on the radio. Interest rates were predicted to be going up a quarter of one per cent tomorrow, said a man, igniting fears of a slump in the economy. I stared at the radio, listening intently to the voice. It seemed like a miracle that I could understand every word he was saying.

I got up, opened the wardrobe. It was full of clothes. It

took me a while to decide what to wear. Choices. I picked up a T-shirt I hadn't seen for a while. On it was Rosa Luxemburg's quote: Movement is nothing ... the goal every-thing. I put it down. Opted for plain white.

I walked out of the door. It was raining.

'Haven't see you for a while,' the guy behind the counter in the corner shop said.

'Been away.'

'Anywhere nice?'

I picked up a copy of *Private Eye*.

'Here and there.'

I walked to the café up the street, grabbed my favourite seat in the corner, away from the loudspeakers.

Some of the papers were scattered on the table. I picked up the *Sunday Mirror*. Tara was still winning the battle against drugs. Kerry had had a couple of setbacks. Her mum didn't like her new fella, they'd had a big fall-out over it. Posh was planning a big family party for Christmas. Britons were still drinking themselves to death. Carole Malone was still calling Cherie Blair a money-grubbing cow. Ketchup gave you cancer. On page 15 there was a story about immi-gration. A Tory backbencher was predicting blood on the streets.

I looked across at the *Mail on Sunday*. The immigration story was the splash.

In the *Observer*, a bloke on a motorbike was heading up through Spain, Portugal and France. He was tired, he said, was really looking forward to getting home. It was raining where he was, too. He sounded like a right miserable sod.

I put down the *Observer*, opened *Private Eye*. 'Leave Cherie alone!' screamed Glenda Slagg. 'She's a great role model for working mums.'

The waitress came over.

'Vat you like?'

'Sorry, haven't looked yet.'

'Vant a minute?'

'No, no. Just give me a sec.'

I picked up the menu. I could understand every word. Knew what everything was. I stared at it with the same rapt wonder with which I'd earlier listened to the man on the radio, looked at it like it contained the secrets of the universe.

The waitress took a little step backwards.

'Bacon sandwich, please.'

'Von bacon sanvitch.'

'No, a sausage sandwich.'

'Von sausage sanvitch?'

'Yes.'

'Ketchup?'

'Definitely not.'

'No ketchup.'

'Where are you from?' I asked her.

She seemed hesitant, guarded, didn't take a step forward again.

'From here,' she said, eventually.

'Doesn't sound like it.'

She paused.

'Originally from Poland.'

'Been here long?'

'Three months.'

'Where in Poland?'

'You know Poland?'

'Was travelling around there a bit earlier this year.'

'From Zamość. You vill not know it. It is small.'

'I was there.'

'You ver in Zamość?!'

She stepped forwards. A huge grin spread across her face.

'You like?'

'I liked very much. It is beautiful.'

'Beautiful. I miss.'

The smile slipped into something else.

'You are from here?' she asked.

'I was,' I said. 'I will be.'

I loaded a change of clothes and some smart shoes into the boxes and pulled off into the early evening rush-hour traffic. I weaved in and out of the cars effortlessly. How different it all felt to six months earlier. The bike was weightless.

'Why were you going so fast?' The policeman showed me the screen on the speed gun. It said 47. 'The limit is 30. Why the hurry?'

'No reason. I don't have any excuses. I'm sorry, that's all.'

'Sorry's not going to save you from three points. Could be an automatic ban if it goes to court.'

He asked for my licence. I handed it over. He walked across to the police car, got on the radio, ran some checks.

He returned to where I was standing.

'Might take some time,' he said.

'Got plenty.' I smiled.

He didn't.

He reached inside his pocket. Photos of his sisters?

He pulled out his ticket book. Licked his index finger, folded back the first sheet.

'What's your job ...' He peered at my licence. '... Michael?'

I hesitated. Had to think. I hadn't been asked that question in a long time.

'Journalist,' I said, finally. I hadn't thought about myself in terms of a job for ages. It felt strange to say the word.

He filled in something on the ticket. I couldn't make it out.

'Date of birth?'

'It's on my licence ...'

'Date of birth?'

I told him.

'Day before me,' he said.

'What year?'

'Same year.'

He looked over at the bike.

'Any good?'

'Just got back from a trip. Six months, 20,000 miles, didn't let me down once.'

He walked over to it, bent down, read some of the stickers.

'You've been all over,' he said. 'Where's this one supposed to be?'

'Latvia,' I replied. 'Got washed off in a storm.'

'And this?'

'Montenegro.' It just said Monte now.

He ran his finger across the pannier, across the flags and the stickers.

'Turkey, Albania, Bulgaria, Poland ...' he said '... Croatia, Romania, Greece, Finland. What's that one?'

'Bosnia.'

'Bosnia. That's dangerous, isn't it?'

'Not when you're there.'

There was a crackling from the car. He walked over to it, reached inside, talked into the handset. He came back.

'All in order,' he said.

He was still holding the ticket book open.

'How's it been?' he asked.

'What?'

'The trip.'

'Long, hard, brilliant, terrible, boring, exhilarating ... you know. Like life, but with better scenery.'

He laughed.

'What's the best place?'

'Impossible to say.'

'Come on.'

'Six months, how could I ...?'

'You must have favourites.'

'Well, Krakow and Naples were fantastic. Sarajevo and Mostar, too, all battle-scarred but surviving. Stockholm,

Athens and Zagreb because of the people I met there. There were the landscapes: the fjords in Norway, the Amalfi coast road, the deserted beaches in Albania, the monasteries in the clouds in Meteora, the deserts in eastern Turkey and the Kurdish people …'

'Sounds incredible.'

'Had its moments.'

'Why?'

'Why what?'

'Why the trip?'

'Does there have to be a reason?'

'I'm a policeman.'

'Fed up, I suppose. Usual shit. Nothing very original.'

'And now?'

'Too soon to tell, I'd say.'

The policeman closed his ticket book and put it back in his pocket.

'I ride a bike,' he said.

'What sort?'

'Beamer as well.'

He pulled out his notebook, scribbled something down, ripped off the sheet and handed it to me.

'What's this?'

'My mobile,' he said.

'Er … thanks.'

'Can I take yours?'

'… sure.'

I wrote it in his notebook.

'I'll give you a call, if that's okay,' he said.

'No problem.'

'Like to talk to you some more.'

'Sure. Anytime. Is that it?'

'It's your lucky day. Ride within the speed limits.'

'Thanks.'

'Talk to you soon.'

*

I parked the bike, opened the boxes, took out my clothes, walked to a doorway, got changed, put the biker gear away in the panniers.

Then I walked around the corner, through a door and down a flight of steps. The *Observer*'s Christmas party was in full swing.

There was the glad-handing and the back-slapping and the congratulations. People I'd never spoken to before came up to me and treated me like a long-lost friend.

Everything looked familiar, but I had the sense that I was a stranger wandering around my old life.

'Find any answers, then?' I was asked time and time again by people with rapt faces, like I'd been outside the cave. 'What was the highlight? What was the most dangerous part? Did you find love?' I knew they didn't just want a list of countries and conquests and tales of exotic food.

I didn't know what to say. I was a rabbit caught in the headlights. I wished I could have delivered. As a proxy knight-errant, I felt like a terrible disappointment.

'What are you going to do next?'

'Same as before,' I wanted to reply. But I couldn't. I wasn't allowed to say that. It wouldn't have been the truth, anyway. Everything was changed. For ever. I just had no idea how to explain.

Eventually, the new friends drifted away and I was left with my close colleagues. Soon, talk reverted to tangled love lives and failed promotions and the price of property. It was a relief.

I wandered up to the bar, ordered a lime and soda.

'Not drinking, Carter?'

It was Jo, my travel editor. Exactly 12 months ago to the minute, it was a combination of her, Stella Artois and my gob that started the whole thing off.

'No. I'm on the bike.'

'You married to it now, then?'

'Feels odd to go anywhere without it,' I said.

'I bet.'

'What you doing for Christmas?' I asked her. That was different. I never ask that.

'Same old, same old. Going to see my folks in Essex. Family get-together. The usual. You?'

'Going up to Brum to see my dad and a mate of mine who's having a hard time. Probably spend Christmas up there. Haven't done it in years.'

'On the bike?'

'On the bike.'

'That'll be nice.'

'I hope so.'

'So, any answers?' Jo said, finally.

'What?'

'From the trip?'

'It's hard to tell exactly. I guess the least you could say is that I learned to ride a motorbike pretty well.'

'I should hope so.'

'It was quite lonely at times.'

'It's good to have a clear out from time to time, though,' Jo said.

'Sure. It's certainly done that. I thought I could hack it all alone. Thought that there lay the key; like somehow withdrawing was the calling of middle-age. But I'd get up, jump on a motorbike, ride 300 miles, cross a border, enter a strange, new town and, yet, travel nowhere. There was always something missing.'

'Missing?'

'It was only when I managed to make meaningful connections with other people that everything changed. Everything. Transformed. I can understand now why some people will pay for a massage just for the physical human contact. That seems such a beautiful idea to me now. I understand now why we grieve so much over lost love, why we make alliances, cling to them, fill internet chat rooms. We are desperate for touch, for contact, for love. Without it we can survive, but we're like plants clinging to a rock. I've always felt ashamed to admit this need to myself, like I was somehow flawed, inadequate. But I see it now: love is really the only thing that makes life worth living.'

'You didn't need to go away to learn that.'

'I did. I really did. I understand now what that was all about. I'd been staring at the tree on the bend, you see.'

'The tree on the bend?'

'It's a long story.'

'Go on.'

'Well, it's a biking thing. It's called target fixation. Just say you're going round a bend and there's a tree on the far side. If you stare at the tree, that's where the bike has to go. It's a natural law. Couldn't be more simple. Other people can stare at the tree, there's not much you can do about that. But you can choose where you look. Ignore the tree, keep your eyes on the road and you'll be fine.'

'That's what you learned in six months?'

'It's enough.'

Just after midnight, I went to the toilet, splashed a bit of water on my face, looked up, smiled, then I walked out, turned left up the stairs, out through the door and down the side street. I opened the pannier, removed my shirt and stuffed it in the box. Then I walked, topless, around to the box on the other side to get my biking gear.

'Strippagram's here, girls,' said a voice.

'Get 'em off.' came another.

I looked up. There was a small crowd of young women standing there, a vision of sparkly party frocks, Santa hats and antlers.

'Get 'em off, matey.'

'No.'

'Come on, you're halfway there. It's Christmas.'

'Get 'em off, get 'em off,' came the chorus.

So I did. Stood there in my underpants in the middle of the street with my jeans round my ankles while the Santa hats and the antlers screamed and wolf-whistled and took pictures with their phones.

They went off howling into the night. And, apart from hurting my back as I bent down to pick up my trousers, nothing bad happened.

# EPILOGUE
# The trip in numbers

**19,950**: miles ridden. I was tempted to make a final circuit of the M25 to hit 20,000. But the lure of my bed won through.

**23**: gifts received, including a frying pan, a map, and a piece of old rope (but excluding the pens and the man-sized boxes of tissues).

**22**: number of ferries taken.

**8**: number of tyres worn out.

**1**: puncture, in Spain.

**1**: fallen off, in Estonia.

**27**: number of countries visited.

**27**: number of countries where I was informed at some stage that the next country was dangerous.

**7**: attacks – three by dogs, one each by a snake, a wasp, a goose and a human.

**Millions:** wasps splattered against my windshield. You could call that a victory.

**93**: email addresses/phone numbers exchanged, with the words 'if you're in London, come and stay'.

**200**: euros paid in fines, including 50 euros to the scooter-riding cop in Barcelona suffering from small-bike syndrome.

**1**: dead polish sheep used as a saddle cover. It didn't have to be Polish, but it did, ideally, have to be dead.

**3,000**: euros spent on fuel. The most expensive fill-ups were in Turkey.

**2**: number of times I lost all my underwear.

**4**: sets of earplugs lost.

**4**: women I met I could have easily have fallen for.

**1**: number of people who definitely fell for me. His name was Hassan, a waiter in Turkey.